CLIENT VIOLENCE IN SOCIAL WORK PRACTICE

Client Violence in Social Work Practice

Prevention, Intervention, and Research

CHRISTINA E. NEWHILL

THE GUILFORD PRESS
New York   London

© 2003 The Guilford Press
A Division of Guilford Publications, Inc.
72 Spring Street, New York, NY 10012
www.guilford.com

Printed in the United States of America

This book is printed on acid-free paper.

Last digit is print number: 9   8   7   6   5   4   3   2   1

Library of Congress Cataloging-in-Publication Data

Newhill, Christina E.
    Client violence in social work practice : prevention, intervention,
and research / by Christina E. Newhill.
        p.   cm.
Includes bibliographical references and index.
    ISBN 1-57230-872-9
    1. Social workers—Violence against—United States—Prevention. 2.
Violence in the workplace—United States—Prevention. 3. Social
service—United States—Safety measures. I. Title.
HV40.8.U6 N48 2003
361.3′2′0289—dc21
                                                              2002151981

About the Author

Christina E. Newhill, PhD, LCSW, is currently an Associate Professor of Social Work at the University of Pittsburgh, and has been a member of the faculty since 1990. She holds a bachelor's degree in sociology from the State University of New York at Binghamton, a master's in social work from Syracuse University, and a doctorate in social welfare from the University of California at Berkeley. Dr. Newhill has over 10 years of community mental health practice experience, primarily in psychiatric emergency and inpatient settings, and teaches in the direct practice mental health specialization. She is Principal Investigator on several research studies focusing on violent behavior and risk assessment and is currently examining the relationship of Cluster B personality disorders, emotion regulation problems, substance abuse, and violent behavior. She has conducted training workshops on violence in the workplace at the local, state, and national levels for many years. Dr. Newhill is also a member of the Academy of Certified Social Workers and the NASW Register of Clinical Social Workers, holds a Diplomate in Clinical Social Work, and is a licensed clinical social worker in the State of California.

Contents

Why Violence Is an Issue for Social Work Practice

A woman goes to a hospital emergency room asking for psychiatric inpatient admission because she feels like she "might explode." After waiting in the lobby for a long time, she leaves and goes to another hospital with the same request but this time says she is afraid she will hurt someone. Again she is told to wait in the lobby. Angry, she goes home, gets a gun, goes back to the original hospital, enters the emergency room and demands to see someone. A social worker, who was just called down to the emergency room to see a distraught family, sees the woman and asks if she can help. The woman draws her gun, takes three people hostage and, without warning, shoots the social worker in the back, killing her instantly. The woman is currently serving an indeterminate sentence in a forensic mental health facility. (Hasch & Guggenheim, 1988, p. A8)

A young social worker, who worked for Child Protective Services in Michigan, went to a client's home to explain how a mother, whose house had been deemed unfit, could get her children back. Two days later, the social worker's body was found beaten and strangled. Two sisters were charged in her murder and police believe that the sisters became incensed when the social worker refused to say who had made the child protection complaint against them because reports of child abuse and neglect are confidential. Agencies that serve abused and neglected children state that such confidentiality is essential or reports of abuse and neglect will not be made for fear of retaliation. ("Lisa's Law," 1998, p. A8)

This book is about violence and social work practice. The preceding true cases are but two of the thousands of incidents of client violence toward social workers that occur every year in the United States. Most of

1

us choose social work as our profession because we want to help other people: to help individuals, families, and communities achieve quality of life; to help foster social justice; to advocate on behalf of those who are oppressed, vulnerable, and at risk; and, in short, to help make the world a better place. When I ask new social work students on their first day of class to tell me why they chose social work as their profession, these are the kinds of things that they usually say. They do not say that they are entering the social work profession anticipating that they may become targets of violence from the very individuals they want to help (Skolnik-Acker et al., 1993; Star, 1984). Rarely does a beginning student fully realize that many clients may not want a social worker's help and that, in fact, they may even attempt to harm us.

Risk as a reality of life in social work practice is not new in this country or internationally. In fact, a 1986 editorial in the British journal *New Society* states that, in the United Kingdom, social workers are the professional group at second greatest risk of violence, following the police ("Violence and the Social Worker," 1986). The British Broadcasting Company's television program "Panorama" of April 18, 1988, stated, "proportionally, more social workers than police have been murdered on duty in England and Wales in the past three years" (as quoted in Norris, 1990, p. 17). In the past two decades many social workers have been killed in the course of their work in the United States, and scores more have been injured. Furthermore, as we begin the 21st century, a variety of indicators suggest that physical and verbal violence by clients toward social workers is increasing across settings (Dillon, 1992).

THE SOCIAL WORKER'S DILEMMA: CARE VERSUS CONTROL

Why do social workers become targets of a client's violent behavior? The answer to this is complex and not entirely clear. Some argue that such violence represents a barometer for our violent society (Dillon, 1992). Long-standing social problems such as unemployment, poverty, racism, and economic inequality can create an environment in which violence can thrive (Young, 1992). Others argue that the answer lies in the unique nature of social work, namely, that our work is both caring and controlling, often involving the responsibilities of interpreting government regulations and dispensing resources. It is through this process "that the client's rage, frustration and helplessness [may] surface" (Euster, 1992, p. A14).

Society uses social workers as agents of both social care and social control, charging us both to protect our clients from society and to protect society from our clients (Townsend, 1985). Deciding whether to re-move a child from a home because of allegations of abuse, whether to in-voluntarily commit a client to a psychiatric hospital on the basis of danger to others, or whether to recommend a couple who wish to be-come foster parents are all examples of this social care–social control dichotomy. As one social worker put it: "I feel like we're the social police—except we don't carry guns or wear bulletproof vests" (personal communication, 1983).

Another issue that plays a role in understanding client violence is the fact that in many ways social work practice has changed since earlier times. Today, social workers on the front lines handle situations and cli-ents that previous generations of workers did not encounter as fre-quently: mentally ill individuals who may not be taking their prescribed medication or may be using street drugs (and who formerly would have been confined to locked state hospital wards); increasingly volatile issues related to mandated reporting of child abuse and neglect; explosive situ-ations involving substance abuse and withdrawal; new intervention roles in domestic violence situations and divorce mediation; police–social worker teams; and the changing nature of the cases seen at our social welfare agencies. MacFadden (1980) likens the position and perspective of the frontline social worker to that of a soldier on the front lines in combat. Thus the increased concern about violence and social work practice has arisen not because social workers are less able to cope than in earlier times but because today's social workers are exposed to a greater number and range of violent situations as a result of changes in our work roles, changes in society, and the evolving organization of the welfare state (Griffin, 1995; Parton & Small, 1989)

CONSERVATIVE SOCIAL POLICIES
AND DESPERATE CLIENTS

A variety of political issues and policy shifts have also created condi-tions that place social workers at risk. For example, the number of people who need public assistance and other social services has in-creased as government has cut back on certain types of institutional support, such as state hospital care and general relief (Abt, 2001). Such budget cuts and the ensuing understaffing of social service agen-cies have led to increased vulnerability for social workers (Hiratsuka, 1988; Petrie, Lawson, & Hollender, 1982; Schultz, 1987, 1989). At the same time, an increasingly conservative political atmosphere has led to a variety of approaches to cutting the welfare rolls, usually termed "welfare reform." Many individuals have been forced off welfare and given only a mixed bag of transitional support; it is not clear that this policy has led to true financial independence and security for most former recipients (Abt, 2001). Currently, the minimum wage is not a living wage. To independently support a single individual, much less a family, on a minimum-wage job is nearly impossible (Ehrenreich, 2001), yet these are the only jobs that many welfare recipients are eligible for. Some states have purposely not provided for adequate mechanisms to evaluate the outcome of welfare reform efforts. Those states that have done so have reported results that, although initially positive, have for the most part been ultimately discouraging. The safety net for those unable or unwilling to care for themselves independently has shredded.

Welfare reform has also led to more aggressive efforts to obtain child support payments from deadbeat parents, usually fathers (Griffin, 1995). Individual citizens, along with politicians, are actively arguing that parents, not taxpayers, should support their children, and these new efforts have produced an unfortunate by-product: violence. For example, in 1992 in Watkins Glen, New York, a father who was enraged over child support payments shot four women working in the local welfare office and then shot himself (Dillon, 1992).

Other parents may become violent in response to the actions of child protection agency investigations. One of the most dangerous actions a social worker can take is removing a child from the parent's home because of allegations of abuse or neglect (Hoy, 1993). Here are some examples:

> In the summer of 1998 in Flint, Michigan, a 35-year-old child protection social worker was threatened because she refused to tell family members who had made a child neglect complaint against them. Police said that when the worker visited the family's home, a man in the house threw rocks at her and smashed her car windshield with his fist. Fortunately, the social worker herself was not hurt but charges are pending against the man. ("Lisa's Law, 1998, p. A8)

> In 1991, Cayuga County, New York, social worker Sabrina Kulakowski was followed to her home by Roy Brown, whose daughter had been placed in a foster home. Earlier Mr. Brown had called the county office threatening to "spray" workers with Uzi rifle fire "to wipe everybody out." When Mr. Brown caught Ms. Kulakowski at her home, he stabbed, strangled and beat her until her skull was crushed. Then he burned her house down. The police matched human bite marks on Ms. Kulakowski's body with Mr. Brown's jaw and he was convicted of killing her in February 1992. He is now serving 25 years to life in prison. (Dillon, 1992, p. C18)

These are some of the clients we see as social workers. They are often desperate, frightened, hopeless, powerless, and angry, and sometimes the only recourse they see is violence. Many social workers also fear that publicity about violence may cause even more attacks to occur. For example, in June 1991, Arnold Bates, a 34-year-old food stamp applicant who was turned down for benefits by a Baltimore welfare office, stabbed to death one of the caseworkers, Tanja Brown-O'Neill. The aggressive public reaction to this tragic incident was shocking and included phone calls to the agency threatening to "take out more of you social workers" (Dillon, 1992). Public reaction often seems to involve blaming the social worker for the violence, suggesting it was justified because the social worker didn't give the client what the client wanted—in essence, blaming the victim (Ryan, 1976). The public often expects clear, quick solutions to complex social problems that, in reality, are not easily resolved (Griffin, 1995). Furthermore, because of confidentiality restrictions, social workers are often unable to explain or defend their actions publicly.

Recognition that these changes have occurred in U.S. social work practice, however, has not been accompanied by adequate systematic investigation into the implications of those changes for the profession. Although the subject of dangerousness has generated a plethora of literature in the past four decades, discussion has primarily addressed the appropriateness of the dangerousness standard for involuntary civil commitment and explored the ability of clinicians to predict violent behavior (Newhill, 1992). Only a few studies address the danger posed by clients toward human services professionals, and only a small proportion of these specifically concern violence toward social workers. The lack of attention to this issue suggests that many social workers may not be adequately informed as to the potential hazards they face in their day-to-day work or provided with systematic training to enable them to skillfully manage those risks (Hiratsuka, 1988). Many social workers remain caught between desperate clients and a government that is perceived by the clients as a cause of their problems or as an entity that cannot or will not help them. The question now is, What can be done to prevent such incidents from occurring while still providing clients with the best services?

PREDICTING VIOLENCE

The prevention of violence requires that one can, on some level, predict who is at risk for behaving in a violent manner. My interest in the issue of how to predict client violence developed as a result of my practice experience in psychiatric emergency and inpatient settings in which the assessment and prediction of client violence was a regular clinical task. Although how to work with violent clients was not addressed in my master's degree program or in any available continuing education classes at that time, I was still expected to know how to assess and intervene with violent clients and to identify which clients were imminently violent and should be hospitalized and which were not. I had to do this without any real guidelines to draw on.

Whether a social worker is evaluating a client for psychiatric hospitalization, assessing an abuse case for child welfare services, or advising juvenile justice staff about whether to place a threatening youth within the general detention center population, the assumption that we possess the expertise to both predict and treat violent behavior is inherent. To be able to assess and predict client violence is an important set of skills that is within the domain of clinical expertise if certain limitations are adhered to. For example, clear evidence exists that clinicians have little to no ability to predict violence over the long term (Monahan, 1981) and, in fact, flipping a coin results in a better rate of accuracy than clinical judgment does (Ennis & Litwack, 1974). However, research has shown that *short-term* predictions are, indeed, within the clinical realm if the clinician has the appropriate knowledge and skill base (Monahan, 1984). One of the key issues to remember is that violence is a *relationship*—a relationship between the individual and the individual's environment (Sarbin, 1967). What this suggests is that social workers must take a systems or ecological approach to the assessment and prediction of violence if we are to practice in this arena competently (Newhill, 1992; Shah, 1981; Silver, Mulvey, & Monahan, 1999).

Using a systems orientation, when a clinician evaluates a client to determine whether he or she is a danger to others, the clinician interprets the client's clinical status within the context of that individual's past, present, and future social environments (Shah, 1981). A positive effect of the systems approach is that it diffuses the perception of human violence as a reified personality trait (Shah, 1981) and instead encourages the clinician to focus on the person's current mental and emotional states, along with his or her current and future environments, with the recognition that these are dynamic, not static, states. Both the systems/ecological approach and the person-in-environment paradigm are hallmarks of the social work perspective (Hepworth, Rooney, & Larsen, 1997), and thus I would argue that social work may be one of the most appropriate disciplines, in terms of philosophical orientation, for assessing and working with violent clients.

Unfortunately, however, if the social worker is not appropriately trained to do a careful examination of the individual, situational, and environmental variables that are risk factors associated with violence, he or she may rely on stereotypes, most often stereotypes related to how the person looks. For example, let's imagine that a clinician is assessing two different clients. Client 1 is a young man who is dirty, disheveled, and smells bad. He is gesturing and talking to himself and glares at the clinician in a manner perceived by the clinician as threatening. The clinician is wary in the presence of Client 1 and decides to see him only in the presence of other staff. In contrast, Client 2 is a young man who is clean-cut, well dressed, articulate, and cordial. The clinician relaxes in the presence of Client 2, takes him into the interviewing office, and asks him what kind of help he needs. Which of the two clients would most clinicians perceive as dangerous? When I have asked my students this question, the majority say "Client 1." However, let's say that Client 2 is, in fact, the notorious serial killer, Ted Bundy. Those who have studied Ted Bundy's criminal career note that he was probably such a "successful" killer because he looked and acted the opposite of what the average person would expect of someone who engaged in such heinous behavior (Doyle & Cave, 1992). Ted Bundy's physical appearance was the epitome of the clean-cut, all-American young man. He was handsome, soft spoken, articulate, well dressed, and mannerly. He did not fit the common stereotype of a "dangerous person." In fact, however, he was extremely dangerous. As social workers, we must guard against common generalizations and stereotypes about violence and dangerousness and, instead, examine what we know about the actual risk factors for violence, along with identifying specific situational contexts that may enhance the probability of violence. To reduce your risk of being a victim of client violence and to provide the best services to clients who have problems with violent behavior, you have to have the right knowledge and skills. This book attempts to provide that knowledge and skill base so that you, as a social work practitioner, are equipped to meet the demands of today's practice world, a world that sometimes involves encounters with danger.

ORGANIZATION OF THIS BOOK

This book is organized into three major sections. Part I addresses the issue of how and why client violence is an issue for social work practitioners. The first half of Chapter 1 introduces the reader to the role of violence in our society, looking at the cost of violence, the role of guns and the gun culture, and violence in our schools, and asks the question: Are we an angry, stressed-out culture? The second half of Chapter 1 addresses violence in the workplace and examines what we know about the nature and causes of workplace violence and the steps that many businesses have taken to reduce violence and to respond constructively to those who are victimized, providing some lessons for us as social workers. Chapter 2 focuses on the main point of the book, that is, client violence toward social workers. It reviews existing studies, both in the United States and internationally, on client violence and social work practice.

Part II addresses issues related to understanding the nature of the different types of client violence and the various risk factors associated with violent behavior. Four of the most common forms of client violence reported by social workers are property damage, threats, attempted assaults, and actual assaults. Using findings from my study of client violence toward social workers (Newhill, 1996), Chapter 3 looks at property damage and threats, particularly the nature of such incidents and what motivates a client to damage property or threaten a social worker. Chapter 4 discusses attempted and actual physical attacks. It examines reported cases in which clients killed social workers in the line of duty, then details nonfatal assaults and explores the motives and provocations for such incidents.

When you are evaluating a client, it is critical that you know what to look for in terms of assessing risk. If one expects a modicum of accuracy in predicting violence, an essential requirement is a thorough knowledge of the risk factors associated with violent behavior. Therefore, Chapter 5 provides an overview of the large body of research that has examined correlates of violent behavior in an effort to improve assessment, prediction, and the development of effective interventions. These risk factors are organized into three major domains: (1) individual and clinical risk factors (including demographic risk factors, high-risk psychiatric symptoms, personality risk factors, substance abuse, and biological risk factors); (2) historical risk factors (including history of violence, social and family history, work history, and history of psychiatric treatment and hospitalization); and (3) environmental and contextual risk factors (including level and quality of social support, peer pressure, the influence of popular culture, identities of the actual or potential victims, and the individual's ability to engage in violence).

Throughout these chapters and the remainder of the book, short case vignettes are used to provide a clinical context for the various topics of discussion. These cases come from three sources: (1) data from my Client Violence (CV) Study (Newhill, 1996); (2) cases from my unpublished Crisis Casebook, which is composed of cases collected from my clinical practice over the past 20 years (Newhill, 1995b); and (3) cases reported by the popular press. All identifying information in the vignettes drawn from the CV Study and the Crisis Casebook has been altered to preserve confidentiality, and most of the vignettes are composite cases drawn from multiple actual cases. Such alteration assures that no one will recognize any specific individuals depicted in the cases, including the individuals themselves. Those cases reported openly in the popular press are not disguised, and the sources are cited.

The information presented Parts I and II show that the issue of safety and violence is not just a perceived issue but a real one for many, if not most, practicing social workers and that there are a variety of both risk and protective factors that can illuminate an understanding of the dynamics of violent behavior. How do we protect ourselves, our colleagues, and our clients? How do we effectively assess a client for risk of violence? What interventions are feasible and effective in working with violent and aggressive clients? And, finally, what prevention strategies are effective in reducing the occurrence of client violence toward clinicians?

To address these questions, Part III provides an integrated instructional package designed to teach all of the key areas of knowledge and skills related to the risk assessment of violent clients, such as ways of approaching and engaging violent clients, intervention modalities for treating violent clients, and strategies to prevent client violence in both office and field settings, including models for developing an agency safety plan and a violent incident report form. The emotional and physical impact of client violence on social workers is also discussed, including the effect that experiencing such violence can have on a social worker's feelings about his or her profession and on his or her practice conduct.

The end of each chapter (except Chapter 12) contains a section titled "Skill Development Exercises." These exercises include discussion questions, case analyses, and role plays that coordinate with the various topics presented in the chapter. The exercises can be used in agency training, in academic classes, or for individual learning. Discussion questions can be posed to a training group as a whole, or participants can be divided into small groups of three to five. Case analyses can be done individually or in small groups, or the cases can be used as illustrations in a training session. Role plays can be used by participants in pairs or in groups of three, in which two individuals participate in the role play and the third person acts as an observer to provide feedback. At the end of the book I provide a model syllabus for a course on "Understanding and Managing Violence and Safety in Social Work Practice."

It is my intention in this book to provide social work students, social work educators, practitioners, supervisors, agency administrators, and policymakers with the kind of guidance that will serve to change the following Scenario 1 to Scenario 2:

SCENARIO 1

A child protective services social worker was asked to make a home visit to investigate a report of suspected child abuse. The social worker took the report and immediately drove out to the client's home. Without hesitation, she walked up to the front door, rang the doorbell, and, when the client answered, identified herself as being from child protective services. The client became angry and began swearing at the worker. The worker insisted on entering the client's home, upon which the client grabbed the worker and tore out a chunk of her hair. The worker fought with the client, managed to escape, ran to her car, and drove away. By the time she got back to the agency, she was shaking and crying. For the next week, she was unable to return to work.

SCENARIO 2

A child protective services social worker was asked to make a home visit to investigate a report of suspected child abuse. Prior to making the home visit, the worker checked carefully in the computerized records to see if previous reports had been filed. No reports had been filed on that particular client, but cross-checking revealed that the client's husband had been accused of abuse 2 years before. At that time, the investigating worker had reported that the husband had threatened him and that firearms were in the home. With this information, the worker told her supervisor that she would make a home visit only if another worker accompanied her and if she was given a cell phone. Both workers drove to the client's home and parked a block away. They surveyed the neighborhood and then cautiously approached the house. They rang the doorbell but stood at the edge of the porch. The client opened the door, the social workers identified themselves, and the client became angry and began swearing at the workers. They immediately turned around and left, called the police from their cell phone, and then waited for the police to arrive. Accompanied by the police, the workers went back to the client's home to interview the client safely. Following the interview, the two workers returned to the agency to complete the next steps of the investigation.

If you compare these two scenarios, you can see several junctures at which either the approach or the intervention was altered to achieve the goal of reducing risk for violence. As a result of these changes, the outcome of Scenario 2, unlike Scenario 1, was that the client assessment was completed safely and both workers were able to continue with the investigation.

SKILL DEVELOPMENT EXERCISES

Discussion Questions

1. Is violence toward social workers simply a barometer for our violent society, or does it stem from the type of work that we do? Explain your answer.

2. How do we as social workers deal with the dilemma of caring for clients while engaging in duties that involve social control, for example, removing an abused child from the parent's home or hospitalizing a client involuntarily?

3. Think about U.S. social policy and how it functions as an underpinning to various social problems, such as violent behavior. What social policy changes might reduce violence risk?

4. Do you think that it is appropriate to expect mental health professionals to predict violence in the short term? Why or why not?

Part I

Violence and Social Work Practice

Chapter 1

Violence in Our Society and in Our Workplaces

VIOLENCE IN OUR SOCIETY

H. Rap Brown, the African American militant activist, once observed that violence "is as American as cherry pie" (Weeks, 1982). Brown made this comment in the 1960s, but, in many ways, things have not changed greatly since then. America continues to be an exceptionally violent society (Dionne, 1999). Our country was born out of violence, and violence has been used repeatedly in our history as a means of effecting change and gaining power. The United States is not unique among countries in this regard, but what is unique are some of our attitudes about violence, the role of violent behavior in American popular culture, and the easy availability of firearms, in particular cheap handguns and high-caliber weapons.

Violent behavior is also a staple of our news media, especially local news broadcasts ("if it bleeds, it leads"; Thirteen/WNET, 2001), and popular entertainment, including movies, video games, and music. Popular entertainment is saturated with violence, much of it gratuitous, that sends the underlying message that violence is an acceptable and effective method to solve problems and a means for gaining respect, power, money, and attention. Although the data on the influence of violent media on aggressive behavior are compelling, they do not completely explain why the homicide rate in the United States is higher than the rates in other countries that import America's violent media (Zuckerman, 1996). Clearly, the reasons for America's exceptional level of violence

15

are more complicated. What we do know is that violence in this country is both a social problem and a public health problem ("Violence and the Public's Health," 1993).

Defining Violence

Before discussing some specific issues related to violence in our society and, in particular, client violence toward social workers, I must first define what I mean by the word "violence." If a social worker states that a client punched, stabbed, or shot him or her, that client's behavior would be clearly defined as violent (Monahan, 1981). If, however, a client *threatens to kill* the social worker, should that be considered violence? Some would argue yes, because threats may lead to physical action (Ervin & Lion, 1969; Flannery, Hanson, & Penk, 1995) and because threats alone can cause trauma in the victim (Newhill, in press). Also, many clinicians experience abusive language from a client as frightening and a form of violence even if it does not constitute an actual threat. Should a definition of violence include only physical action and not verbal action? Sarbin (1967) argues that a definition of violence should be limited to physical behavior involving action. Others define violence as including only injury or death to *persons* (see, e.g., Rubin, 1972) and not damage to property, whereas others (see, e.g., Mulvihill & Tumin, 1969) include damage to either persons or property. It is not clear where threats fit in these definitions.

The working definition of violence utilized by the National Commission on the Causes and Prevention of Violence (Mulvihill & Tumin, 1969) addresses the direct application of force resulting in some form of injury or destruction to persons or property. This definition includes physical attacks, threats, and property damage and appears on the surface to be a good one; however, a couple of issues confound its acceptance. The first is the issue of legality. If one ignores whether the act is legal and examines only the act itself, then certain legal injuries, such as surgical procedures, would be categorized as violence. Or, if one looks only at legality, then certain legal actions, such as government-sanctioned genocide of a selected group of people, would not be considered to be violence. Furthermore, what about unintentional or accidental damage, such as injuries resulting from a plane crash? Would such events be considered "violence"?

Let's look at how a well-established dictionary, a source that, presumably, would be ideologically neutral and objective, defines violence. *Webster's Third New International Dictionary* (Gove, 1971) states that violence may be defined as

Exertion of any physical force so as to injure or abuse (as in warfare or in effecting an entrance to a house) . . . an instance of violent treatment or procedure . . . injury in the form of revoking, repudiation, distortion, infringement, or irreverence to a thing, notion, or quality fitly valued or observed . . . intense, turbulent, or furious action, force, or feeling . . . vehement feeling or expression. (p. 2554)

This definition seems to include a wide range of incidents, including physical attacks, threats, and property damage, and comes close to the definition of violence to be used for the purpose of this book and the definition used in my Client Violence Toward Social Workers Study (hereafter referred to as the CV Study) (Newhill, 1996).

Putting all of this together, then, I define violence as including *intentional* (not accidental) incidents of actual physical attacks, attempted physical attacks, threats, and property damage. An *actual physical attack* is defined as an incident in which an individual directly lays hands or a weapon on another individual with the intent to harm; an *attempted physical attack* is defined as an incident in which an individual attempts to intentionally physically attack another individual but does not make actual physical contact; a *threat* is defined as a verbal or written threat to harm another individual or a deliberate threatening physical gesture (including stalking) from one individual toward another; and *property damage* is defined as an incident in which an individual intentionally damages another individual's personal property or property the individual was using at the time of the incident (Newhill, 1996). As can be seen, these definitions include both physical action and threats of physical action, along with harm to both persons and property.

Why is achieving a good working definition of violence important to social work practitioners? It is important because only when we define violence clearly will we be able to talk about it clearly, develop appropriate safety plans, and report, accurately and meaningfully, incidents that do occur. We have to define what we are talking about before we can do anything about it.

The Cost of Violence

The cost of violence to our society is tremendous. It includes the pain and suffering of the victim and the victim's family; medical expenses to victims; lost productivity due to injuries; expenditures for mental health services to deal with trauma reactions; expenditures for police, social services, courts, investigations, and incarcerations; and financial support of victims (e.g., through public assistance, domestic violence shelters, foster care for victimized children, etc.).

In 1990, the U.S. federal and state prison systems alone spent $11.5 billion on incarceration (Greenfield, 1992), with an estimate of $75 billion for all criminal justice expenditures (Lindgren, 1990). The Bureau of Justice Statistics reported that in 1999, the number of adults in the United States who were under the direction of federal, state, and local correctional supervision rose 3% to a record high of 6,288,600 individuals. This figure includes those in jails and prisons, plus those on probation or parole. Reasons for this increase include toughened sentencing standards, an increase in community supervision, and the building of more prisons ("Record Number of Adults in Prison," 2000).

In addition to these costs, one may calculate victim loss in dollars. The National Crime Victimization Survey of 1992 estimated that cost to be $17.6 billion (Klaus, 1994). Because not all violent crime is detected or reported, such figures are underestimates. Clearly, violence exacts a heavy cost to individuals, families, communities, institutions, government, and our society as a whole.

The Role of Guns

What we have today in America is a lethal combination of a violence-prone culture and a gun culture that supports "gun laws that are more permissive than in any comparable nation" (Dionne, 1999, p. A21). Fifty-two percent of the approximately 25,000 murders that occur each year in the United States involve handguns (American Psychological Association Commission on Violence and Youth, 1993). This number contrasts to only 128 yearly handgun murders in Canada, 97 in Switzerland, and 60 in Japan (Handgun Control, 1995). In fact, the number of people killed by guns in a typical week in the United States is greater than the number of people killed in all of Europe over the course of a year (Bellesiles, 2000). The United States also provided more than half of all weapons sold on the worldwide market during 2000, particularly to developing countries (Shanker, 2001).

It is true that our constitution includes an amendment that specifies the right to bear arms. Constitutional scholars, however, have argued for decades that the intent and proper interpretation of the amendment is that it provides American citizens with the right to organize a militia with arms as a means to preserve democratic freedom should the government evolve into autocratic tyranny. The founding fathers did not intend the amendment to mean that every citizen has the individual right to own multiple handguns, nor, at the time the amendment was formulated, did they anticipate the level of firepower available today. Furthermore, Americans have not been armed to the teeth since the birth of our nation. In colonial America, gun ownership was rare and strictly regulated by the government. Only since the Civil War and the age of industrialization has gun ownership become increasingly common, with the gun culture central to America's identity (Bellesiles, 2000). The notion that the gun has always been an important part of American history and American culture is largely a myth.

A 2000 *Washington Post*–ABC News national survey reports that nearly one in four Americans say that they have personally been threatened with a gun, with 10% of adults reporting that someone has taken a shot at them at least once. Nearly half of all Americans—45%—stated that they keep at least one firearm in their home (Morin & Deane, 2000). "I think [the survey] shows that . . . gun ownership . . . is about as mainstream as one can get in America," said Bill Powers, director of public affairs for the National Rifle Association (Morin & Deane, 2000, p. A22). Nevertheless, two out of three of the poll respondents said that gun laws should be strengthened.

Recently, however, in a reversal of "decades of official government policy on the meaning of the Second Amendment, the Justice Department told the Supreme Court for the first time [on May 6, 2002] that the Constitution 'broadly protects the rights of individuals' to own firearms' " (Greenhouse, 2002, p. 30), incorporating the view of Attorney General John Ashcroft. Rather than interpreting the Second Amendment as protecting a collective state right to organize a militia, Ashcroft stated in a letter to the National Rifle Association last year that it "unequivocally" protects the *individual right* to keep and bear firearms (Herbert, 2002).

The current status of gun-related violence in our country consists of both good news and bad news. The good news is that although the media highly publicize grisly shootings, and although most Americans are given the impression that gun violence is in the rise, statistics show that the number of shooting deaths in the United States has actually dropped in recent years. The number of gun-related deaths dropped to 32,436 in 1997 from a high of 39,595 in 1993. The bad news is that in 1995, the latest year for which statistics are available, 5,280 children under the age of 19 died from firearms injuries, representing a significant increase from the previous decade (Johnston, 1999). Furthermore, 57% of individuals who commit suicide kill themselves with a gun (Slaby, 2001). Thus, as social workers, our efforts to encourage nonviolent alternatives to problem resolution and safety for ourselves, our clients, and our communities is juxtaposed against a litany of messages in our culture that encourage the expression of violence.

Violence in our Schools

Violence among young people in our society is currently a topic of renewed discussion, sparked by a series of school shootings perpetrated by preteen and adolescent males that have occurred over the past 6 years. In particular, the mass murder and suicides committed by Eric Harris and Dylan Klebold on April 20, 1999, at Columbine High School in Littleton, Colorado, in which 14 students and a teacher were killed and numerous other students seriously injured, has brought the topic of violence once again into the forefront of public and political debate (Johnson & Brooke, 1999). This debate, however, has primarily taken the form of attempts to pinpoint blame by rounding up the usual suspects (and a few new suspects) and engaging in much chest-thumping and hand-wringing without much coordinated substantive action as a society. Who or what can we blame? Violent Internet Web sites? Violent movies? Violent video games (e.g., "Doom" and "Quake")? Heavy metal nihilistic rock music? Poor parenting? Television? Negligent teachers and school administrators? Large schools? Too much testosterone? Youth? Gender? Access to firearms?

In actuality none of these factors *alone* is sufficient to cause what happened at Columbine High School or to explain the cause of most other incidents of violent behavior. Violence is a *multifaceted multidimensional phenomenon* resulting from the interaction of a combination of factors. There is no simple unidimensional linear explanation or linear solution. The school shootings that have occurred recently do contain some common threads that, tied together, form a lethal combination. These threads include: an easy access to firearms with sophisticated knowledge of how to use them; the stresses of adolescence in kids who do not know how to handle them in a healthy, nonviolent way and who have not received the adult attention and guidance to learn healthy coping strategies; and a tacit tolerance by adults for violence among adolescent peers (Lewin, 1998a). Adults sometimes forget how cruel adolescents in middle and high school can be and the terrible psychological and physical toll that bullies can extract from their victims (Hudgins, 1999). It is far too common for kids to be pushed around, shoved into lockers, and beaten up by other kids. The vast majority of kids who are victimized in this way and who are treated as outcasts do not act out violently in revenge. But they do sometimes "suffer real fear at the hands of others their age" (Hudgins, 1999, p. A22), and it is up to adults to intervene and stop such behavior. Unfortunately, many times adults simply drop the ball, and the child is left to cope as best he or she can.

It is also significant that all of these shootings have been perpetrated by boys. When something goes wrong for girls, they tend to strike inward and harm themselves (Simmons, 2002). For boys, the tendency is to strike outward toward others. The reality, too, is that Eric Harris and Dylan Klebold, no matter how violent their thoughts and no matter how many violent video games they played or how much they were taunted by classmates, would not have been capable of taking so many lives with so little effort in so short a period of time without the level of firepower they had at their disposal (Glassner, 1999). Guns per se did not directly cause whatever motivated their actions, but guns served as the mechanism by which they were able to act on those thoughts and cause the deaths of other people. The types of guns they had access to enabled them to kill many people very quickly. As Thomas Friedman (1999) commented:

> The idea that two high school kids were able to amass an arsenal that included an Intratec fingerprint-resistant, high-volume assault weapon; a Hi-Point 9-millimeter carbine; a sawed-off pump-action shotgun, and a sawed-off double barreled shotgun should make anyone who opposes gun control ashamed. (p. A31)

The focus of this book is not guns and gun control; however, it is important to note that weapons often make the difference between simply thinking violent thoughts, making threats, or even injuring someone and taking action that leads to a fatality. "The vast majority of shooting victims arrive at the hospital as a result of a trivial altercation that turned deadly because the combatants could easily resort to weapons" (Johnston, 1999, p. 5). When the Founding Fathers conceptualized the right to bear arms, whether as a militia or individually, they were envisioning heavy, awkward muskets, not handguns or automatic weapons. We as Americans must think long and hard about whether our current interpretation of the right to bear arms is worth this kind of loss of life. If one were to replay the Columbine scenario and substitute slingshots for the guns, the outcome would be drastically different (Lewin, 1998a).

Taking Action

In response to public, media, and governmental concern that school violence is a pressing national problem, many states have commissioned studies to determine the incidence and prevalence of school violence and to draft legislation to guide school policy development (Furlong, Babinski, Poland, & Munoz, 1996; James, 1994). Most of the research on school violence has focused more attention on students and less on parents, teachers, or other school personnel such as school social workers (Astor, Behre, Fravil & Wallace, 1997), although research has shown that 92% of the public supports violence training for school personnel (Elam, Rose, & Gallup, 1994).

To address the lack of data on the issue of school violence from the perspective of school personnel, the National Association of Social Workers, in collaboration with researchers at the University of Michigan, undertook a study of school social workers to learn their perceptions and experiences with school violence (Astor et al., 1997). The researchers found that the social workers tended to minimize the violence that they reported had occurred in their schools. This finding is consistent with the retrospective reports acknowledging that "red flags" had occurred prior to some of the school shootings but had been ignored or minimized by parents, school officials, and law enforcement personnel. For example, law enforcement officials in Littleton, Colorado, admitted that they had done little to follow up on a complaint that one of the teenage killers "talks often of making pipe bombs and using them to kill numerous people" (Brooke, 1999).

It is important, however, to put all of this into a broader perspective. In spite of the well-publicized incidents of violence in our schools over the past few years, school is still one of the safest places for a child or adolescent, and, in fact, violence in our schools overall has not risen over the past few years (Lewin, 1998b; Stolberg, 1999). What is new is that young white males in our hinterland have committed several multiple murders on school campuses over the past 3 years. White kids killing other white kids in affluent suburban schools attracts a lot of media attention.

An Angry Culture

What is it that supports and feeds our violent society? Some have argued that part of it is that we are living in an angry culture that has been evolving for decades. In Paddy Chayefsky's script for the 1976 movie *Network*, Howard Beale, a news anchor at a fictitious television network, is fired for threatening to commit suicide on the air with the purpose of improving declining news show ratings. As ratings continue to fall, the vice president of programming states that, to improve, the news show must provide what the American people want, saying: "The American people want someone to articulate their rage for them. . . . I want angry shows." Howard Beale is rehired in the role of host for a variety show that attempts to articulate the public's rage: "Howard must be an angry prophet denouncing the hypocrisy of our times," as one of his colleagues puts it. At one point during the show, Beale raises his fists and tells his audience that he is "mad as hell and I'm not going to take it anymore!" The audience goes wild; people all over America open their windows and yell, "I'm mad as hell, and I'm not going to take it anymore!" Immediately, the ratings soar, and Howard Beale is elevated to media-star status. Eventually, however, Beale and his show self-destruct, illustrating how damaging such collective amorphous rage can be.

Today, we have coined a variety of terms for different types of public rage, perhaps in an attempt to explain the violence surrounding us and, with that explanation, to feel as though we have some measure of control. We have "road rage" to name and explain human acts of violence on our roadways. How does one explain an incident in which a young man is stabbed to death by another young man whose car he passed? Road rage. Or what could be the motive behind the murder of a 32-year-old woman who is shot in the head after her husband cut off another man in traffic? Road rage. But does road rage really exist as a unique phenomenon? In answer to my question about whether he ever had feelings of wanting to harm others, a former client said:

> "I have big time road rage. Big time. If somebody cuts me off or disrespects me somehow, watch out. Nobody has that right . . . uh-uh . . . I stand up for myself, you know what I mean? Drop of a hat, man, I'm ready to fight. Good thing I don't keep a gun in my car. I mean, I'd use it."

I responded to his statement by pointing out that sometimes people make mistakes. For example, someone might cut him off in traffic without meaning to. He scratched his head, considered that possibility, and then concluded that it didn't matter. Disrespect was disrespect. The legitimate consequence, regardless of the motive, was to express revenge. Where does such entitlement to revenge come from? Experts say that it is typically sparked by a fragile, exaggerated sense of honor, extreme oversensitivity to slights, and lack of a sense of proportion (Kaminer, 1995). Exactly what this means is discussed in Chapter 5.

Some argue, however, that although altercations between drivers on our roadways may be fairly common (although there is no national database to confirm this), *fatalities* caused by angry drivers are still very rare, at a rate of about one death per year in this country on average (Glassner, 1999). This finding underscores one of the primary obstacles to violence research in general, the *low base rate* (Monahan, 1981). This term means that violence is a comparatively rare event. This is true whether one is talking about a school shooting or a roadway fatality due to an angry altercation or a bank robbery. It is this rarity that makes violence difficult to predict.

Rage and anger do play a role in violent behavior, however, and a thorough exploration of where such rage comes from would constitute another book. The roots of human rage are multidimensional and individually shaped and lie in a variety of sources, from the long-term consequences of antiauthoritarian attitudes in the 1960s to the cynicism toward government, politicians, and social institutions that began with the Watergate scandal in the 1970s to the greed-is-good mantra of the 1980s. The problems have continued with the increasing chasm between the "haves" and the "have-nots" in the 1990s, as our social safety net has shredded in the name of welfare reform and more conservative social policies have taken hold. Finally, of course, there was the terrible September 11, 2001, terrorist attack, which resulted in trauma for thousands of immediate victims and family members and a pervasive sense of vulnerability for the American people as a whole (Goode & Eakin, 2002). All of these issues and events form the social fabric within which we and our clients live and work. Societal trend watchers have suggested, though, that there are additional qualitative aspects of late 21st-century life that have contributed to the development of an "angry culture."

James Gleick (1999) suggests that our modern age of information technology has one key quality: acceleration. Everything in life runs faster than ever before, and the effort to accommodate such pressure creates stress that makes people irritable and angry. One of the strange paradoxes of modern life is that, although we fill our lives with time-saving strategies and devices, we feel more rushed than ever (Gleick, 1999). This sense of pressure and acceleration can be accommodated to a degree, but for some people, it contributes to dissatisfaction with life and anger that, under certain circumstances, may lead to violence.

Leslie Charles (1999) identifies 10 aspects of modern life that affect us individually and collectively and that, she argues, help explain this sense of acceleration and play a role in the creation of a cultural "anger epidemic." These aspects include the following:

- *Compressed time*: the constant experience of having too many things to do and too little time to do them in.
- *Communication overload*: he constant bombardment of information simultaneously from multiple sources 24 hours a day.
- *Disconnectedness*: being physically or electronically connected to others but without meaningful emotional intimacy that is nurturing and supportive (the role of positive social support in preventing violence is highlighted in Chapter 5).
- *Cost*: not having enough money and other resources to live comfortably while living in a society of unbridled consumerism, entitlement, and enormous wealth for a relatively small proportion of the population.

- *Competition*: increasing demands to achieve status, power, and profit with fewer resources available to achieve them.
- *Customer contact*: too many people to deal with, especially in the service area (including social work services), and contacts that are cold, unpleasant, uncaring, and frustrating, leading to an "assembly-line" feeling (managed care may be an example).
- *Computers*: coping with the pressure of learning to use various kinds of technology, increasing dependence on computers to function at home and work, as well as being constantly on call due to e-mail, faxes, cell phones, pagers, beepers, and so forth.
- *Change*: social and technological change that moves at a pace faster than the ability of many people to adapt comfortably.
- *Coming of age*: significant changes in the nature, experiences, and expectations of the various life cycle stages due to both sociological influences and changes brought by medical and health care advances.
- *Complexity*: coping with all these aspects.

In Charles's (1999) analysis, these 10 aspects of modern life can lead to a general atmosphere of stress, irritability, frustration, anger, and hostility, and these particular emotions often underlie and precede violent behavior.

VIOLENCE IN OUR WORKPLACES

The violence we find in our society also manifests itself in our work environments. Violence in the workplace has become a critical issue in the United States for a wide range of workers, including jitney and bus drivers, convenience store clerks, nurses, teachers, probation and parole officers, security guards, white-collar office workers, and social workers. For the purpose of this discussion, the term "workplace" is defined as "the primary physical location where an individual works, involving any time an individual is at work or on duty" (Seeck, 1998, p. 3), including time spent in the field and traveling to and from work.

Although violence has always been inherent in certain occupations, such as law enforcement, correctional work in jails and prisons, security work, and military combat, violence is now reported in occupations traditionally assumed to be "safe," such as social work. Johnson and Kinney (1993) report that approximately 111,000 acts of workplace violence occurred in 1992, a rate of about 425 per workday. Serious incidents of workplace violence can cost an employer $250,000 or more, and it is estimated that the annual cost to employers overall is about

$4.2 billion. Thus the problem of workplace violence is both a business problem and a problem of liability (Dunkel, 1994).

Although many employers, both public and private, have taken substantial steps to establish policies and strategies to ensure employee safety, social service agencies still lag behind the efforts of much of the corporate world. Until recently, the topic of violence as a workplace safety issue was rarely addressed in either the social work practice literature or social work education. In fact, most of the literature in this area is still confined to psychiatry, business, and legal sources. Yet it is social workers who are most often on the front lines in high-risk settings such as children and youth services, emergency room services, criminal justice services, drug and alcohol services, and mental health services. Furthermore, social workers often work in high-risk environments such as in clients' homes and shelters and out on the streets, sometimes during the highest risk evening and night hours. Thus, when one looks at the reality of social work practice today, the fact that violence is an issue for the profession is not as surprising as it might seem at first glance. Unfortunately, safety measures are often put into place only *after* a violent incident takes place . A good example is a comment from one of the CV Study respondents:

> "We had been asking for a security guard to be hired for our walk-in clinic for some time now. It wasn't until a client tore out a handful of my hair as we were trying to escort him down to the inpatient unit that administration finally listened. I was glad we got the guard but am resentful that I had to pay the price for it."

As I discuss in this chapter, social services and the social work profession can learn much from the corporate world and, unfortunately, from the many workplace tragedies that have prompted businesses to take workplace violence seriously.

Prevalence of Workplace Violence

In 1993, the U.S. Bureau of Labor Statistics reported that there were 1,062 work-related homicides in the United States, with homicide being the second leading cause of death in the American workplace for that year (Harrison & Gillen, 1996; U.S. Department of Labor, 1994a). Firearms are the lethal weapon in 75% of workplace deaths (Labig, 1995), with robbery being the primary motive (U.S. Department of Labor, 1994b). Handling money at work during evening or night hours is the kind of situation at highest risk for workplace homicide. Two of the most dangerous lines of work in this regard are prostitution and jitney or taxicab driving, because both involve being in an enclosed area alone with a stranger, often at night, handling cash transactions, and being unprotected by the presence of others or by being in a public space. During the first half of 2000, almost one dozen cab drivers were murdered in New York City alone. Although social workers generally do not handle cash transactions with clients, they are often in the similar position—particularly with home visits—of being in an enclosed area (the client's home) with a person (the client) whom the worker may not know well, or who may even be a stranger, without having others around. The advantages of a team approach to home visiting cannot be underestimated, and this precaution is discussed in detail later.

Nonfatal workplace violence is much more common than workplace fatalities across occupations, including social work. The Northwestern Life Insurance Company (1993) released a study that reported that one out of every four workers was harassed, threatened, or attacked on the job between July 1992 and July 1993. This study has been criticized for its small sample size and low response rate, but it is an indicator that suggests the prevalence of nonfatal workplace violence (Seeck, 1998). Statistical data related to workplace violence is collected by several federal agencies, including the Federal Bureau of Investigation (FBI), the National Institute for Occupational Safety and Health (NIOSH), the Occupational Safety and Health Administration (OSHA), and the Bureau of Labor Statistics. There are also a variety of state and private organizations that collect workplace injury data (U.S. Department of Labor, 1994a, 1994b; White, 1996). There is, however, no national database that tracks workplace violence data specifically for social workers.

How does the United States compare with other countries in the incidence and prevalence of workplace violence? The good news is that the United States actually has a *lower* incidence of work-related violence than many other countries, according to a survey conducted by the International Labor Organization (ILO), a United Nations agency. This survey, the first multinational effort to examine the prevalence of workplace violence around the world, was conducted jointly in 1996 by the Dutch Ministry of Justice, the United National Interregional Crime and Justice Research Institute, and the Home Office of the United Kingdom (Grimsley, 1998). The survey was prompted by a series of violent international events in 1996, including an elementary school shooting in Scotland that left 16 people dead; a mass murder in a national park in Tasmania, Australia that left 35 people dead; and an armed hostage-taking situation in Paris, France, that involved teachers and students at a school (Grimsley, 1998).

For the survey, in-person and telephone interviews were conducted with random samples of workers 16 and older from 33 different countries regarding whether they had been victims of crime or had experienced any assaults at work over the previous year. If so, they were asked to describe the event, the circumstances surrounding it, and how it affected them. The ILO defined the term "assault" as a frightening threat or physical attack. The combined sample size across countries totaled 130,000 respondents. Findings included the following:

- The types of incidents reported by respondents included rape, sexual harassment, battering, kicking, biting, punching, stalking, stabbing, shooting, verbal threats, burning of the victim's flesh, dousing the victim with toxic chemicals, and attempted murder.
- Male workers in the United States were assaulted less often than male workers in several other countries. Only 1% of American men reported threats or attacks at work, as compared with 1.7% of the men in Sweden, 3.2% in Uganda, 3.6% in the Netherlands, and 6.1% in Argentina.
- Although American women reported higher rates of assault (4.2%) than women in many developing nations (e.g., only 1.1% of Indonesian women reported assaults), women in several other countries, including Finland, France, Argentina, Uganda, and Northern Ireland, reported much higher rates of assault (Grimsley, 1998).
- No occupation was free from reports of crime and violence (Grimsley, 1998).

What these findings suggest is that violence in the workplace is not just an American problem; it is a global problem affecting all occupations across many countries and cultures. Vittorio Di Martino, senior specialist on working conditions for the ILO, cautioned that it is difficult to make direct comparisons across different countries because the nature and prevalence of certain crimes differ from country to country; also, cultural variance can affect how and whether certain crimes and assaults are reported (Grimsley, 1998). For example, kidnapping wealthy executives for ransom is a common crime in many Latin American countries but happens only rarely in the United States. Or, in countries torn by civil war or tribal animosities, general lawlessness may be present that goes well beyond the workplace. Also, in some cultures, the acceptance of sexual harassment and abuse of women is deeply ingrained, and thus such incidents are not viewed as worthy of being reported. In contrast, in countries in which sexual harassment and abuse have received public attention that identifies them as unacceptable and in which women can turn to the law for protection, women are more likely to report such behaviors.

Classifying Workplace Violence

Some of the agencies that collect data on workplace violence classify such violence into different types to facilitate interpretation of the figures. OSHA, for example, identifies three types of workplace violence: Type I, Type II, and Type III (Kraus & McArthur, 1996). *Type I* violence is the most common and involves the kind of high-risk setting described (previously, that is, robbery of a late-night or 24-hour small business, such as a convenience or liquor store. *Type II* violence includes incidents in which an employee is assaulted by someone who is receiving services from the employee's workplace, that is, the individual is a client or patient. Client violence toward a social worker would be classified as a Type II incident. Finally, *Type III* violence involves incidents in which the perpetrator him- or herself has some kind of employment-related connection with the workplace. The person may be a coworker, an ex-employee, or a supervisor. In the CV Study survey, no questions were asked directly about violence by coworkers; however, some respondents volunteered information that they had experienced violence at the hands of social work or other colleagues. For example, one respondent reported an incident in which she was persistently stalked by an coworker whom she had supervised previously. The suspected motive, according to the respondent, was probably anger and retaliation because of earlier supervisory conflicts over job performance.

Another classification scheme divides workplace violence into two types: internal and external (Maxey, 1997). *Internal workplace violence* is defined as incidents in which the perpetrator is familiar with supervisors and coworkers. A fired employee who returns to the workplace and kills his supervisor or coworkers is an example of an internal incident of workplace violence. *External workplace violence* is defined as incidents in which the violence is perpetrated by third parties who are unfamiliar with the people who work there, as in the case of a bank robbery committed by individuals who do not work for the bank.

Incidents of client violence toward social workers typically fall within the internal violence category, even in situations in which the incident occurs during the first contact with the worker. The random killing with an instrumental motive, such as robbery, in which the perpetrator is completely unfamiliar with the social worker or the agency, is rare simply due to the nature of the business of social service versus, for example, a liquor or convenience store. Nearly half of workplace homicides occur in food-related businesses, particularly those with transient traffic and close proximity to money. Robberies, for example, commonly occur as workers lock up a restaurant for the night or make money drop-offs (Maxey, 1997).

Obtaining drugs is often a motive for attacks on nursing personnel in hospitals, particularly emergency rooms. Like food businesses, emergency rooms serve transient traffic and have direct access to drugs as part of their normal course of business. By and large, social workers are not in the business of handling large sums of money during the night, nor are they medical professionals likely to be handling drugs that are desirable to addicts. Social workers do work in emergency services, however, and are exposed to the risks inherent in serving clients who are in crisis.

Causes of Violence in the Workplace

Workplace violence is not just a reflection of our violent society but involves the interaction of our society with specific dynamics of the modern workplace, which have significantly changed over the past 20 years. As noted, we have always expected violence to occur in certain types of jobs that are inherently dangerous and have been traditionally male dominated, such as law enforcement or the military. Employees in such professions expect and are trained to handle dangerous situations (Kelleher, 1997). What is new is that workplace violence increasingly occurs in occupations that have not been traditionally viewed as dangerous places to work and that are more likely to be female dominated, such as nursing, teaching, and social work.

What are the specific dynamics in the workplace that play a role in workplace violence? Johnson and Kinney (1993) argue that workplace violence is a cultural trend activated by a number of social and economic factors. In a healthy society, a variety of social control forces serve to inhibit destructive behaviors by the members of the society. Such forces include an economic system that supports full employment with adequate wages, along with an adequate safety net for those who cannot work, a legal system that prevents crime and creates a protective environment for all citizens, and a cultural system that promotes orderly behavior and discourages disorderly behavior. Violence is more likely to occur when these social control processes, which operate as protective factors, are absent or ineffective. The probability is enhanced when certain critical risk factors are also present.

Risk factors that enhance the probability of violence occurring in the workplace emanate from our increasingly hyperactive, competitive, market-driven economy. Such factors include an acutely overstressed population of workers, changing and unstable family and community structures, and innumerable self-proclaimed victims produced by what author Robert Hughes calls "the culture of complaint" (Dunkle, 1994; Hughes, 1992).

This market-driven economy, combined with the constant glamorization of violence by popular culture, an overabundance of inexpensive firearms, and massive economic changes over the past two decades that have had a major impact on average workers, can produce a lethal situation (Johnson & Kinney, 1993). Furthermore, the contemporary workforce is increasingly emphasizing multiculturalism, diversity, and gender equity, amounting to a revolution in the modern workforce and contributing to the number of scapegoats for anger, as well as to mixed signals and differing values that can spark conflict. Because valuing diversity and cultural competence is deeply ingrained in the social work value base, open acknowledgment of the existence of racism, sexism, and other discriminatory forces within our ranks is particularly emotionally charged.

The rapid transition to a high-tech global economy also plays a significant role in workplace violence. Aggressive corporate downsizing, in particular, is creating a multitude of "psychologically walking wounded who have seen their job prospects and self-respect evaporate" in the name of global competition and profit (Dunkel, 1994, p. 40). Businesses that downsize while still enjoying good profits create particular anger in workers. Whereas in the 1970s, 80% of all displaced workers could find comparable replacement jobs, now the total is around 25% (Johnson & Kinney, 1993). For people whose sense of self-worth and identity is primarily rooted in their jobs or careers, fear of or actual loss of a job or being laid off are extremely traumatic events. Men, in particular, are vulnerable due to deeply held cultural expectations of what it means to be a successful man, and, although comparatively few men respond with violence, many men feel cheated and let down by a system they had trusted (Faludi, 1999). Mark Barton, who in July 1999 murdered his family and then killed nine people at the brokerage firm where he did day trading, stated in a suicide note: "I wake up at night so afraid . . . I have come to hate this life and this system of things. I have come to have no hope" (Sack, 1999). These factors have implications for prevention. When we think about preventing violence, we usually immediately think of making the physical workplace environment more secure, for example, installing metal detectors or hiring security guards. But these measures will not affect many of the factors noted here, which play key roles in the development of a violence-prone workplace setting.

Corporate Responses to Incidents of Workplace Violence

How do corporate businesses respond in the wake of an incident of workplace violence? Responses run the gamut, from a complete lack to good constructive responses. Sometimes the response is to blame the victim. For example, an employee of a prominent Fortune 500 company in

Washington was gang-raped in broad daylight in the firm's parking lot. Because her attackers threatened to kill her if she reported the crime, the victim was hesitant to file a police report. Her supervisors, however, refused to improve security until she filed a report. Finally, a friend of the victim's stepped in and complained, noting that the most unresponsive of the supervisors were the women. Why? The friend's conclusion was that the underlying dynamic was *denial*—that is, if you blame the victim, you can avoid acknowledging that you too are vulnerable (Dunkel, 1994). Social workers are hardly immune to denial; in fact, the role of our collective denial as an obstacle to preventing client violence is discussed more fully in Chapter 2.

Increasingly, however, many companies are providing support, including on-site counseling and temporary leave for victims and witnesses of workplace violence. Providing counseling at the work site is often preferable to off-site help because many workers see the workplace and their coworkers as family, and getting support from them, along with the counseling, is better than being alone at home (Bizjak, 1988).

Sometimes it takes a while for workers to recover psychologically, and anniversaries of traumatic events can be particularly difficult. Recognizing this fact, the U.S. Post Office in Edmond, Oklahoma, has given employees the day off on the anniversary of a mass murder that occurred there and has continued to provide counseling as long as employees need it. Immediately after the massacre, the Edmond Post Office repainted the offices, rearranged the desks and furniture, and brought in new supervisors as a way of symbolically starting over (Bizjak, 1988).

How management responds in the wake of an incident of workplace violence is a very critical factor in helping the victimized worker to recover from the trauma. A callous or dismissive response can be very damaging. After being threatened by a client, a former social work colleague asked her supervisor for help. The response from the supervisor was "if it's too hot, get out of the kitchen." Needless to say, this was not a helpful response and, in fact, undermined the colleague's confidence in herself as a social worker.

CONCLUSION

The dynamics of violence as a central element of our society is but one of many factors relevant to understanding client violence toward social workers. A violent society is also often an angry society lacking in stability, security, connectedness, and a strong sense of community. Many of our clients are living extraordinarily difficult lives and must struggle with multiple challenges and problems every day. They may be struggling with poverty, mental illness, drug addiction, family troubles, legal hassles, and living in a dangerous disintegrating community. Sometimes we can help, but, unfortunately, sometimes we cannot. Most of the time our clients recognize what we can do and what we cannot do and are remarkably understanding of the limitations of what we are able to offer.

Violence in the workplace is a concern that cuts across occupations, countries, and cultures. Although the majority of workers still will not experience violence on the job, the number of workers who do has been significant enough to prompt the business community to take steps in the direction of both prevention and intervention. Although there has been some research in this area, there is still a lot we do not know about the incidence, prevalence, and nature of workplace violence. For example, there is still no comprehensive national database that tracks workplace violence and professional social work practice. However, we know enough to conclude that such violence should be taken seriously, and much can be done to both protect workers and intervene with potentially violent clients, customers, and coworkers to prevent the occurrence of more incidents without compromising the quality of our services. The success of such efforts, however, is also dependent on society's willingness to look at some of the social and economic risk factors that contribute to the development of this phenomenon. This will require some painful soul-searching and changes in how we as a society choose to operate, particularly in terms of the balance between individual rights and the common good.

SKILL DEVELOPMENT EXERCISES

Discussion Questions

1. Do you agree with H. Rap Brown's observation that violence "is as American as cherry pie"? Why or why not?

2. What is the cost of violence for your particular agency? What is the cost of violence for your community? Has your agency or community taken any steps to reduce this cost?

3. To what extent do guns play a role in violence in our society? Should we institute more stringent gun control, and, if so, what should such a policy look like? If not, how do you think society should manage gun-related violence?

4. Does your agency have a safety policy? If so, what does it consist of? If not, why hasn't a safety policy been developed in your agency? How could the development of such a policy be approached?

5. Are we an angry culture? Why or why not?

6. On pages 24–25, several sources of pressure in everyday life in the United States are discussed. Is it possible for us individually or collectively to reduce some of these pressures? If so, how?

7. To your knowledge, have there been any incidents of client violence toward staff in your agency? If so, what were the circumstances and how did the agency respond to the incident?

Chapter 2

Overview of the Incidence and Prevalence of Client Violence toward Social Workers

Over the past two decades, more than two dozen studies have addressed the issue of client violence toward social workers, with the bulk of the studies published since 1988. The United Kingdom led the way in investigating this topic, and, since then, several studies have been conducted in the United States that collectively provide a good picture of the incidence and prevalence of client violence toward social workers.

It is somewhat difficult to compare results across studies because of methodological variations in time frame, sample source, the way violence is defined, types of violence examined, and types of respondents. In general, the studies utilized one or the other of two time frames: violence experienced during a discrete time period (usually 1 or 2 years prior to the study) or violence experienced at any time during the respondents' careers. Time frame is critical to consider when comparing prevalence rates across studies because a prevalence rate for the preceding year will usually be lower than a career prevalence rate.

Another area of methodological variance is the sample source. Some studies use national random samples—usually drawing from a professional organization membership list, such as the National Association of Social Workers (NASW)—whereas other studies use samples from smaller geographic areas, such as a particular city, county, or state. There are also differences in how investigators define violence and which types of violence they choose to investigate. Some studies look only at assaults, others examine threats and/or verbal abuse, others include property damage, and still others study lawsuits and sexual harassment. Some studies address individual practitioners, other studies examine agency reports of violence, and still others address specific respondent subgroupings, such as social work students, children and youth–child protection caseworkers (many of whom are not professionally trained social workers), social services workers in general (both professionally trained social workers and those without formal social work training) and professionally trained social workers. Finally, there are studies that examine human services professionals in which social work is represented as one of several disciplines (most typically psychology, psychiatry, and nursing) included in the sample.

In this chapter, I provide a brief overview of the various studies, highlighting what I believe to be the most relevant findings for you, the practitioner. This section is followed by a discussion of findings from the CV Study that are most applicable to practitioners in terms of understanding what kind of client violence actually occurs in the real world. At the conclusion of the chapter, Table 2.3 summarizes all of the studies on client violence toward social workers in chronological order. The table is organized by study authors, sample source, time frame studied, type of violence studied, and study results and is designed to facilitate a quick review of the research for the reader.

OVERVIEW OF THE LITERATURE

International Studies

Several comprehensive surveys and direct interview studies have been conducted by researchers in the United Kingdom on client violence toward social workers. One of the first efforts to simply identify the topic of client violence as relevant to social work practice was an article (Prins, 1975) examining the management of dangerous clients, with a range of case examples that illustrate common scenarios in which violence may occur, along with suggestions for preventive intervention. Beginning in the mid-1980s, a number of empirical studies were then conducted with the purpose of obtaining practical data on the incidence and prevalence of violence toward social workers in the United Kingdom.

These empirical investigations were spurred by the recognition that attacks against working people were no longer confined to those involved in combat or law enforcement; furthermore, client violence represents a violation of every citizen's right to work in a safe environment (Norris, 1990). Representatives from the British Health Ministry argued that social work exists for the protection and empowerment of those who are most disadvantaged and vulnerable in society, and thus "an attack on those whose task is to help the disadvantaged is an attack on the disadvantaged themselves, even if the attacker comes from within their ranks . . . as such, it is a matter of serious political concern" (Harman, 1990). These efforts, in combination with the murders of several British social workers in a short period of time, spurred the British government to establish a Department of Health and Social Security Advisory Committee to investigate and monitor violence in the social services (Department of Health and Social Security [DHSS], 1988).

With these events as a platform, a number of studies were undertaken in the mid- to late 1980s in the United Kingdom that made significant contributions to understanding the nature and prevalence of client violence. Brown, Bute, and Ford (1986) collected data via a mailed survey questionnaire of social services departments in the Wessex area of the United Kingdom. They found that 53% of the social service staff had been victims of assaults or had been threatened with violence in the 3 years prior to the survey. Field workers, residential care workers, and day care staff were most at risk, probably due to the fact that these workers typically spend more *time at risk*, that is, in face-to-face contact with clients who are often in crisis (Brown et al., 1986)

One of the most systematic investigations was a three-stage project conducted by Rowett (1986). Rowett dispatched a questionnaire to 132 social services departments across the United Kingdom, followed by a mailing to every social worker with direct client contact in one county. Finally, structured interviews were conducted with 60 assaulted social workers and 60 nonassaulted social workers from the same county. In these interviews, Rowett asked the social workers to describe in detail the most serious incident they had experienced and to describe any physical injuries as a result of the incident. Although the majority of reported incidents were considered to be minor, Rowett found a rise in the reported incidence of assaults at each successive stage in the research, suggesting that many assaults are not formally reported to supervisors or administrators and that the actual incidence rate of client violence toward social workers is probably far higher than officially assumed (Rowett, 1986).

Another study, commissioned by the British social service trade union, National and Local Government Officers Association (NALGO), looked at the level of violence experienced by different types of social workers (University of Southampton Department of Social Work Studies, 1989). In this investigation, which was a combination of questionnaires and direct interviews, researchers examined threats and assaults experienced by field and other professional social workers and paraprofessional social services staff. They found that just under 38% of the social workers had experienced or had a colleague who had experienced at least one incident of violence in the 3 months prior to the study. The NALGO study also found that the threat of violence was mainly directed at professional (specialist) social workers, with the number of threats to paraprofessional staff, for example, social work assistants, much lower.

Findings from this body of research led to direct corrective action by the British Association of Social Workers and the British government, clear evidence that violence toward social workers is viewed as an important concern in the United Kingdom. Reporting protocols have been developed in an attempt to combat the bureaucratic obstacles to reporting such incidents, and training programs have been created throughout the United Kingdom to equip social workers with the necessary knowledge and skills to protect themselves while still providing uncompromised service to clients (e.g. Eccles & Tutt, 1987; Wiener & Crosby, 1986).

Informed by the British studies, a study of assaults on social work staff was undertaken in 1990 by a large statutory authority covering a number of social service areas in Scotland (Leadbetter, 1993). This study consisted of four components: a correspondence investigation of what social services departments were doing in the area of managing and preventing violence to staff; a series of interviews with social workers who had experienced a client assault to investigate their perceptions of and reactions to the assault and any other incidents of violence; an analysis of incident reports of violence toward social work staff over a 3-year period; and a "diary study" with staff in three adolescent residential treatment programs to investigate the extent of underreporting of incidents, that is, the extent to which incidents described in the diaries are not reported to management.

Leadbetter (1993) found that total violent incident reports over the 3-year period showed increases in each successive year, with physical assaults predominating over verbal abuse or threats. This finding, however, may reflect reluctance by workers to report nonphysical abuse rather than a higher actual occurrence of physical assaults. Similar to the previous studies in the United Kingdom, the studies in Scotland found that residential staff, particularly those working in children's homes, were most at risk for assault and that male staff across settings were disproportionately represented among assaulted staff. The explanation for the gender difference is unclear, but there are many speculations as to why males are more at risk. For example, Leadbetter suggests that males' enhanced risk may reflect the fact that men use a more confrontational approach, which may be viewed as provocative by certain clients, or that men are more likely to be assigned to settings or to particular clients in which risk of violence is high. It may also reflect a greater willingness of men to report violent incidents.

The intent of the final component of Leadbetter's (1993) study, the diary study, was to explore the relationship between reported and nonreported assaults. Staff were given diary sheets listing a variety of assaultive and abusive behaviors that fell within the range of incidents subject to formal reporting. They filled out the sheets at the end of each day over a 2-week period. On average, each staff member reported 19.3 incidents in their diaries during the 2-week period, yet not one of the incidents was reported via the formal violent incident report procedure. The figures obtained from the formal violent incident reports, however, constitute the basis on which management makes decisions about safety. This finding highlights one of the major suspected problems with assuming that data obtained from incident reports accurately reflect the incident rate of violence by clients toward staff: the issue of underreporting of incidents. This problem is discussed in more detail later in the book.

Guterman, Jayaratne, and Bargal (1996) conducted a cross-national study of American and Israeli social workers to compare incidence rates of workplace violence and victimization. The authors argue that cross-national comparison data can serve to provide clues about culturally based risk factors for violence. Guterman and colleagues mailed questionnaires to random samples of American and Israeli direct-practice social workers and asked respondents whether they had experienced any of six forms of client violence or victimization over the past year: physical threats, physical assaults, threats of a lawsuit, lawsuits filed, verbal abuse, and sexual harassment. Respondents were asked to check a "yes" or "no" box next to each type of violence or victimization listed. Across types of violence and victimization, 48.8% of Americans and 47.4% of Israelis reported at least one incident of some kind over the previous year, with verbal abuse the most common type reported. These findings suggest that victimization by clients crosses national boundaries in similar ways, and thus Americans do not appear to face disproportionate risks of physical violence as compared with Israelis. However, no data were gathered to address the nature and context of the incidents, thus limiting the researchers' ability to examine possible cultural differences in expression of violence.

Finally, in a recent Canadian study (MacDonald & Sirotich, 2001), a random sample of 300 social workers from the 1996 membership directory of the College of Certified Social Workers in Ontario was surveyed regarding reporting behavior of social workers who have been targets of client violence. The researchers found that a majority of the respondents had experienced some form of violence from clients (most commonly verbal harassment) at some point in their careers but that approximately one-fourth did not formally report the incident to management. The most common reasons given by respondents for not reporting an incident were that they perceived the incident as not serious enough to warrant reporting or that "they considered violence a part of the job" (p. 111).

U.S. Studies

The research addressing client violence toward human service professionals in the United States began by addressing professionals in disciplines other than social work, such as psychiatrists (Madden, Lion, & Penna, 1976; Ruben, Wolkon, & Yamamoto, 1980; "Psychiatrist Identifies Physical Clues," 1986), and hospital nursing staff (Lanza, 1983; Levy & Harticollis, 1976; Lion, Snyder, & Merrill, 1981). Four studies, however, looked at allied disciplines that included social work.

In 1972, Whitman, Armao, and Dent (1976a, 1976b) conducted a questionnaire survey among psychotherapists in psychiatry, psychology, and social work in Cincinnati, Ohio. They asked respondents about the number of clients seen during the year prior to the survey who the therapist felt posed a physical threat to others, the number who the therapist felt posed a physical threat to the therapist him- or herself, and the number who actually assaulted the therapist. Eighty-one percent of the social workers reported that they perceived at least one patient they had seen as a threat to others, 35% reported at least one incident in which they felt threatened personally, and 20% were actually assaulted. Whitman and colleagues (1976a) concluded that "the more patients a therapist reported as posing threats to others, the more patients he felt posed a threat to himself; and the more patients he felt posed a threat to himself, the more patients actually assaulted him" (p. 428).

Bernstein (1981) investigated client violence aggregated across the four disciplines of psychiatry, psychology, social work, and marriage, family, and child counseling in San Diego County, California. Bernstein found that 14.2% of the respondents reported being assaulted by clients at least once and that 35.6% were threatened by a client at least once. In another study, Carmel and Hunter (1989) reviewed reports of staff injury caused by patients in a state mental hospital. Their study, which included psychiatrists, psychologists, social workers, and rehabilitation therapists, reported a rate of 1.9 injuries per 100 professional staff members over a 1-year period.

Finally, Seeck (1998) examined the occurrence of violence in the workplace among psychologists and social workers in West Los Angeles, California. Seeck asked about respondents' safety concerns, appropriate safety training, whether the respondent had experienced certain types of violence (i.e., threats, assaults, or stalking), and whether the respondent or his or her employer utilized safety precautions. Unlike many other studies, Seeck's study found that the vast majority of the psychologists (98%) and the social workers (93%) in her sample reported that they did not worry about their safety with clients. A little more than one-third of the social workers and the psychologists reported that they had been threatened by a client, but more psychologists than social workers reported being actually assaulted and stalked by clients. Most of the assaults reported were not serious and included hits, bites, kicks, or punches without the use of weapons. In all of these cross-discipline studies, generalizability was limited, because each study surveyed individuals within a relatively limited geographic area.

Schultz (1987, 1989) examined client violence via a small random survey of social service workers in a rural state. The survey consisted of 19 forced-choice items that were designed to elicit information on the types of violence experienced, the location of violent incidents, insurance coverage, in-service training on client violence, and job orientation to violence. Fifty-five percent of the study respondents reported that they had experienced violence, defined as physical assaults, threats, or property damage. Shultz concluded that violence by clients toward workers was relatively common, with verbal threats being the most frequent, and occurred most often in corrections, health and mental health services, and services for persons with disabilities (Schultz, 1987).

Four studies of client violence toward child and youth–child protection workers have been published, three based in the United States and one based in Canada. The first study surveyed line workers and supervisors employed by the Montana Department of Family Services (Horejsi, Garthwait, & Rolando, 1994). The authors reported that threats and physical violence directed against child protection workers were fairly common occurrences, with 97% of the sample reporting that they had been screamed or cursed at by a client at least once in the previous year. In Skiba and Cosner's (1990) investigation of Pennsylvania child protective services workers, almost half reported verbal assaults, and just over one-fourth described a physical assault by a client. Newhill and Wexler (1997), in a study of 111 child welfare social workers, reported that 75% of the child and youth social workers reported that they had experienced at least one incident of client violence, defined as property damage, threats, and attempted or actual physical attacks, at some point during their careers, with male clients most often identified as the aggressors. Finally, Snow (1994), in a pilot study of Canadian child and youth care workers, found that attempted and actual assaults by residential treatment clients were frequent and resulted in a variety of negative consequences for staff members.

Two studies specifically assessed client violence toward social work students. One investigation, an informal survey of social work graduate students at the University of Southern California, found that client violence was one of the three most prevalent treatment issues in the students' field placements (Star, 1984). Regardless of agency setting, virtually every student was called on to work with at least one overtly or potentially violent client or situation. The other study, a survey of 121 social work students and 96 social work field instructors at the University of Georgia, reported that more than one-fourth of the students had directly experienced some type of violence during their field placements (Tully, Kropf, & Price, 1993). Of the field instructors, 62% reported verbal abuse from clients, 42% reported being threatened by a client, and 24% reported a physical attack from a client.

To date, with the exception of Guterman and colleagues' (1996) cross-national study and the CV Study, there have been only seven studies of client violence that specifically sampled professionally trained social workers in the United States. Three of the studies—Mace (1989), Seeck (1998; discussed previously), and Beaver (1999)—are unpublished doctoral dissertations.

Mace (1989) examined the effect of attitude and belief on social workers' judgments concerning potentially dangerous clients and investigated the prevalence of client assaults, representing the first national random sample study to address client violence toward professional social workers in the United States. The source of Mace's sample was the 1987 *Register of Clinical Social Workers*. Mace found that almost 27% of the sample (N = 799) reported being assaulted by a client at some point during their careers and that about 40% personally knew another professional in the field who had been assaulted by a client. The majority of the assaults were "simple" assaults, defined as assaults with no injury, although 6% of the sample reported missing work or seeking medical treatment as a result of the assault.

As an outcome of the activities of the Committee for the Study and Prevention of Violence Against Social Workers of the Massachusetts chapter of NASW, Skolnik-Acker and colleagues (1993) conducted a statewide survey to examine the nature and extent of work-related violence and its impact on social work practice. The survey consisted of 27 closed-ended questions addressing demographics, setting of the assault, type of assault (physical attack, threat, or property damage), use of weapons, and impact of the assault on the social worker physically and emotionally.

The authors report a curious discrepancy among findings for physical assaults and threats. When respondents were asked if they had experienced an assault, 28% said "yes." The three most common types of assaults were pushing, grabbing, and hitting. However, when asked to describe the effect of a physical assault, 50% described emotional and physical responses. Thus almost half of those who said they *had not* experienced an assault described the impact of an assault. The same phenomenon occurred when the authors inquired about what they refer to as "verbal assaults." Although 77% of the respondents described the impact of a verbal assault, only 63% indicated that they had experienced a verbal assault. The authors' explanation is that these discrepancies may reflect "the well established clinical observation" that to get an accurate picture of a phenomenon, one must ask the same question in more than one way (Skolnik-Acker et al., 1993). Perhaps some experiences that were not labeled as physical or verbal assaults by the social worker were still experiences viewed as affecting the worker in some manner. It is difficult, however, to interpret which figure accurately represents the incidence rate for those types of violence. Nineteen percent of the respondents reported property damage, with 33% reporting more than one incident.

Jayaratne, Vinokur-Kaplan, Nagda, and Chess (1996) conducted a national random survey of 1,200 members of NASW that addressed a variety of practice issues including job stress, psychosocial strain, burnout, social support, and violence and harassment on the job. Data related to violence were obtained via a series of closed-ended questions that asked each respondent whether he or she had experienced any of a list of specific violent behaviors. Among the respondents, 43% reported verbal abuse, 17.4% reported physical threats, 15% had been threatened with a lawsuit, 6% reported sexual harassment, 2.8% experienced actual physical assaults, and 1.1% had been sued. The authors concluded that the data suggest that violence and harassment in the workplace is a national phenomenon (Jayaratne et al., 1996).

In the fourth study, Rey (1996) surveyed 300 randomly selected licensed social workers and 150 agency directors in a western state to determine the extent of client violence toward social workers, agency directors' attitudes toward client violence, and agency directors' knowledge about client violence. Eighty-nine percent of the social workers reported verbal abuse by a client, 60% had been threatened, 47% had had property stolen, 45% had been "harassed via telephone," 24% had "had objects thrown," 23% reported that they had been physically attacked, and 19.3% had had property damaged. Eighty-two percent of the social worker respondents reported that they were fearful of workplace violence, and 47% had witnessed violence at their agencies.

Rey (1996) found that the social workers were more aware of safety measures, for example, policies and procedures for checking and back-up, than were their agency directors, suggesting that procedures to ensure safety are not handed down from the top but, rather, are developed informally by staff. In spite of the relatively high level of violent incidents that were formally reported (76%), only 15% of the agency directors indicated that they were aware of employee victimization. The author provides a range of suggestions for training to prevent violence and concludes by stating that a key component to coping successfully with client violence is high professional self-esteem, including a "refusal to accept violence as a condition of life for our clients or ourselves" (p. 33).

In the fifth study, Astor, Behre, Wallace, and Fravil (1998) examined violence and school social work. The issue of school violence has been a prominent one in our society, as noted in Chapter 1, and one that the public views as the most important problem our schools are facing today (Elam et al., 1994). In response to this concern, Astor and colleagues conducted a national survey of school social workers that investigated personal reports of victimization, precautions taken to prevent violence, training to prevent school violence, and the involvement of school social workers with violence intervention. The authors found that minority social workers were more likely to view the community surrounding the school as dangerous; however, minority social workers were also more likely to work in poor inner-city settings than were white social workers. Many of the respondents expressed fear for their personal safety, ranging from 31% in rural schools to 71% in inner-city schools. Most of the respondents indicated that they were involved in one or more programs serving aggressive youths and their families, including making home visits, crisis intervention, social skills training, and services using traditional social work practice methods, although many of these efforts are not formally labeled as school violence prevention programs by the school districts.

Lyter and Martin (2000) surveyed agencies serving as practicum sites for schools of social work in the eastern United States to learn more about the incidence of violence in social work practice and the strategies used by agencies to promote safety. Fifty-two percent of the respondents reported that at least one of their social workers had reported that violence was directed at him or her by a client during the previous 2 years. Forty-one percent of the incidents were described as verbal assaults, 34% as "intimidation," and 25% as physical assaults. The incidents occurred in a wide range of settings, including the worker's office (46%), the community (22%), and the client's home (19%). The majority of the agencies had not restricted or altered their services because of safety concerns; however, the remainder had taken a number of precautions, including using security guards and surveillance cameras, restricting or eliminating home visits, making home visits only with teams of workers, using alarms or cell phones, and employing law enforcement as backup for home visits.

Finally, Beaver (1999) conducted a national survey of 1,500 direct-practice social workers, drawn from the NASW membership roster, that addressed frequency of client violence, worker characteristics, and the impact of worker job satisfaction, burnout, and health. Beaver used a closed-ended survey instrument consisting of 66 items within 7 sub-scales. Beaver listed seven types of violence and asked respondents to check off whether they had experienced each of the types during their careers or during the previous year. The items included: physical assault by a client, threat with physical harm by a client, verbal abuse by a client (including threats of lawsuits or loss of job), sexual harassment by a client, personal or agency property damage by a client, and physical assault or threats against family members by a client. Sixty-five percent of Beaver's respondents reported having experienced client violence at some point in their careers, with 23% reporting an incident of client violence within the previous year.

THE CV STUDY

The primary goal of the CV Study, on which this book is based, was to examine the extent, nature, degree, and impact of client violence toward social workers (Newhill, 1992, 1995a, 1996, in press; Newhill & Wexler, 1997). As described previously, other studies have provided solid data on what proportion of social workers experience certain types of violence, but no other American study has examined in detail exactly what such incidents entailed. For example, what behaviors and emotions did the client exhibit during a violent incident? How did the social worker respond? How did the social worker feel during and after the incident? To what extent did the incident change the social worker's approach to his or her practice and feelings about the profession? Such information is important in providing an accurate context for understanding how and why client violence occurs. This knowledge, in turn, can inform the development of preventive strategies that practitioners and agencies can use. After all, the whole point of this line of research is to develop an effective approach to reducing risk.

For the study, anonymous questionnaires were sent to random samples of social workers from Pennsylvania ($N = 800$) and California ($N = 800$), with a follow-up mailing to nonrespondents 3 weeks later. The original mailing included the questionnaire; a cover letter explaining the project, the voluntary nature of participation, and procedures to ensure anonymity; and a precoded return postcard. Respondents were asked to mail the postcard separately when they returned the questionnaire to reduce follow-up costs and preserve anonymity. Respondents were identified through a computerized random selection procedure from each state's NASW membership directory. Eleven hundred and twenty-nine usable questionnaires were received, thus achieving a 71% return rate.

The eight-page questionnaire (see Appendix 1) included both closed-ended and open-ended items developed on the basis of issues reflected in the literature and direct recommendations from clinicians. Questionnaire completion time varied from approximately 15 minutes to 1 hour, depending on the extensiveness of the respondent's personal experience with client violence, including actual or attempted physical attacks, threats, and property damage. Respondents were asked to indicate whether they had experienced any of these three types of client violence at any time during their careers. If they had, respondents were asked to provide detailed narrative descriptions of what happened during and after the incidents. If multiple incidents had occurred, respondents were asked to specify how many incidents they had experienced and to describe the most serious one.

Who Were the Respondents?

Fifty-three percent of the sample was from Pennsylvania, and 47% was from California, with demographic indicators, such as gender, race, and practice affiliation suggesting that the pooled sample of both states was representative of the national NASW membership as a whole. Respondents were overwhelmingly female (80%), Caucasian (87%), and in their mid-40s, and they had been in practice for an average of 15 years. Eighty-eight percent possessed an MSW as their highest degree. Almost two-thirds (65%) characterized their sole practice function as direct services, 16% reported administrative or supervisory responsibilities, and 20% described other kinds of activities (e.g., planning, research, consultation) or a combination of functions, including direct practice.

Social Workers' Experiences with Client Violence

Fifty-eight percent of the sample ($N = 660$) reported that they had directly experienced one or more incidents of client violence at some point in their careers. Twenty-five percent of the sample reported property damage, 50% reported threats, and 24% reported attempted or actual physical attacks. Half of the respondents who reported violence experienced *more than one type* of client violence. Of those who experienced violence, 43% reported property damage, 86% reported threats, and 42% reported attempted or actual physical attacks. The type or combination of types of client violence reported is given in Table 2.1.

To put these numbers into a practice context, following are some composite narrative examples of the kinds of incidents that the social workers described:

> *Property damage*: "The client tore the telephone out of the wall and slammed it on the floor, breaking it. He also kicked in the TV."

TABLE 2.1. Types of Incidents of Client Violence Reported by All Respondents in Sample

Type of incidents reported	Percent of respondents
No incidents reported	41.5%
Property damage only reported	5.1%
Threats only reported	21.5%
Attempted or actual physical attacks only reported	2.3%
Property damage and threats reported	7.4%
Property damage and attempted or actual physical attacks reported	0.8%
Threats and attempted or actual physical attacks reported	9.5%
Property damage, threats, and attempted or actual physical attacks reported	11.9%

Threat: "The client was enraged over a decision we had made. He threatened to get a gun, come to the hospital, and kill all the staff and himself."

Attempted attack: "I was facilitating an inpatient DBT [dialectical behavior therapy] group, and one of the clients was very angry and kept saying insulting things to the others in the group. I tried to set limits but finally had to ask the client to leave the group and take a time-out in her room. She got really angry, walked over to me, and then tried to slap my face. I left the group and asked a couple of male staff to help escort her to her room."

Actual attack: "I told the client I would have to hospitalize him. Without warning he leaped across the room, jumped on me, and began trying to strangle me. The police pulled him off before I got badly hurt. I did have bruises on my neck, though, and I was really freaked out by it."

Respondents' Knowledge about Colleagues' Experiences with Client Violence

Sixty-three percent (*N* = 710) of the respondents stated that they knew of social work colleagues who had experienced at least one incident of client violence. On average, this group of respondents knew of four colleagues whose property had been damaged by clients, five colleagues who had been threatened by clients, and three colleagues who had experienced attempted or actual physical attacks. This knowledge of the experiences of other colleagues affected respondents' perceptions and feelings about violence, even if they had not experienced violence directly themselves. For example:

> "I had a colleague who was threatened by a client who was going to court. Somehow the client was able to get past the metal detector at the courthouse, entered the courtroom with a gun, and shot three sheriff's deputies and tried to shoot the judge and lawyers. My colleague was in the courtroom but wasn't shot at. Just knowing about the incident was very scary for me."

Perceptions and Attitudes about Client Violence and Social Work Practice

All respondents were presented with four statements reflecting opinions about client violence and were asked to rate the extent to which they agreed with each statement. As can be seen in Table 2.2, the majority of the social workers considered violence toward social workers to be a significant issue for the social work profession in general but not necessarily in their own practices. Although most respondents didn't see violence as a significant issue in their own practices, more than half often worried about their own safety, and most of the respondents admitted that they preferred not to see violent clients. For example, one respondent commented:

> "We live in an increasingly violent society, and this is reflected in our clients. I won't put my life at risk and have chosen a population to work with that I can feel safe with."

Both personal experiences with client violence and knowing of incidents that had occurred to others significantly influenced respondents' views of the importance of the issue for the profession. Respondents who had personally experienced one or more incidents of client violence were significantly more likely to view client violence as an important issue for the profession than those who had not personally experienced client violence. Eighty-three percent of those who had personally experienced client violence viewed it as a significant issue for the profession, whereas only 72% of the respondents who had not experienced client violence did. Furthermore, those respondents who indicated that they knew of social work colleagues or social work coworkers who had experienced client violence significantly more likely to agree with the statement that client violence is an important issue for the profession than those respondents who did not know of any colleagues who had

TABLE 2.2. Respondents' Opinions and Feelings about Client Violence

Statement	Agree	Neutral	Disagree
I consider client violence toward social workers to be a significant issue for the social work profession.	78%	16%	6%
Client violence toward social workers is a significant issue in my own practice.	31%	20%	49%
I sometimes worry about my own safety while working with clients.	52%	15%	33%
I prefer not to work with clients who are or may be violent.	60%	19%	21%

experienced client violence. Only 30% of those respondents who *did not* know any colleagues who experienced client violence thought that client violence was a significant issue, whereas 68% of those who knew colleagues who had been victimized thought so. Those respondents who personally experienced client violence were also significantly more likely to agree that client violence is a problem in their practice than were those without that experience. Those who had personal experience with client violence were also significantly more likely to worry about their own safety.

Finally, on the statement addressing avoidance of violent clients, some interesting findings emerged. Those respondents who had experienced client violence themselves were significantly *less likely* to prefer not to work with clients who are or may be violent than those who had never experienced any incidents. Respondents who had *not* experienced client violence themselves were significantly *more* likely to avoid violent clients, whether or not they knew of a colleague who had experienced violence. What this suggests is that direct exposure to client violence does not lead to the avoidance of violent clients.

CONCLUSION

Reviewing all of the studies described herein clearly suggests that the issue of violence as a serious and legitimate social work practice concern both here and abroad is firmly established. The question now is: How will we as individual social workers, as colleagues, as agencies, and as a profession respond to this issue? The remainder of this book attempts to address this question by, first, describing in detail the kinds of violent incidents that occur in real-life practice, why they happen, and how work-

TABLE 2.3. Summary Chart of Client Violence toward Social Workers Studies

Study	Sample	Time frame	Type of violence studied	Findings
Whitman et al. (1976a, 1976b)	101 psychiatrists, psychologists, and social workers in Cincinnati, OH	Year prior to survey	Perceived physical threats, actual assaults	81% of the social workers perceived at least one client as a threat; 35% were personally threatened; 20% were actually assaulted
Bernstein (1981)	Psychiatrists, psychologists, social workers, and marriage, family, and child counselors in San Diego County	Any time during career	Threats and assaults	In aggregate across disciplines, 14% of respondents were assaulted at least once; 36% were threatened at least once
Star (1984)	Social work graduate students at University of Southern California	Any time during field placement	Extent that students were called on to work with violent clients	Almost all the students, regardless of setting, were called on to work with potentially or overtly violent clients
Brown et al. (1986)	United Kingdom: social service departments	3 years prior to survey	Assaults and threats collectively	53% of respondents experienced at least one incident during 3-yr period
Rowett (1986)	132 U.K. social service agencies (three-stage study)	Any time during career	Most serious incident experienced	At each successive stage, reported incidence of violence rose
Schultz (1987, 1989)	150 social service workers in a rural state in United States	Any time during career	Physical assaults, threats, property damage	55% of sample reported experiencing violence, with verbal threats as the most frequent type

50

Study	Sample	Time frame	Type of violence	Findings
University of Southampton (1989)	All types of social service staff in United Kingdom	3 months prior to study	Threats and assaults	38% of social workers directly experienced an incident or knew of a colleague who had
Carmel & Hunter (1989)	Reports of staff injuries caused by clients in a U.S. state hospital	Year prior to study	Physical injuries	Rate of 1.9 injuries per 100 professional staff
Mace (1989)	National sample of NASW register of clinical social workers in United States	Any time during career	Assaults	28% of sample reported at least one assault (71% were simple assaults with no injury)
Skiba & Cosner (1990)	Children and youth workers in PA	Any time during career	Physical assaults and verbal assaults	Almost half of sample reported verbal assaults; more than one-fourth reported physical assaults
Leadbetter (1993)	Social service agencies and individual social workers in Scotland	Four-component study with varying time frames	Threats, verbal abuse, assaults; any type of incident in the diary study (2-wk period)	On average, 19.3 violent incidents recorded by each respondent in the 2-week diary study
Tully et al. (1993)	Social work students and field instructors at University of Georgia	Any time during field placement	Various types of violence, including verbal abuse, threats, physical attacks	26% of students experienced some form of violence; of field instructors, 62% reported verbal abuse, 42% reported threats, 24% reported physical attacks
Skolnick-Acker et al. (1993)	Random sample of Massachusetts NASW members	Any time during career	Verbal assaults or threats, physical assaults, and property damage	28% of sample reported assaults, 63% reported threats/verbal assaults, 19% reported property damage

TABLE 2.3. (*continued*)

Study	Sample	Time frame	Type of violence studied	Findings
Horejsi et al. (1994)	Line workers and supervisors at Montana Department of Family Services	Year prior to study	Physical assaults, threats, verbal abuse	Threats and physical violence directed toward child protection workers is common; 97% of sample reported verbal abuse
Snow (1994)	Child and youth care workers in Canada	Unclear	Attempted and actual assaults	Both attempted and actual assaults were frequently reported
Newhill (1996)	Random sample of NASW members in two states (PA, CA)	Any time during career	Actual and attempted assaults, threats, and property damage	57% of sample reported at least one incident of client violence: 25% had property damaged; 51% were threatened; 25% were assaulted
Guterman et al. (1996)	Cross-national study of American and Israeli social workers	Year prior to the survey	Physical threats, assaults, threat of lawsuit, lawsuits filed, verbal abuse, sexual harassment	49% of Americans and 47% of Israelis reported at least one incident of some kind over the past year
Jayaratne et al. (1996)	National random survey of U.S. NASW members	Year prior to survey	Physical threats, assaults, threat of lawsuit, lawsuits filed, verbal abuse, sexual harassment	17% reported physical threats, 3% assaults, 15% threat of lawsuit, 1% lawsuits filed, 43% verbal abuse, and 6% sexual harassment
Rey (1996)	Licensed social workers and agency directors in one state	Any time during career	Actual assaults, objects thrown, threats, verbal abuse, property stolen or damaged	23% assaulted, 24% reported objects thrown, 50% threatened, 89% verbally abused, 47% reported property stolen, 19% reported property damaged

Author (year)	Sample	Time frame	Variables	Findings
Newhill & Wexler (1997)	Child and youth–child protection social workers in PA and CA	Any time during career	Attempted physical assaults, actual physical assaults, threats, property damage	75% of sample reported at least one incident of client violence
Seeck (1998)	Psychologists and social workers in West Los Angeles, CA	Any time during career	Threats and assaults	15% of psychologists and 12% of social workers reported assaults; more than one-third in each discipline reported threats
Astor et al. (1998)	National sample of NASW school social workers	Unclear	Perceptions of safety, training in violence prevention	Perception of safety varied depending on location of school; most respondents were involved in programs serving aggressive kids or prevention programs
Lyter & Martin (2000)	Agencies serving as practicum sites for eastern U.S. Tri-State Consortium	Up to 2 years	Incidence of violence in social work practice and safety strategies employed	52% of agencies reported that at least one social worker experienced client violence directed toward him or her, most strategies often in the worker's office setting
Beaver (1999)	National random sample of direct-practice social workers from NASW roster	Previous year *and* at any point during career	Assault, threat, verbal abuse, sexual harassment, personal or agency property damage, assault or threat toward family member	65% of sample reported experiencing client violence at some point in career; 23% reported experiencing client violence during the past year
MacDonald & Sirotich (2001)	Random sample from Canadian College of Certified Social Workers roster	At any time during career	Verbal harassment, sexual harassment, racial/ethnic harassment, stalking, threats, and assaults	88% of sample reported verbal harassment; 64% threats of physical harm; 29% assaulted with no injury; 8% assaulted with injury

ers and agencies actually respond to incidents. Then, using this information, I outline clinical assessment, intervention, and prevention strategies that you can use to reduce your and your agency's risk of experiencing client violence.

SKILL DEVELOPMENT EXERCISES

Discussion Questions

1. *Before* reading Chapter 3, read the following statements on attitudes about client violence and discuss to what extent you agree or disagree with them and why. *After* reading Chapter 3, look at the statements again. Have any of your attitudes changed as a result of learning about the studies that have been done on client violence?

   - I consider client violence toward social workers to be a significant issue for the social work profession in general.
   - Client violence toward social workers is a significant issue in my practice.
   - I sometimes worry about my own safety while working with clients.
   - I prefer not to work with clients who are or may be violent.

2. Have you ever personally experienced an incident of client violence? To the extent that you are comfortable, share with discussion group participants what happened to you. How are you feeling now about what happened to you?

3. Have any of your colleagues experienced an incident of client violence? Discuss what happened and how your agency handled the incident. Do you think the incident could or should have been responded to differently? If so, why?

Part II

Issues Related to Risk Assessment of Violent Clients

Chapter 3

Understanding Client-Initiated Property Damage and Threats

This chapter addresses the nature and motivation for two types of client violence that social workers commonly experience: property damage and threats. The previous chapter gave an overview of the prevalence of client violence toward social workers as reported by existing studies, but we do not yet have a clear detailed picture of what kind of violence occurs. What exactly do clients do when they threaten a social worker or damage the social worker's personal property or agency property? How serious are these acts of violence? What kind of harm usually occurs? Finally, what motivates a client to strike out like this toward a social worker? Throughout this chapter and the remainder of the book, short case vignettes are used to provide a clinical context for the various topics of discussion. Let's look at each of the types of violence and what the CV Study social workers reported happened to them.

PROPERTY DAMAGE

Little attention has been paid in the professional literature to the problem of property damage by clients, even though it is a relatively common occurrence. The reason may be that, in general, incidents of property damage are less distressing to victims than other forms of client violence, because they do not involve damage to people. As one respondent in the CV Study commented: "Property damage can be repaired or replaced. It's not the same as violence to a live human being."

Property damage is, however, a form of violence, and it can leave a mark on victims. It is not uncommon, for example, for victims of property damage to feel violated and intruded on, even if the property can be replaced or its monetary value reimbursed via insurance. It's akin to the feelings often reported by victims of burglary. Feelings of being harmed are particularly common if the property has personal meaning. For example:

> "The client grabbed my sterling silver bracelet and ripped it off my arm, breaking the bracelet. I was upset because it had been a birthday gift from my great aunt and therefore had sentimental value and couldn't be replaced."

What Kind of Property Damage Occurs?

In the CV Study, most respondents reported that they had experienced multiple incidents of property damage over the course of their careers, rather than a single incident. On average, respondents experienced eight separate incidents, with 15% reporting "multiple" or "numerous" incidents, particularly if their clientele included adolescents. As one respondent noted:

> "In residential care with adolescent boys, damage to property occurs constantly—I can't even count how many times. They write graffiti on the walls, punch holes in walls, and smash up furniture. They're there because they have problems, and many are just so angry and frustrated about everything in their lives that they take it out on the furniture. I look at it this way—it's better than taking it out on each other."

An examination of the descriptions of property damage that the respondents provided showed eight distinct types of damage (see Table 3.1).

Respondents were not asked a specific question about their perception of the client's motive for damaging the property; however, from the content of the respondents' descriptions, the primary motive for the client seemed to be anger, with the property damage serving as a mechanism for the expression of that anger.

To bring the statistical figures into context, following are some composite case examples describing what actually happened in cases of property damage for the four most common categories. As noted in Table 3.1, the most common type of property damage was direct damage to the agency's property:

TABLE 3.1. Nature of Property Damage

Type of property damage	Percentage of cases[a]
Directly damaged agency property	61%
Threw property, resulting in destruction of the target or object thrown	24%
Damaged the social worker's automobile	16%
Threw property, resulting in mild damage to the target or object thrown	10%
Defaced agency property	9%
Damaged the social worker's personal property	8%
Stole property	7%
Set a fire/committed arson	5%
Other	6%

[a]Percentages add up to greater than 100 because many respondents reported more than one type of property damage for a single incident. For example, one incident involved a client who sprayed graffiti on the clinic walls (defaced agency property), punched a hole in the wall (damaged agency property), and threw a chair, breaking one of the legs (threw property, resulting in mild damage to the object thrown).

- Client punched holes in the walls and broke a window.
- The client damaged two computers, broke several pieces of furniture, broke the office door window with a stick, and tore the pages from several books.
- Client tore the telephone out of the wall and slammed it on the floor, breaking it. He also kicked in the TV.
- The client was brought to the emergency room in restraints after he had shot up his home. The doctor, against my advice, had him released from restraint. The client promptly destroyed the examining room.

In the second most common type of property damage, the client threw a piece of property, which resulted in the destruction of the target or of the object thrown:

- Client threw a rock and a typewriter through a plate glass window, destroying the window and the typewriter.
- Client threw several chairs and small tables and broke them.
- Client destroyed a wall by hitting it with a chair and his fists. The wall was destroyed on the office side and damaged on the outside and had to be rebuilt.

The third most common type of property damage was to the social worker's own car. Many social workers who are required to do outreach work, field visits, or home visits must use their own cars, and thus clients identify the cars as good targets for property damage:

- One time on a home visit, a client smashed my car window.
- My car was parked in the agency parking lot, and the client shattered one of my car windows.
- Client vandalized my car, taking less than $100 worth of property; another client slashed three of my tires.

Finally, in the fourth most common type of property damage, the client threw a piece of property, resulting in mild damage to the target or the object thrown:

- Client threw a chair, breaking one leg.
- Client threw a brick at a window, chipping and mildly cracking the window.

In about one-fourth of the reported incidents, certain tools were used by the client for the purpose of damaging the property. In those cases, sticks, clubs, or knives were the most common tools. For example, a respondent reported: "I work in a residential treatment facility. The kids there often use sticks to smash windows, and then they climb through them to escape." Other tools used included rocks, furniture, ashtrays, fire, bombs, spray paint, markers, crayons, and garbage.

Overall Extent of Damage

Respondents were asked to provide details about the most severe incident of property damage that they experienced, including the overall extent of damage. Extent of damage was categorized as mild, moderate, severe, or unclear (see Table 3.2). "Mild damage" describes incidents in which the damage could be easily repaired without professional help and that involved little monetary loss. For example, "Once a client tore up my file cards on my desk." "Moderate damage" required some professional help to repair or was not costly to replace or repair. For example, "Client 'tagged' the walls with gang graffiti, which required professional repainting." "Severe damage" refers to extensive damage that was expensive to repair or was not repairable and represented a costly loss. For example, "The client intentionally flooded the bathroom, causing extensive damage to the residential dorm rooms below." Finally, "unclear

TABLE 3.2. Overall Damage for Incidents Reported

Overall extent of damage	Percentage of cases
Mild damage	18%
Moderate damage	28%
Severe damage	40%
Unclear	14%

damage" describes incidents in which the severity of damage could not be determined. For example, "The client messed up my office."

In summary, although the topic of property damage by clients has not been examined extensively, it is a form of client violence that can have significant consequences. Such consequences include the monetary loss incurred by damage or loss of property and the emotional consequences related to loss for the owner of the property. We can still only speculate about motives for property damage, but they appear to be predominantly related to anger, for which property damage serves as a mechanism for expression. There is some evidence that when an agency decides to utilize certain deterrent measures, such as pressing charges for property damage, such incidents may decrease. This evidence is addressed in Chapter 9. Now let's turn to the most common form of client violence, which is threats toward social workers.

THREATS

Although the literature on threats toward clinicians is relatively sparse compared with the literature on assaults (Lion, 1995), studies suggest that threats are a very common occurrence across human services settings and are far more common than property damage or assaults (Bernstein, 1981; Haffke & Reid, 1983; Whitman, et al, 1976a). In the CV Study, fully half of all the respondents had experienced at least one threat at some point in their careers, and, of those respondents who experienced some form of client violence, 86% had experienced one or more threats. Furthermore, of those individuals in the CV Study who experienced threats, the majority experienced multiple threats. Only one-fourth of those threatened had experienced only one threat; the average number of threats experienced was 17, ranging from 1 threat to more than 100. When asked how many threats he had experienced, one respondent stated, "How many stars are in the sky?"

Nature of the Threats

The nature of the incidents of threats reported by respondents in the CV Study is given in Table 3.3. As the table indicates, the most common type of threat was a "nonspecific verbal threat." This type of threat involved statements that were not specific in method or outcome but clearly menacing in intent. For example, one client said to the social worker, "I don't get mad . . . I get even." What exactly he intended to do was not clear, but the statement inspired fear in the social worker.

The next most common threat was to kill the social worker. Approximately half of these threats specified a method for killing, for example, "I'll cut your throat." Even those threats not specifying a means were often menacing:

> "The client threatened to kill me in five years when he was off parole. Told me I would never even know it was him."

The third most common threat was of physical harm other than killing. Such threats included threats to beat the worker up, hit the worker, and so forth. For example:

> "Client was angry, hostile, threatened to beat me up and then physically prevented me from leaving the interview room."

Finally, the fourth most common threat involved a threat with a weapon; the presence of the weapon enhanced the power of the threat. For example:

> "The client threatened to run me over with his car. He had already run over his girlfriend and was on parole for that, so I knew he was capable of it."

Following are more case examples that illustrate the other types of threats. Reading such examples can help provide a real-life context for the experiences of many social workers.

> *Threatening moves* (these threats did not involve a specific verbal threat, but the client physically moved in such a manner that the social worker felt threatened): "I was the social worker for a man with severe mental illness who had a long history of violence toward staff. After I told him I was leaving my job, he stood very close to me, screamed, and raised his fists in front of my face. To interrupt his thought processes, I offered him a candy bar and a ciga-

TABLE 3.3. Nature of Threats

Type of threat	Percentage of respondents[a]
Nonspecific verbal threat	25%
Threat to kill the social worker	23%
Threat of physical harm	23%
Threat with a weapon	19%
Threatening moves	15%
Threat to hit or kick the social worker	14%
Client rageful, agitated	14%
Angry verbal abuse	11%
Threat to harm, stalk the social worker's family	6%
Threat to kill him- or herself and staff members	5%
Letter, phone threat	4%
Holding the social worker (with or without others) hostage	3%
Threat of others harming the social worker	3%
Sexual threat, rape	3%
Other	11%

[a]Percentages add up to greater than 100 because many respondents reported more than one type of threat behavior occurring for a single incident. For example, one incident involved a client who was verbally abusive toward the social worker, engaged in threatening moves, and threatened to kill the social worker.

rette. That seemed to help because he calmed down and was willing to talk with me about my leaving. Staffing had been cut drastically, and I was often alone with the patients with no backup. I resented being placed in this situation by an agency that had no conception or concern of how dangerous it is to work with severely mentally ill clients when staff is cut to the bone (and beyond)."

Threatened to hit or kick the social worker: "I was evaluating a client when she threatened to hit me—fortunately I had left the office door open so I exited to get help—she then went out into the waiting room, picked up a lamp, and threatened to hit me with it."

Client rageful, agitated: "The patient was highly delusional and paranoid. He began cussing at me and waving his guitar around. I told him he was not to hurt me and he left—still raging. I called the police."

Angry verbal abuse: "Client swore at me and called me names because I wouldn't give him more money. I was his temporary conservator."

Threat to harm, stalk the social worker's family: "I saw a client who had a serious history of violent behavior and found out he lived only four doors from me. He began to stalk me and my husband and said he knew that he and I were meant to be together, and he had this delusion that we would get married and live together. I dealt with this in treatment but, finally, I had to move from my home."

Threatened to kill him- or herself and staff: "Client was enraged over a decision we had made. He threatened to get a gun, come to the hospital, and kill all the staff and himself."

Letter or phone threat: "The client sent five threatening letters to me and my family plus a year and a half of telephone threats to my home and office directed at both me and my family. The letter and phone threats to my wife involved sexual offers. I turned it in to the phone company, but the clinic where I worked did nothing to help me. He also followed my car and tried to run me off the road. I was then fired because they said the client's behavior was my fault."

Held the social worker (with or without others) hostage: "We received a telephone threat from a client that if his children were not returned to him from protective custody that he would harm staff. Subsequently he and his friends appeared at the office armed with rifles and held us hostage until the sheriff's deputies arrived."

Get others to harm the social worker: "The client made an anonymous phone call to a hot line saying he knew of a gang member who was trained by the Medellin cartel in Colombia and was on his way to our county to kill me. The hot line advised our police, who then advised me so I could take steps to protect myself. At the time I was working for child welfare—threats happen all the time in my work."

Sexual threat, rape: "Months after it happened, I found out that one of our clients had told inpatient staff that he planned to kidnap and rape me. Apparently, one staff member made a joke about it and this was very upsetting to me. I had had numerous contacts with the client without any idea that I was potentially in danger. I should have been immediately warned."

Motives for Threats

Dubin and Lion (1992) comment that "threats rarely occur in a vacuum" (p. 20). Threats occur within a situational context, and an examination of this context can provide clues as to what the client's motive may be. Knowledge of the motive can then suggest target goals for both prevention and intervention when a threat occurs. Threats often represent a variety of psychological underpinnings, including disappointment, perceived or actual rejection, a spurned desire for closeness, rage stemming from loss, a sense of betrayal, or a power struggle with the clinician (Dubin & Lion, 1992; Kaplan & Wheeler, 1983). Threats may also signify anger over limit setting, frustration stemming from an inability to obtain resources to meet pressing needs, or an effort to force compliance in a request (Newhill, in press).

Verbal threats can be divided into two broad classes: (1) "hot threats," defined as those characterized by a rapidly escalating process driven by emotion; and (2) "cold threats," defined as those threats that indicate a plan for future aggression (Dubin & Lion, 1992). Unlike hot threats, cold threats are often delivered without emotion and often have an eerie and creepy frightening quality about them. For example:

> "I was working in the prison system . . . the client said to me in a very cold voice, 'You can run, but you can't hide. I'll get you.' "

Table 3.4 summarizes the distribution of motives for threats in the CV Study.

In 44% of the threats, respondents indicated that no identified motive or an unclear motive was present. In some cases, the social worker reflected that the threat seemed to "just come out of the blue" and was completely unanticipated. In other cases, the worker reported that there probably was a motive but that it could not be pinpointed. For the rest of the threats, however, the client's motive for the threat could be clearly identified.

In 14% of the threats, the motive was related to a child welfare or child protection issue, usually having to do with an abuse or neglect investigation or removal of the children from the home. For example:

> "I was alerted to the probability that I would be assaulted during a home visit with children where the father was planning to abduct the children and take them out of the country. Plans were made for another social worker to accompany me on the visit, but that fell through. The father ended up not trying to abduct the children because he didn't have any money for gas, but told me later that he had a baseball bat behind the chair and had planned to hit me over the head with it."

In 12% of the cases, the cause of the threat was anger at "the system," that is, anger at the staff, agency, or system at large for various reasons. In many of these cases, services that the client was receiving

TABLE 3.4. Motive or Cause of Threat

Motive or cause of threat	Percentage of respondents
No identified motive	34%
Child welfare or child protection situation	14%
Client was angry at "the system"	12%
Motive unclear	10%
Client was upset about therapy	7%
Client was confronted about his or her behavior or limits were set regarding his or her behavior	6%
Client wanted specific action or information	5%
Client wanted to be left alone	1%
Other (e.g., client was psychotic or delusional)	12%

were not achieving the goals the client wanted. In frustration, the client threatened the social worker, who may or may not have been involved in the services received but who was a readily available target. For example:

> "I was a medical social worker, and the elderly spouse of one of the hospitalized patients was afraid of the possibility that his wife was dying. Her health was deteriorating, and he cited me as the person who was responsible for her deterioration. He told me 'I know where you live, where you eat lunch, the car you drive . . . and I'll get you.' I understood his anger and tried to talk with him and allow him to vent his feelings but, at the time, he could only vent them by means of the threat."

In 7% of the threats, the client was angry about sensitive personal issues related to services or therapy. Sometimes the situation related directly to the content of therapeutic issues raised in treatment:

> "I was seeing a client at a child guidance clinic. We were discussing her concerns when she suddenly got off her chair and raised her arm as though she was planning to strike me after I asked a question which struck an 'emotional chord.' "

In other cases, the source of the client's anger may be outside the therapeutic relationship, but the anger is brought into the therapy session and expressed toward the social worker:

"I was working with a 14-year-old boy who returned from a family visit quite upset because the family didn't want him to return home the next weekend. He came to my office threatening to kill himself or kill me if I tried to stop him."

Finally, some threatening situations involved anger over the suggestion that the client should receive services or a referral for services:

"The client had chronic schizophrenia, and his psychiatrist felt he should participate in day treatment. I brought this up to the client, and he became very agitated and threatened to 'knock my block off' if I made him go. I felt sorry for him because he had really bad negative symptoms and the thought of having to go to day treatment was just too stressful for him."

In 6% of the threats, the motive was related to the client being confronted about his or her behavior or to limits being set on his or her behavior. Such situations ranged from reporting misconduct to reprimanding clients directly for problematic behavior. This was a common motive for threats in settings such as residential treatment or inpatient services. Here are some examples from different types of settings:

"I was the case manager for a client in supportive housing. I was reprimanding the client for setting a chair in his apartment on fire. Unknown to me, the client was off his medication and thought I was his brother, whom he did not like. Fortunately, another case manager came along and helped."

"The client was a 16-year-old girl. Because I had disciplined her for assaultive behavior, she threatened to have her old gang murder me and my family."

"The client said, 'I'll get you at your home,' after an incident where I reported the client to his caseworker at the welfare office because I discovered he was receiving public assistance under two or three different names."

In 5% of the threats, the client threatened to harm the social worker if he or she didn't reveal certain information or take certain actions. These threats arose from such actions as refusing to tell the client who involuntarily committed him or her; refusing to tell an abusive husband the address of the domestic violence shelter where his wife was staying; or telling the client that he or she was not eligible for certain services or resources, such as public assistance. For example:

"The client was angry at not getting what she wanted. She began yelling, stood up, clenched her fists and tensed her arms, stating how many men and women she had assaulted, how she had maimed or hurt them and got what she wanted. Implied that I would be harmed if she did not get what she wanted immediately. . . . There have been other incidents where clients had weapons, the threat wasn't so immediate as in this case, because this woman client was about 300 pounds and very strong and aggressive."

In 2% of the threats, the client didn't want to participate in therapeutic activities or wanted to be left alone:

"I was working in a partial hospitalization program. I knew the client would be kicked out of the program if he didn't start participating, so I began to push him to come to group. He kept saying 'no' and finally yelled at me and shook his fist, threatening to punch me. I backed off."

Finally, in 12% of the threats, a wide range of other motives were described: The client was responding to psychotic symptoms such as threatening voices; the client was under the influence of drugs and alcohol; or the client was compromised in some way that affected judgment and ability to control his or her behavior.

The ability of the social worker to identify a motive behind the threat is useful in two important ways. First, determining the client's motive helps the social worker target intervention efforts meaningfully to help de-escalate the anger and potential for violence. Second, identifying a motive helps to engender empathy on the part of the social worker toward the client. Many motives are quite understandable, and even when limits have to be set on the client's behavior, expression of empathy helps make such limits more palatable to the client, thus preventing the therapeutic alliance from unraveling and even, in some cases, serving to enhance the worker–client connection. I discuss the use of empathy in more detail in Chapter 7.

Threats and Weapons

In 19% of the threats reported in the CV Study, the client used a weapon in making the threat. Of these, 32% used guns, 20% used knives, 15% used sticks, 4% used more than one type of weapon, and 29% were categorized as "other." This "other" category included: furniture (e.g. chair, couch, table, lamps, etc.), a broom, a picture frame, a nameplate, cars, ashtrays, tools (including a chain saw, pickax, and a weed eater), a paint scraper, a bottle, lye, a frying pan, a ceramic cup, an electric wheelchair, a crutch, a briefcase, food, and HIV-infected blood. All such incidents were threats and not actual or attempted assaults. The weapons were not used, but they certainly served to enhance the power of the threat. For example:

> "While I was walking through the waiting room to call my own client, another client, who was an alleged perpetrator of sexual abuse of his child, pulled a gun on me and demanded the whereabouts of his daughter. I was terrified."

In summary, threats represent the most common form of client violence toward social workers. Threats cover a wide range of form, content, motive, and intent. Identifying the client's motive is the first step toward tailoring a response that will not only deal constructively with de-escalating the threat but can also serve as therapeutic intervention. Chapter 4 looks at assaults toward social workers and the motives behind this type of client violence.

SKILL DEVELOPMENT EXERCISES

Case Analysis Exercises Involving Property Damage

Exercise 1

A respondent in the CV Study commented: "Property damage can be repaired or replaced. It's not the same as violence to a live human being." Property damage is, however, a form of violence and can leave a mark on victims. With this in mind, read Vignette 1, and then discuss the three questions:

> Vignette 1
>
> The client grabbed my sterling silver bracelet and ripped it off my arm, breaking the bracelet. I was upset because it had been a birthday gift from my great aunt and therefore had sentimental value and couldn't be replaced.
>
> - How would you feel if this incident happened to you?
> - How would you respond to the client?
> - What kind of agency response do you think would be appropriate in this scenario?

Exercise 2

Read Vignette 2, and then discuss the three questions:

Vignette 2

In residential care with adolescent boys, damage to property occurs constantly—I can't even count how many times. They write graffiti on the walls, punch holes in walls, and smash up furniture. They're there because they have problems, and many are just so angry and frustrated about everything in their lives that they take it out on the furniture. I look at it this way—it's better than taking it out on each other.

- Do you agree with the social worker's stance on the boys' behavior?
- Do you think this kind of property damage should be accepted as something that "goes with the territory" in residential care with adolescent boys?
- How should residential care staff handle such behavior? What kind of response would be most therapeutic for the clients involved?

Case Analysis Exercises Involving Threats

Exercise 1

Read the following brief descriptions of threats and, for each one, discuss how *you* would feel if the threat was directed toward you and what your immediate response might be. Have you ever experienced a similar situation in your practice? If so, how did you and others handle it?

- The client said to me, "I don't get mad, I get even."
- The client was angry and hostile and threatened to beat me up and then physically prevented me from leaving the interview room.
- The client threatened to run me over with his car. He had already run over his girlfriend and was on parole for that, so I knew he was capable of it.
- The client was enraged over a decision we had made and threatened to hurt me.

Exercise 2

Review Table 3.4 summarizing client motives for threats. Then think about any incidents of client threats that have happened to you or to one of your colleagues. Can you pinpoint what the client's motive was for each incident? Does the motive suggest anything specific in terms of what an appropriate intervention might be?

Chapter 4

Understanding Client-Initiated Physical Attacks

Unlike property damage and threats, physical attacks by clients on clinicians have been studied fairly extensively, especially attacks on psychiatrists. Studies that have examined client violence toward psychiatrists have reported that, on average, 40% of psychiatrists relate having been assaulted by a client one or more times during their careers (see, e.g., Bernstein, 1981; Haffke & Reid, 1983; Hatti, Dubin, & Weiss, 1982; Madden, Lion, & Penna, 1976; Ruben et al., 1980; Tardiff & Maurice, 1977; Whitman et al., 1976a, 1976b). Those few studies that have examined physical attacks on social workers have generally shown comparable (Newhill, 1996) to lower (Beaver, 1999) prevalence rates than those reported for psychiatrists. Although the majority of physical attacks by clients are not fatal, fatal attacks have occurred, and they often receive considerable press coverage.

FATAL ATTACKS BY CLIENTS

The professional literature has reported a number of anecdotal cases involving fatal attacks by clients on psychiatrists, although statistics regarding the homicide rate for psychiatrists at the hands of patients do not exist within either the American Medical Association or the American Psychiatric Association (Dubin & Lion, 1992). The incidence and prevalence of murders of social workers by clients is also unknown. Although anecdotes about such cases are often reported in social work professional newspapers or general newspapers, there is no national

71

database that could provide information to help us understand the context surrounding such incidents and, perhaps, serve to inform the development of preventive measures. The following cases, in reverse chronological order, have been reported in the professional and popular press over the past two decades. All of the cases involved direct-services social workers, and most of them occurred in child welfare or mental health settings.

Lisa Putnam (1998)

Lisa Putnam, a 28-year-old social worker, worked for the Child Protective Services branch of the state Family Independence Agency in Macomb County, Michigan, just north of Detroit. On May 20, 1998, Ms. Putnam went to a client's home to explain how a mother whose house had been deemed unfit could get her children back. Two days later, Putnam's body was found beaten and strangled. Two sisters were charged in her murder, and police believe that the sisters became incensed when Putnam refused, for reasons of confidentiality, to say who had made the child protection complaint against them. Agencies that serve abused and neglected children state that such confidentiality is essential because without it reports of abuse and neglect would not be made for fear of retaliation. Ms. Putnam's mother, Barbara Case, was constantly worried about her daughter's safety because of the nature of her work: intervening with angry clients, working in unsafe environments, and dealing with sensitive issues such as whether to remove a child from his or her home. Currently, Ms. Case is advocating for the passage of "Lisa's law," which would require that social workers make client home visits only as a team, not alone ("Lisa's Law," 1998).

Steven Tielker (1997)

Forty-one-year-old Steven Tielker, a social worker who specialized in working with both victims and perpetrators of sexual abuse, was killed on April 28, 1997, by a client, Gary Wright, who was on probation for child molestation. Wright, 45, had requested a meeting with Tielker and Wright's probation officer, 38-year-old Donald R. Knepple, who was also killed in the incident. The shootings occurred about a half-hour after Wright arrived at the Fort Wayne, Indiana, Family and Children's Services agency to meet with Tielker and Knepple. Following the murders, Wright ran to the back of the building, entered an open office, and fatally shot himself, according to Sgt. Bill Walsh of the Fort Wayne Police Department. Steven Tielker was a clinical supervisor at Family and Children's Services and had received his MSW from Indiana University.

Tielker was highly committed to helping victims and perpetrators of sexual abuse and, along with his regular job at the agency, was active in a sexual abuse task force run by Fort Wayne's Center for Nonviolence, which aims to empower victims of abuse. An editorial in the Fort Wayne *Journal Gazette* noted the sad irony in the fact that Tielker was a champion of nonviolence, and yet he died as a victim of the very phenomenon he sought to eradicate ("Good Guys Show Support," 1997). Although Wright had been convicted of three counts of felony child molestation in 1996, he had an active gun permit at the time of the incident ("Counseling Session Ends in Shootings," 1997).

Rebecca Binkowski and Barbara Synnestvedt (1993)

In 1993, two Michigan social workers were killed by clients. On February 3, Rebecca Binkowski, a 25-year-old MSW student at Western Michigan University, was stabbed to death while she was giving a client a ride in her car. Ms. Binkowski worked as a resident manager at a Kalamazoo Township apartment house for people with mental illness. A tenant in the apartment, 24-year-old David Stappenbeck, was convicted of her murder. Ms. Binkowski didn't know her client was dangerous, although he had a history of violence and had attempted to burn down the residence in which he was living. It was only after Binkowski's family sued the agency for which she had been working that the agency initiated safety training and put in place a lengthy violence assessment for clients. Western Michigan University's School of Social Work has established a scholarship in honor of Ms. Binkowski.

Just two months later, 46-year-old Barbara Synnestvedt, who was a social worker at the W. J. Maxey Training School for juveniles near Whitmore Lake, Michigan, was found beaten and strangled in an employees' lounge. A 19-year-old man, Jermell Johnson, who was sent to the Maxey School following a conviction for rape, was convicted of first-degree murder in her death and sentenced to life in prison in July 1999. In the aftermath of these two horrific murders, the Michigan chapter of NASW took steps to address the issue of social worker safety in both agencies and schools of social work ("Slayings Stir On-Job Fears," 1993).

Robbyn Panitch (1989)

On February 22, 1989, Robbyn Panitch, a 26-year-old social worker in Los Angeles County, California, was stabbed to death by a client in her office at Santa Monica Mental Health Center (Simon, 1989). Ms. Panitch was talking to her fiance on the phone at the time the client burst into her office unannounced and attacked her with a knife. Her fiance, hearing her screams over the phone, immediately called the front desk, and police were notified. By the time two male employees were able to disarm the client, Panitch had been stabbed 31 times in the face and neck. She died within 2 hours. Her assailant, 26-year-old David Smith, told police that he murdered Ms. Panitch because he thought she looked like a childhood friend whom he believed was the Antichrist. Smith also complained that he was tired of living on the street and was angry at Ms. Panitch for not finding him a shelter. In fact, she had made a reservation for him at a shelter and referred him to it, but he had never gone. Smith had threatened Ms. Panitch previously, and she had tried to get him hospitalized, but the evaluating psychiatrist had refused to admit him. There were no security guards or alarm systems at the Santa Monica Mental Health Center, and the center was operating with only half of its staff in spite of increasing caseloads. Staff members had expressed concerns about safety, but mental health administrative personnel claimed that because of budget cuts, they had no money to hire security guards. Following Ms. Panitch's death and a strong professional and public outcry, money was allocated to improve security. As one of Ms. Panitch's colleagues, Reevah Simon, LCSW, commented:

> I knew Robbyn mainly through her work with the Association of Psychiatric Social Workers . . . she was intensely dedicated to the welfare of patients and improving the lot of her co-workers. It is a terrible irony that it is only the ultimate sacrifice of her life that may lead to the achievement of her goals. I am sure that it is only Robbyn's death that has spurred all the publicity and media attention; that led to the Board of Supervisors finally making security a priority after years of futile pleading by employee unions. . . . (1989, p. 5)

In December 1991, David Smith was convicted of first-degree murder. A Santa Monica Superior Court jury determined that Smith was sane at the time of the killing and was able to tell the difference between right and wrong. Although the jury recognized Smith's diagnosis of paranoid schizophrenia, they also concluded that Smith knew society's rules and made a choice not to follow them. Smith now faces life in prison. NASW's board of directors established a fund in Ms. Panitch's name, in memory of social workers killed in the line of duty ("Drifter Is Judged Guilty," 1991).

Linda Rosen (1988)

In Pittsburgh, Pennsylvania, another social worker, 27-year-old Linda Rosen, was shot and killed by 31-year-old Edith Anderson in the psychiatric emergency waiting room at St. Francis Medical Center (Hasch & Guggenheim, 1988). Ms. Rosen was interviewing Ms. Anderson to determine what kind of help she needed when the client suddenly pulled out a gun. Ms. Rosen immediately turned and ran away, calling for security guards. At that point, Ms. Anderson began shooting. After killing Ms. Rosen, Ms. Anderson took three people hostage. The skillful intervention of two city police officers ultimately saved the hostages' lives. The officers managed to establish rapport with Ms. Anderson and persuaded her to release the hostages and give them the gun. Ms. Rosen's mother stated that she often worried about her daughter's safety at work, but Ms. Rosen told her mother that her mother loved her work and that she didn't need to worry (Behrer & Evans, 1988).

Ava Gawronski (1982)

A 32-year-old social worker, Ava Gawronski, suffered second- and third-degree burns over 70% of her body, and her husband was killed, as the result of a fire set to their home by one of her former clients, William John Clark (Sobel, 1982). Clark stated that he did it because he wanted to make his therapist suffer the way he had suffered when she cut off his counseling. His original plan was to set Gawronski's house on fire, drive her and her family out of the house, and then shoot Gawronski's husband in front of her. A few months earlier Clark had attempted to rape Gawronski and tried to force her car off the freeway. Following the attempted rape, Gawronski discontinued treatment with Clark. The court noted that Clark was of "superior intelligence" but evidenced a "peculiar mental state." Convicted of multiple charges, he was given the death penalty ("Death Penalty Upheld," 1990).

What can we learn from reviewing these cases? They do suggest some of the factors that surround circumstances in which social workers have been murdered by clients. Certain dynamics, such as loss and rejection, probably played roles in some of the cases. In others, the dynamics are not clear, and one can only guess at the client's motivation. Problems related to poor safety precautions within the agency setting, such as lack of security guards or metal detectors, and inadequate staffing, leading to staff members working alone, also are apparent in some of the cases. However, similar circumstances surround incidents in which murders do not take place. The most important thing to note, fortunately, is that fatalities are rare. They do occur, but what data are available suggest that such occurrences are still highly unusual. Far more common are attempted and actual physical attacks that may lead to physical injury but not death. Such injuries cover a wide range, from those that do not require any medical attention to those that require hospitalization. How common are these? What exactly occurs? And, finally, what motivates a client to physically attack a social worker?

THE NATURE OF ATTEMPTED AND ACTUAL PHYSICAL ATTACKS

Twenty-four percent of the social workers in the CV Study reported that they had experienced one or more attempted or actual physical attacks by clients. It was most unusual for a respondent to report having experienced attacks without also reporting having been threatened. Eighty-eight percent of the respondents reporting attacks also reported threats. Seventy-nine percent of those respondents who reported attacks also said that they knew of social work colleagues or coworkers who had experienced some form of client violence, on average, they knew 10 colleagues who had also experienced physical attacks by clients. In contrast, those reporting no attacks knew, on average, only one colleague who had experienced an attack. What this suggests is that social workers who experience attacks know of others who experience attacks because they and their colleagues work in similar high-risk settings.

Respondents who reported attacks were asked how many attempted and how many actual physical attacks they recalled experiencing over the course of their careers. The number of attempted attacks experienced ranged from 1 to 50, with an average career prevalence of 4.6 incidents. The number of actual attacks experienced ranged from 1 to 25, with an average career prevalence of 2.2 incidents. Several respondents did not provide a number but said, instead, that they had experienced "a few" or "multiple" attacks. As one respondent noted:

> "I've spent my career working on inpatient units and psychiatric emergency teams and conduct psychiatric evaluations for the police and the courts. This work has exposed me to numerous assaults . . . but I have been lucky. I have never been seriously hurt, but violence is a part of emergency services. It is routine. I just wish to be adequately compensated for the dangerous job I do."

Those respondents reporting attacks were then asked to choose the most serious attempted or actual attack and to describe the nature of that incident in detail. Not surprisingly, 71% of the respondents chose an actual attack as the most serious. Fifteen respondents (29%) who had experienced actual attacks chose an *attempted* attack as the most serious. Judgments of seriousness involve a variety of factors, including not just actual physical outcome but also psychological stress and trauma and elements relating to the nature and context of the event. For example, an individual may view a mild slap to the arm (an actual attack) as less serious than an unsuccessful attempt to shoot the individual (an attempted attack). Table 4.1 identifies the various kinds of attacks that the respondents reported.

The most common type of attack was one in which the client kicked or hit the social worker. The majority of these were actual physical attacks. One respondent said:

> "The client wanted to be admitted to the hospital. I informed him we couldn't based on our assessment, and I offered him other community resources. Without warning, he hit me quite hard in the eye."

In the second most common attack, the client lashed out or flailed wildly at the social worker in an agitated rage. If the client made physical contact with the worker, it was considered an actual attack; if no

TABLE 4.1. Nature of Attempted and Actual Physical Attacks

Type of attack	Percentage of respondents[a]
Kicked or hit the social worker	45%
Lashed out at the social worker in a rage	28%
Charged or cornered the social worker	23%
Jumped on or pushed the social worker	21%
Tried to or actually did hurt the social worker with weapon	13%
Tried to strangle or put a choke hold on the social worker	11%
Threw an object that hit the social worker	9%
Bit or spit at the social worker	8%
Harmed self or others in addition to attacking social worker	8%
Scratched social worker or pulled out his or her hair	7%
Tried to stab or actually stabbed social worker	7%
Grabbed social worker or tore his or her clothes	6%
Sicced attack dog on the social worker	4%
Head- or body-slammed the social worker	4%
Tried to shoot the social worker	3%
Sexually assaulted the social worker	2%
Kidnapped social worker or held him or her hostage	1%
Other	16%

[a]Percentages add up to greater than 100 because many respondents reported more than one type of physical attack occurring for a single incident. For example, during one incident a client cornered the social worker, kicked her, and then spit at her.

physical contact was made, it was considered as an attempted attack. For example:

> *Actual attack*: "The client had been verbally abusive and threatening to staff in dorm [of adolescent residential treatment center]. I had gone to dorm to meet with client. He was quite agitated, and I do not feel that I was as empathic as I had usually been with him. His anger escalated, he began flailing his arms, and then the client took a punch at me, just grazing my nose since I ducked. Staff then restrained him."

> *Attempted attack*: "The client, who was 8 years old, was upset about his home visit with his parents. When I picked him up to return him to his foster home and asked him about the visit, he became very angry and began hitting his head. When I tried to stop it, he flailed out at me and said 'I hate you, I hate you,' but didn't end up hitting me. I just kept talking to him and eventually he calmed down. I felt very sorry for him because the family situation was really bad."

The third most common type involved the client charging and cornering the social worker. This either constituted an attempted attack if the worker was able to escape or escalated into an actual attack if the worker was unable to escape:

> *Attempted attack*: "I couldn't arrange for welfare for the client because he wasn't eligible. As I went into another office, he followed and took a swing at me—a female staff person intervened and the client appeared unwilling to attack a female, although he was after me for sure."

> *Actual attack*: "The client jumped out of her chair, ran toward me, and backed me into a corner as if to attack me—I tried to duck and get away, but she grabbed me by the hair and pulled out a huge chunk of it clean out of my head."

In the fourth most common incident, clients jumped on or pushed the social worker:

> "As our interview was ending, I was pushed and then slammed into a bookcase with a full body slam by the client. I turned it around and held her against the wall—male staff came and restrained her."

Finally, in the fifth most common incident, the client tried to or actually did hurt the social worker with a weapon.

USE OF WEAPONS

Only a few of the studies addressing client violence toward social workers have looked at the use of weapons (see, e.g., Rey, 1996). Several studies, however, have looked at the use of weapons in assaults and threats toward psychiatrists (see, e.g., Bernstein, 1981; Hatti et al., 1982; Madden et al., 1976) and psychiatric residents (Black et al., 1994). Studies have also examined the prevalence of use of weapons in certain settings, such as psychiatric emergency rooms (McCulloch et al., 1986) and forensic hospitals (Hunter & Love, 1993) . In a summary of this research, Dubin (1995) concludes that threats and assaults toward psychiatrists usually involve weapons, most particularly knives, guns, or other objects commonly found in offices, such a furniture or ashtrays.

The issue of the client's intent is also critical to consider. A client may threaten a clinician with a gun or knife but not have any intention of actually using it. Instead, the motive is to ensure that the clinician will take what the client has to say seriously, with the weapon serving as leverage. For example, I recall being called out by the police to see a client who was standing in his yard threatening to stab himself with a butcher knife. When I arrived and began listening to his concerns, the client revealed that he didn't really want to stab himself but that nobody was listening to him and appreciating the emotional pain he was suffering. With a weapon, he figured that people would take him seriously. Once he felt that he was taken seriously and empathized with, he put the knife down.

In the CV Study (Newhill, 1996), 23% of the reported physical attacks involved weapons. The most common weapons clients used were knives (22%) and furniture (22%), followed by rocks or other blunt objects, sticks, and firearms. Unusual weapons used included a cherry bomb, a German shepherd attack dog, sulfuric acid, a water gun, hot coffee in a mug, a broken bottle, and a belt. For example:

> "I was a new MSW assigned to a client who had brain injury from an accident, and he kept attacking women. During one session, I could see I was no longer connecting with him, and so I decided to end the session. I went to open the door but he wouldn't leave. He then grabbed me, tried to kiss me, and put a knife to my throat—I stayed calm, told him I knew he didn't want to hurt me, pulled his arm away, and ran."

In many of the cases, the clients used as weapons whatever was handy at the time of the incident. In other words, the attacks were not premeditated and the clients were not armed initially, but they picked up whatever was within their immediate reach. This fact clearly points to the importance of paying attention to the places in which one interviews or intervenes with clients and of making sure that objects that can be used as weapons are not readily available. This subject is discussed in more detail in Chapter 9, which addresses strategies to prevent violence. The most common weapons used, however, were not external objects; they were the client's hands and feet, and several respondents reported being injured as a result of such attacks.

CLIENT MOTIVE OR PROVOCATION IN INCIDENTS OF ATTEMPTED OR ACTUAL PHYSICAL ATTACKS

What motivates a client to attack a social worker? To understand clients' motivations, we have to understand certain aspects of our roles as social workers. As noted in an earlier chapter, our role is often both caring and controlling. Social workers, in the eyes of many clients, wield enormous power. The social worker may have the power to decide whether to take away a client's children in response to allegations of abuse, to involuntarily hospitalize a client and thus temporarily take away that client's civil liberties, to probe into the most private and sensitive regions of a client's life and self, or to determine whether a client is eligible for services that provide food, clothing, or shelter. When we think about our relationships with clients, we cannot deny issues related to power and control. In spite of our commitment to developing equal partnerships with clients and respecting clients' worth and dignity, the reality is that we hold power over our clients' lives, and we must recognize that and respect their position in the hierarchy. In examining the CV Study respondents' comments about the client's motives for the attacks, we find that the issues of power, control, freedom, and choice are embedded throughout. Table 4.2 provides the breakdown of the various client motives identified:

Table 4.2 shows that the most common situation reported was an attack that the social worker described as completely unprovoked or unexpected. For example:

> "I was seeing a 7-year-old child in therapy who had a history of severe abuse. We were sitting on the floor together playing a game, and suddenly he became upset and kicked me very hard in the stomach. I pulled myself together, told him that therapy had to be a safe place, and ended the session. I was very surprised that I didn't see it coming and scared too because I was three months pregnant at the time."

TABLE 4.2. Client Motives in Incidents of Attempted or Actual Physical Attacks

Motive or provocation for attack	Percentage of respondents[a]
No information given	26%
Attack was completely unprovoked and/or unexpected	11%
Client was psychotic, delusional, paranoid, etc.	11%
Client was trying to escape (e.g., get out of inpatient or run away from group home)	7%
Client was angry or upset at staff, agency, system, or community for various reasons	7%
Client was angry because he or she was confronted about his or her behavior and given limits	5%
Client attacked in response to a child welfare or child protective services situation	5%
Client attacked in response to being upset over a sensitive issue in therapy or treatment	4%
Client attacked when worker tried to intervene in a fight between client and someone else	4%
Client was under the influence of drugs or alcohol	4%
Client attacked because he or she didn't want to participate in therapeutic activities and wanted to be left alone	2%
Client felt threatened by other sources or for other reasons	2%
Other	6%
Missing	9%

[a]Percentages add up to more than 100% due to rounding.

"The police brought in a guy who was found walking naked in a downtown park. I sat down across from him in the interviewing room (after we got him some clothes), asked him his name, and when I looked up, he punched me really hard in the face. The cops then restrained him. I was really shaken up. I never saw it coming. He had been very withdrawn and passive before it happened. I look back on it and I don't know what I could have done differently."

These kinds of events happen in practice. In both cases, the respondents reflected back on the incidents and could not determine an overt motive. In their reflections they also were unable to identify how they could have prevented the incident. It is this type of incident that incites the greatest anxiety in clinicians because it involves an attack that seems unprovoked and unanticipated, and thus clear lines to prevention are not easily identified.

The most common motive that could be identified as a reason for an attack was that the client was psychotic. Furthermore, in many so-called unprovoked attacks, psychosis or drug intoxication is often the underlying cause, although it may not be apparent at the time of the incident. Although community follow-up studies have reported that individuals with schizophrenia have lower rates of violence than clients with other types of mental illness (e.g., Steadman et al., 1998), other studies have reported a link between schizophrenia and other psychotic disorders and violence (Hatti et al., 1982; Madden et al., 1976; Walsh, 2002). What can be concluded from these conflicting data? In part, we may be seeing an artifact of the settings in which most of the studies have been conducted: psychiatric inpatient units, in which a significant proportion of the patient population has schizophrenia and in which, because of the nature of our civil commitment criteria, those who are a danger to self or others have been involuntarily hospitalized.

In addition, it may be that clients with schizophrenia are less likely to engage in violence overall. However, in clinical situations with patients ill enough to be hospitalized, aspects related to psychosis and transference may enhance risk. As clinicians, we may not fully realize how many clients with schizophrenia are constantly bombarded with critical negative auditory hallucinations (Ault, 1999). The client can't turn these voices off as we can turn off a radio, and therefore he or she may resort to responding to the voices behaviorally. For example, if the client is hearing a constant barrage of voices telling him or her that the clinician intends personal harm, the client may behave violently in self-defense:

> "The client was hallucinating and was afraid I was going to harm her . . . she picked up a steak knife and tried to stab me. Her sister was able to intervene and got the knife away from her."

In inpatient settings, attacks by psychotic patients are common in situations in which staff members are attempting to physically control patients through restraint or seclusion (Carmel & Hunter, 1989). Male staff members, in particular, are often called in to participate in such tasks and thus are disproportionately placed at risk:

> "I was helping staff put a psychotic client into seclusion. He didn't want to go and was scared. In the process of struggling with him, he hit me. I wasn't upset, though—this goes with the territory on inpatient units."

Chapter 5 discusses settings and practitioners that are most at risk for client violence.

The process of civil commitment can lead to violence with both psychotic and nonpsychotic clients. In such procedures, the client is involuntarily placed in the hospital and, as a consequence, is temporarily stripped of certain civil liberties. For some clients, civil commitment actually provides relief, but for others, it is a threatening experience, as illustrated in the following example:

"I was evaluating a delusional psychotic client for possible involuntary hospitalization. I was in the process of writing out the hospitalization papers when he suddenly hit me. I believe he was responding to internal stimuli—hearing voices telling him I was going to harm him, and he was also scared of going into the hospital. Although I understood what was going on with him, I was extremely upset and physically hurt."

The third most common motive for attempted and actual attacks was the client's desire to escape from a confining situation, such as an inpatient unit or a group home:

"I had a client who was getting really agitated and had to be escorted to the seclusion room. I was in front of him with two staff on either side of him. Suddenly he exploded, saying he didn't want to be put in seclusion. He swung his leg around and kicked me in the lower back."

The following example involves a very resourceful, clever social worker:

"The client had run away from her foster home and called me to come pick her up and take her back. When I picked her up and began driving, she pulled a knife on me and told me that she didn't want to go back and ordered me to drive to another part of the state. I did as she requested and then pretended that I was having a seizure. I began swerving the car back and forth, hoping someone on the highway would see me and call in a reckless driver to the police. The child got scared, and finally gave up and handed me the knife. I drove her back to the office and called the police."

Another common motive for assaults involved situations in which clients were angry or upset at clinic staff, the agency, "the system," or the community because they didn't get what they wanted or got something they *didn't* want, such as civil commitment, extension of foster care, and so forth. For example, the very nature of our civil commitment criteria creates a situation with high risk for threats or assaults to occur; the client must be judged to be a danger to self or others or gravely disabled. I worked in psychiatric emergency services for many years, and a major part of our job was making decisions about involuntary hospitalization. It was not unusual for a client to come in asking for admission to the hospital. When the client was told hospitalization was not indicated, sometimes he or she would become very angry and say something along the lines of: "What do I have to do to get into the hospital? Hurt someone? Hurt myself?" On occasion, the individual would then threaten or assault someone to gain admission to the hospital. The opposite situation occurred, as well. Some clients who needed hospitalization didn't want it, and, when told they would be hospitalized against their will, they would become threatening and even assaultive.

Although only 5% of the CV Study respondents indicated that the motive for the attack involved the client's anger at being confronted about his or her behavior, given limits, given a "consequence," or made responsible for his or her behavior, this is a common motive cited in the literature (see, e.g., Schwartz & Park, 1999). This motive was most commonly identified in cases involving adolescent clients. For example:

> "The client had been banned from the building because of previous behavioral problems. He tried to enter the building and was stopped by security. I went down to talk to him to explain why he could not come in. He then punched me in the mouth."

> "The client didn't want to go into the time-out room. I told him why he was given a time-out, and he got angry and tried to hit me."

Understanding the relationship of motive to action is critical for developing both strategies to prevent violence and constructive interventions when violence occurs. Reviewing the variety of motives identified in the CV Study suggests that certain themes cut across different motives. Clients want freedom, choices, control of their own destinies, respect, and preservation of self. When these needs and desires are threatened, and the client is unable to generate effective nonviolent alternatives, the client may then be vulnerable to resorting to violence to achieve his or her goals. There are times in practice at which clients cannot exercise full self-determination, but affirming the client's worth and dignity and communicating respect is always possible. In Chapter 8, I discuss how this approach can be operationalized and how we can work with our knowledge about motive to inform our practice.

CONCLUSION

This chapter reviewed what we know about the nature of attempted and actual physical attacks by clients on social workers, both fatal and nonfatal. Actual attacks are most likely to be reported and also most likely to cause injury to the clinician involved. The data from the CV Study have provided additional information on the prevalence of attacks on social workers, the nature of these attacks, the use and role of weapons, and the motives underlying such incidents. Next I look at the individual, psychosocial, and environmental risk factors that are associated with interpersonal violence.

SKILL DEVELOPMENT EXERCISES

Discussion Questions

Chapter 4 describes a number of fatal attacks against social workers. Victims include Lisa Putnam, Steven Tielker, Rebecca Binkowski, Barbara Synnestvedt, Robbyn Panitch, Linda Rosen, and Ava Gawronski, all of whom were direct-services social workers in child welfare or mental health settings. Review each of these cases, and discuss the following questions:

1. What do you think motivated the client to attack the social worker?
2. Are there any common circumstances that cut across the situations presented?
3. What, if any, steps could have prevented the attack from occurring?
4. What steps should agencies take to prevent such attacks from occurring in the future?

Case Analysis Exercise

For this exercise, choose either of the two vignettes, read the vignette, and then address the case analysis questions.

Vignette 1

I was a new [female] MSW assigned to a client who had brain injury from an accident, and he kept attacking women. During one session, I could see I was no longer connecting with him, and so I decided to end the session. I went to open the door but he wouldn't leave. He then grabbed me, tried to kiss me, and put a knife to my throat—I stayed calm, told him I knew he didn't want to hurt me, pulled his arm away, and ran."

Case Analysis Questions

1. What thoughts and feelings did the social worker probably have during and immediately after the physical attack?
2. What do you think specifically triggered the attack?
3. How do you feel about the social worker? Do you empathize with her?
4. Should this client have been assigned to a male worker instead of a female worker? If so, how could the female social worker have therapeutically approached transferring the case to a male worker?
5. How do you feel about the client? Do you empathize with him? Why or why not?
6. What colleague or agency responses would be helpful to the victim?
7. What colleague or agency responses would not be helpful to the victim?

Vignette 2

"A" is a white male, approximately 30 years of age, who was brought to the admitting office of the state hospital by two sheriff's deputies after he was found walking naked down the middle of a highway at 3:00 A.M. Leaving "A" in the patrol car, the deputies first talked with the social worker, "B," stating that although "A" was passively cooperative, he was mute. They found no identification with him and thus had no information as to who he was or where he was from. "B" got some pajamas from the inpatient unit, and the deputies were able to gain "A"s cooperation to dress himself prior to evaluation. Upon evaluation, "A" sat down in a chair at one end of the large admitting office with both deputies standing by approximately 2 feet away from him. The social worker sat at the opposite end of the room. Addressing "A" directly, the social worker told him her understanding of why he had been brought in, stating that the deputies were concerned because he had been found with no clothes on and was perceived to be in danger because he was walking down the middle of a highway. "A" stared at the social worker and did not respond. She then asked, "Could you tell me what your name is?" Instantly, "A" screamed and leaped across the room, knocked the social worker off her chair, and began to strangle her. Although the deputies were close by and reacted promptly, "A"s grip was so strong that it was a few seconds before they could pull him off. In just those few seconds the social worker almost lost consciousness. Following the assault, "A" was immediately hospitalized as a danger to self and others. The social worker suffered severe bruising of the throat, although she did not suffer any long-term physical injuries (Newhill, 1995a).

Case Analysis Questions

1. What thoughts and feelings did the social worker probably have during and immediately after the physical attack?
2. What thoughts and feelings do you think the client may have had during and immediately after the physical attack?
3. What do you think specifically triggered the attack?
4. How do you feel about the social worker? Do you empathize with her? Why or why not?
5. How do you feel about the client? Do you empathize with him? Why or why not?
6. What colleague or agency responses would be helpful to the victim?
7. What colleague or agency responses would not be helpful to the victim?

Chapter 5

Risk Factors Associated
with Violent Behavior

As noted in Chapter 1, assessing and predicting violence is one of the most challenging practice tasks for a social worker to tackle. However, most of us—at one time or another—are faced with assessing a violent or aggressive client, and we must know what to look for as we attempt to determine the most effective intervention to reduce the chance of future violent behavior. The question of whether clinicians can or cannot reliably predict violence today is complicated, although it has received considerable research effort over the past 30 years. Unfortunately, this research has concluded that clinicians are generally inaccurate when predicting future violence (Monahan, 1981) and most often err toward false positive predictions, that is, predicting that a client will be violent when, in fact, the client *does not* behave violently. The reason is that clinicians want to avoid false negatives at all cost—that is, predicting that a client *will not* be violent when in fact the client *does* behave violently.

How does one avoid this situation and increase the accuracy of assessment and prediction? The cornerstone to accomplishing this, along with providing effective violence reduction intervention, is knowing how to properly assess the client within the context of his or her individual attributes, history, and environment. By relying on a thorough knowledge of the risk factors associated with violent behavior, a clinician can determine which aspects of the client's situation suggest that there may be an elevated risk for future violence. This knowledge, then, shapes the development of an appropriate intervention.

Identification of risk factors is rooted in a large body of research that has examined correlates of violent behavior in an effort to improve assessment, prediction, and the development of effective interventions. These risk factors may be organized into three major domains: individual and clinical risk factors, historical risk factors, and environmental and contextual risk factors. All of these domains must be considered when conducting a risk assessment or providing treatment to violent clients. It is important to bear in mind that these factors *elevate* risk, but they are not automatic linear predictors of violence. That is, a client may evidence a particular risk factor, or even several risk factors, but that does not mean that that particular client will automatically behave in a violent manner. Violence is what we call a *low base-rate phenomenon*, meaning that in the range of all possible human behaviors, violence is a comparatively rare event. However, certain risk factors do represent "warning flags," and the more warning flags a client has, the greater is the risk that future violence may occur; thus some kind of intervention to address these warning flags is warranted. Some of these risk factors are unchangeable, such as biological sex, but others can be mediated via various clinical and environmental interventions, many of which social workers can provide.

This chapter provides an overview of these risk factors, including a discussion of how and why each factor is associated with violence. Later, I use this knowledge to discuss assessment and intervention strategies. Table 5.1, at the end of the chapter, organizes the various risk factors into an outline that can be used as a reference for clinical assessment.

Let's begin by imagining that you, the reader, are the triage social worker for a psychiatric emergency clinic that serves as the gatekeeper for the local locked inpatient unit. You see a wide range of clients in your work, and a common task is evaluating clients for involuntary hospitalization. One day the police bring a client in for evaluation at the request of his family:

> The client, "Bob," is an 18-year-old single Caucasian male, brought to the emergency room by the police after threatening to kill his uncle. The client's family has accompanied the police, and they tell you that Bob has been causing problems in the family for a long time. They describe him as always being difficult (he was diagnosed with attention-deficit/hyperactivity disorder and conduct disorder as a child), but things became considerably worse after a motorcycle accident 2 years ago, in which he suffered a traumatic brain injury. Bob has few friends, and those friends he does have use drugs and have been in and out of juvenile hall. Bob was arrested once at age 16 for simple assault. Bob has performed poorly in school, particularly since his injury, and is preoccupied with listening to heavy

metal music and playing the video game "Doom." The family thought all this would eventually pass and Bob would "straighten out," but recently Bob has become very suspicious and guarded. He has made strange comments about family members trying to harm him and, for whatever reason, has specifically focused his suspiciousness on his uncle, who lives with the family and has always had a close relationship with Bob. Bob's mother says that she found empty vodka bottles and marijuana in Bob's room, and when she confronted him about it, Bob became very defensive and angry and threatened to hit her (although he didn't follow through on the threat). Concerned about the drugs, Bob's father searched Bob's room and found two rifles and ammunition under his bed. When confronted with this, Bob became even angrier and blamed his uncle for "ratting" him out (although the uncle claims he had no idea that Bob had the guns). Bob then made a threat to kill his uncle. Bob is a tall, disheveled young man who is very angry over what has happened. He agrees to come in to your office but says "I don't know why I'm here—I don't need a damn social worker."

Most clinicians would be concerned about seeing a client like Bob and disconcerted, in particular, about his threats to harm others. But how does one go about assessing the true violence risk for this young man and, based on that, determine whether psychiatric hospitalization or some other disposition would be warranted? In Bob's biopsychosocial history, as summarized, a number of risk factors for violence are apparent, and being able to identify what these are and incorporate a knowledge of how and why each represents a risk factor is a critical aspect of developing a competent risk assessment and determining an appropriate disposition. After a review of these risk factors, we will revisit the case of "Bob" and specifically identify the risk factors embedded in the case description. Table 5.1 can be useful as a reference when conducting a violence risk assessment.

INDIVIDUAL AND CLINICAL RISK FACTORS

Demographic Risk Factors

Certain demographic variables, for example, age, gender, race, and socioeconomic status, have been shown to be strongly associated with arrests for violent crime (Klassen & O'Connor, 1994), and examining arrest rates for certain demographic groups has been a common way of determining violence risk. Using arrest rates as a measure of potential or actual violence, however, is problematic because some violent behavior does not result in an arrest and because sometimes innocent people are arrested (Link & Stueve, 1994). Also, the extent to which a particular demographic variable is associated with risk is often shaped by the degree to which other predisposing, moderating, or directly contributing variables interact with it (Klassen & O'Connor, 1994). So, for example, if one controls for socioeconomic status, the association of race with violent crime disappears. With these caveats in mind, let's consider what we know about each of the aforementioned demographic variables as a risk factor for client violence.

Age

Research consistently shows that younger individuals, especially those between 15 and 40 years of age, are at greatest risk for violence, and that the peak period of risk comes between 15 and 24 years old. Why is this the case? What we know is that late adolescence and early adulthood is the time of onset or identification of a number of psychiatric disorders that can serve to enhance risk, for example, certain mood and psychotic disorders, substance abuse, and personality disorders. Also, certain types of harmful behaviors, such as violence toward self or others, often begin to be exhibited for the first time between late adolescence and early adulthood (Stone, Stone, & Hurt, 1987). In the CV Study, more than three-fourths of the clients who engaged in property damage were under 40 years of age; 34% were adolescents. In actual and attempted physical attacks, 68% of the clients were under 40 years of age; 27% were adolescents. Clients who made threats were somewhat older, and only 18% were adolescents; however, most were still under the age of 40.

In general, as individuals age, rates of violence fall (Swanson, Holzer, Ganju, & Jono, 1990). For example, in a community follow-up study of psychiatric patients, the proportion of those over the age of 40 who reported having committed violent acts was one-third the rate of violent acts reported by clients aged 25 to 40 (Steadman et al., 1994). However, at the other end of the life cycle, risk for violence rises again. Studies of the relationship between age and violence have shown that individuals over the age of 65 commit more assaultive behavior than middle-aged individuals, although not as much as those of young age. Violence by elderly individuals is usually related to severe organic impairment, such as dementia, resulting in poor impulse control and disorganized cognitive functioning (Petrie et al., 1982; Tardiff, 1989). In the CV Study, elderly clients were most likely to engage in physical attacks, rather than threats or property damage. However, respondents who reported physical attacks by elderly clients often indicated that, because of the client's age, the violence was not expected:

"I was exiting a locked [psychiatric inpatient] ward with my arms full of books when a tiny senile woman reached up and grabbed me by the throat to make me let her out. I was surprised and bewildered—I couldn't believe this tiny lady was attacking me."

Part of the social worker's surprise in this example was related to the client's gender, along with her age. One doesn't expect small elderly women to be violent.

Gender

A remarkably consistent finding in studies of gender and violent crime is that males are disproportionately represented among those arrested for violent crime, at a rate of approximately 9:1, and this has not changed over time (Barash, 2002; Englander, 1997). Although there has been a gradual increase in violent crime by females over the past three decades, and although some argue that gender differences in aggression are exaggerated (Bjorkqvist, 1994), crime statistics still show that the vast majority of those who commit the most serious violent crimes, such as rape, robbery, aggravated assault, and murder, are male (Englander, 1997). "Violence may or may not be as American as cherry pie, but it is as male as can be" (Barash, 2002, p. B7).

The number of women who are violent offenders is not negligible, however. Fourteen percent of violent offenders are women, and these women have, in many ways, been invisible in terms of public discourse and scholarship (Ness, 2000). Part of this may be "society's discomfort with the idea of girls and women committing violent acts," while at the same time the criminal justice system shows a greater willingness to incarcerate women (Ness, 2000, p. 14). Most of the research on violence toward others by women has emerged from investigations of family violence. The first wave of research in this area clearly identified such violence as emerging from male attempts to dominate and control women, and women's violence was seen as a defensive action against such dominance (Brownmiller, 1975; Counts, Brown, & Campbell, 1972; Dobash & Dobash, 1979; Pagelow, 1984; Walker, 1989). Studies of homicides by females have shown some interesting patterns. Females are more likely to kill family members (usually male), whereas males are more likely to commit acquaintance or stranger homicides (A. Brown, 1987; D'Orban, 1990; Ewing, 1987; Goetting, 1988a; Jones, 1981; Morris & Blom-Cooper, 1964; Wolfgang, 1958).

Studies that have looked at gender differences in violence toward others by psychiatric patients in the community (generally using arrest or recommitment records as outcome measures) have found males to commit more reported acts of community violence than females (Rossi et al., 1986; Tardiff & Sweillam, 1985). One investigation, however, that used more direct measures of clinical prediction and self- and collateral reports of community violence toward others found that the rates of male and female violence were fairly equivalent (Lidz, Mulvey, & Gardner, 1993). One of the striking findings of this study, though, was the apparent inability of clinicians to accurately *predict* violence toward others by female patients. Although violence in male patients was predicted at significantly better than chance levels, clinicians substantially *underestimated* the level of violence by females, and also used the wrong cues in choosing cases thought likely to be violent.

A subsequent study attempted to determine the reason for the observed gender differences in predictive accuracy and found that females who engaged in violence were younger and more likely to be diagnosed with an affective disorder than were the males. Most important, the *situational factors* were different: Females were more likely to be involved in violence in the home with family members, whereas male violence occurred both inside and outside of the home (Newhill, Mulvey, & Lidz, 1995). This gender difference in situational factors fits the patterns of homicide observed more than 40 years ago by Wolfgang (1958) and may result from continued differences in opportunity structures for males and females. Men may simply be more likely to spend greater amounts of time outside of the home and in contact with acquaintances and strangers than many women are. From a clinical assessment perspective, these results emphasize the importance of taking the possibility of male and female violence equally seriously, along with taking different situational and environmental contexts into consideration, depending on gender.

Race

Studies examining the association of race and violence show mixed results. Klassen and O'Connor (1989) found racial differences in rates of violence in a sample of psychiatric patients; however, other studies have found no differences on the basis of race (Craig, 1982; Klassen & O'Connor, 1987; Newhill et al., 1995; Thornberry & Jacoby, 1979). Studies that have found differences based on race report that these differences disappeared when other variables such as educational level or diagnosis were controlled (Rossi et al., 1986; Tardiff & Sweillam, 1980).

When we look at the research as a whole, race does not appear to predict violence, although the stereotype that certain racial groups are more prone to violence than others has, unfortunately, persisted. For example, numerous studies over the past decade "[have] confirmed that police disproportionately stop and search minorities," a practice often referred to as "racial profiling" (Cole & Lamberth, 2001). Those who defend racial profiling argue that certain minority groups, particularly African Americans, are more likely to commit certain criminal offenses, for example, illegal drug trafficking, than whites. However, studies of racial profiling have shown this assumption to be false. Police stops find no differences in so-called "hit rates"—defined as the percentage of searches that find evidence of lawbreaking—for minorities versus Caucasians (Cole & Lamberth, 2001). Since the September 11, 2001, terrorist attacks, racial profiling of people of Middle Eastern descent has renewed debate over this practice. As social workers, we must be careful that we do not subscribe to racial profiling in our assessments of clients. When we lack adequate knowledge about the true risk factors for violence, it is more likely that we will fall back on stereotypes, such as racial profiling assumptions, to guide a client assessment.

Socioeconomic Status

A number of studies have shown that individuals who live in lower socioeconomic strata are more likely to be exposed to environmental conditions that can enhance violence risk (Harris & Varney, 1983; Klassen & O'Connor, 1989; Quinsey, Warneford, Pruessen, & Link, 1975; Silver et al., 1999; Tardiff & Sweillam, 1980). Living in poverty usually means a greater probability that one will be a victim of violent crime, be forced to live in a dangerous neighborhood, and be exposed to violent group norms—the so-called subculture of violence theory conceptualized decades ago by Wolfgang and Ferracuti (1967). Living in poverty also means a high likelihood of living in poorly maintained housing and of being forced to attend poorly constructed and maintained schools, which have older playground equipment that can raise the risk of childhood accidents, perhaps causing head injuries that can lead to neurological impairment. In short, individuals with lower socioeconomic status are more likely to live in situations that cause them to be exposed to or develop other risk factors for violence (Meloy, 1994).

Clinical Risk Factors

The Association of Mental Disorder and Violent Behavior

Is mental illness associated with violent behavior? This question has been the subject of an enormous body of research over the past 50 years, and the most current answer to this question is that mental illness does appear to have a *small but significant relationship* to incidents of violent behavior (for reviews, see Appelbaum, 1994; Eronen, Angermeyer, &

Schulze, 1998; Monahan, 1992; Mulvey, 1994). The vast majority of individuals diagnosed with mental illness are not violent. However, certain small subgroups of individuals with mental illness do evidence a connection between their psychiatric symptoms and violent behavior (Eronen, Tiihonen, & Hakola, 1998; Steadman et al., 1998). For example, Steadman and colleagues (1998) reported that individuals recently discharged from psychiatric inpatient care with major mental illness and substance abuse problems have a significantly higher rate of community violence than individuals with major mental illness who do not have substance abuse problems. Risk is further enhanced if the individual does not comply with his or her prescribed medication regimen and lives in a violent neighborhood.

These findings converge with other studies that have shown higher rates of violence for individuals with substance abuse problems and personality disorders, particularly antisocial or borderline personality disorder (Else, Wonderlich, Beatty, Christie, & Staton, 1993; Hare & McPherson, 1984). Even when psychotic clients are violent, underlying personality features rather than psychotic symptoms are often—although not always—primarily responsible for some of the violent behavior. For example, the presence of the personality trait called psychopathy in individuals with schizophrenia significantly increases the risk of violence (Nolan, Volavka, Mohr, & Czobor, 1999). Psychopathy is characterized by superficial charm, egocentricity, incapacity for love, guiltlessness, lack of remorse and shame, a sense that social rules do not necessarily apply to oneself, lack of insight, and failure to learn from experience (Hart & Hare, 1997; Millon, Simonsen, Birket-Smith, & Davis, 1998; Simonsen & Birket-Smith, 1998; Skeem & Mulvey, 2001).

Certain aspects of psychosis, however, do appear to be associated with violence (Walsh et al., 2002). Link, Andrews, and Cullen (1992) developed a 13-item psychotic symptoms scale that identified certain aspects of psychosis as being linked with a higher rate of violence. They found that violence is more likely to occur "when psychotic symptoms cause a person to feel personally threatened or involve the intrusion of thoughts that can override self controls" (Link & Stueve, 1994, p. 155). This is illustrated in the following composite case example:

> The client's sister came to the psychiatric emergency service asking for help with her brother. The brother has a long history of paranoid schizophrenia and had been making threats over the past week. When the mobile crisis team arrived at the brother's house, he was very agitated, stating that devils were going to kill him and that his sister was a devil. When asked how he knew this, he said the

devils had taken over his brain and told him he was going to die. He then pulled out a knife and tried to stab his sister (Newhill, 1995b).

High-Risk Psychiatric Symptoms and Violence

Certain clinical symptoms that cut across diagnostic categories have been shown to have a positive association with violence. However, the evidence for this is complex, and this complexity must be understood by the clinician when evaluating a client's risk for violent behavior. The three symptoms discussed here include delusions, hallucinations, and violent fantasies.

Delusions. The *Diagnostic and Statistical Manual of Mental Disorders* (DSM-IV-TR; American Psychiatric Association, 2000) defines a delusion as "a false belief based on incorrect inference about external reality that is firmly sustained despite what almost everyone else believes and despite what constitutes incontrovertible and obvious proof or evidence to the contrary" (p. 821). Delusions are one of the most common symptoms evidenced in psychotic illnesses, and approximately 90% of individuals with schizophrenia experience delusions at some point in their illness (Lucas, Sainsbury, & Collins, 1962; Taylor, Dalton, & Fleminger, 1982). The judgment as to whether an individual's belief constitutes a delusion requires that the assessment take into account the individual's culture, ethnicity, religious beliefs, and political beliefs. Delusions are clinically subdivided according to their content, with some of the most common types being bizarre, delusional jealousy, erotomanic, grandiose, mood-congruent, mood-incongruent, delusions of being controlled, delusions of reference, persecutory, somatic, thought broadcasting, and thought insertion (American Psychiatric Association, 2000, p. 821).

Clinical wisdom holds that the persecutory (paranoid) type of delusion is more likely to lead to violence than other types of delusions, and, in fact, there is evidence to support this. Not all mentally ill individuals who are delusional are violent, but those who are violent are most likely to have the paranoid type of delusions and to be in a period of crisis. Evidence for the association between delusions and violence is also indirectly provided by the association of violence with paranoid psychotic illnesses, such as the paranoid subtype of schizophrenia, delusional disorder, and other paranoid states, illnesses in which paranoid delusions are usually a hallmark symptom. These paranoid psychoses are far more commonly associated with violence than are nonparanoid psychoses. The primary reason for this association is that the client views the target of the delusion as someone who intends to harm the client, with the consequence that the client feels personally threatened and thus must defend him- or herself. This defense, then, may include violent behavior (Hafner & Boker, 1973a; Tardiff & Sweillam, 1980).

Hallucinations

The DSM-IV-TR defines a hallucination as "a sensory perception that has the compelling sense of reality of a true perception but occurs without external stimulation of the relevant sensory organ" (American Psychiatric Association, 2000, p. 823). Individuals who experience hallucinations vary as to the extent to which they recognize the experience as a hallucination. Hallucinations occur in a wide range of mental disorders, and transient hallucinations can occur in individuals who have no mental disorder. Hallucinations can involve any of the sensory organs—auditory (sound), gustatory (taste), olfactory (smell), somatic (physical experience within one's body), tactile (touch), and visual (sight)—and may be categorized as mood congruent or mood incongruent. The most common type of hallucination is the auditory hallucination, in which there is a false perception of sounds, usually voices (American Psychiatric Association, 2000). Although it is a false perception, brain-imaging techniques have shown that the brain reacts to auditory hallucinations in a similar way as to actual voices. In schizophrenia, it is common for an individual to report that he or she hears several voices engaging in an ongoing commentary about the individual, which is often critical in nature.

Sometimes auditory hallucinations involve voices telling the person to do something. This type of hallucination is referred to as a "command" hallucination, and many clinicians assume that it is this type of hallucination that is most often associated with violent behavior. Although past research has suggested that most patients with command hallucinations are able to ignore them, even if the hallucinations have violent content (Goodwin, Alderson, & Rosenthal, 1971), a more recent study of 103 patients with major psychiatric disorders found that those patients who experience command hallucinations that tell them to harm others are more than twice as likely to be violent than those who do not have such hallucinations (McNeil, Eisner, & Binder, 2000). McNeil and colleagues (2000) found that command hallucinations continued to be a significant predictor of violence, even when the analysis took into account other risk factors, such as substance abuse and the client's gender.

Violent Fantasies. The bulk of the research and clinical literature on the association of violent fantasies with violent behavior falls into three areas: (1) the assessment and treatment of violent sex offenders (Holmes, 1991; Prentky et al., 1989); (2) the role of fantasy in homicide, particularly multiple homicides (e.g., Gresswell, 1991; Nieves, 1999); and (3) the role of violent media in the development of aggressive fantasies (duBois, 1997; Martin & Fine, 1991). The big question that underlies all of this work is whether violent fantasies reduce aggression or reinforce it. The catharsis hypothesis argues that violent fantasies release the individual's aggressive drives, reduce aggression vicariously, and thus prevent actual violence from occurring (Lorenz, 1966). Later research, however, suggests that the opposite is true. Rather than dispelling violent impulses, violent fantasies often reinforce aggression and serve as a rehearsal mechanism for actual violent behavior. Furthermore, exposure to violent stimuli, for example, repeatedly watching violent movies or playing video games, can lead to increased levels of aggressive responses, particularly in males (Hess, Hess, & Hess, 1999).

Prentky and colleagues (1989) reported that fantasy plays an important role as an internal drive mechanism for repetitive acts of sexual violence in serial sexual homicide but a lesser role for those offenders with only one reported victim. Gresswell (1991) explains this by arguing that multiple murder can be viewed as an addictive activity, with violent fantasies serving to feed the addiction and increase the probability that the individual will continue to engage in violent behavior. Gresswell suggests that interventions based on the addiction model for treatment may aid clients seeking help to control their fantasies and assist them in avoiding acting them out. The following composite case example provides an illustration:

> Jose, a 33-year-old married Hispanic male, came to the psychiatric clinic asking for counseling. Jose had a history of multiple sexual assaults, including forcible rape; he was recently released from prison on parole; and he was registered with the state as a mentally disordered sex offender. Jose stated that he recently got married and was asking for help because his fantasies of hurting and humiliating women had gotten out of control, and he was acting out against his wife. The day before Jose almost killed his wife during sex. His wife threatened to leave him but was willing to stay if he got help. Jose admitted that he was more likely to act on his fantasies when using alcohol or cocaine, but even when he was not under the influence, he felt he could not control his behavior. Jose was referred to a sex offender treatment group, which was based on the 12-step addiction model. This all-male group utilized a highly confrontational style, combined with support and positive reinforcement of nonviolent behavior and maintenance of sobriety. At last contact, Jose said he was doing better, had not behaved violently toward women, and

had managed to stay out of jail, although he still experienced violent fantasies occasionally (Newhill, 1995b).

In sum, the literature suggests that certain types of violent fantasies can play a role in instigating violent behavior for some individuals and that engagement in activities that reinforce the fantasies may enhance the risk that the individual will move from fantasy to action.

Personality Features and Violence

Everyone has a personality, whether or not they also have a diagnosable mental disorder. In terms of violence risk, certain personality features can lay the foundation for aggressive behavior in some individuals. These features include *anger, emotional dysregulation*, and *impulsivity*. These features are also referred to as "dispositional risk factors," defined as "those that reflect the individual person's predispositions, traits, tendencies, or styles" (Monahan & Steadman, 1994, p. 19), and can become exacerbated if the individual also has a mental illness or a substance abuse problem.

Anger. Anger is not inherently dysfunctional (Novaco, 1994), and all of us experience anger from time to time. To understand the genesis, role, and purpose of anger, one must move away from viewing anger as a kind of negative irrational force to viewing it as a normal emotion that is best understood within its situational or environmental context. To do this, one must assume a systems-oriented approach that recognizes that anger is a dynamic phenomenon that waxes and wanes depending on the circumstances (Robins & Novaco, 1999). In other words, to understand a particular individual's experience of anger, that experience must be viewed in terms of how it is embedded within the individual's interpersonal relationships and environment. Sometimes anger serves an adaptive function within an interpersonal system and is a mechanism for assertion and affirmation of self. Other times, however, the expression of anger leads to negative consequences, including violent behavior.

The assumption that anger is the emotional source for violent behavior seems intuitive to most clinicians. It is not unusual to hear a client claim that he or she hit someone or threatened someone because he or she was angry at that person. But to what extent does anger actually *predict* violent behavior and thus operate as a reliable warning sign? Novaco and Renwick (1998) examined anger as a predictor for assaultiveness among forensic hospital patients, utilizing clinical staff ratings and patient self-reports. Staff ratings of patient anger were obtained via two instruments: the Ward Anger Rating Scale and the

Psychotic Inpatient Profile. The researchers found that patients who scored high on both scales were significantly more likely to be involved in and to perpetrate incidents of violence toward others during the 18-month follow-up period. They also found that the anger scores were significantly related to whether or not the patient was discharged from the hospital. Thus anger appeared to have a significant impact on an individual's behavior, along with influencing treatment decisions (Novaco & Renwick, 1998).

In another study of violence among patients with mental illness, Craig (1982) found that, of all the psychiatric inpatient admissions in one county during a 1-year period, 11% of the patients had engaged in assaultive behavior before admission and that anger was the factor most strongly associated with assaultiveness. Other studies have shown similar findings (e.g., Kay, Wolkenfeld, & Murrill, 1988; Segal, Watson, Goldfinger, & Averbuck, 1988). This body of research clearly suggests that anger represents a risk factor for violence, although violence can occur without anger and anger can occur without resulting in violence (Novaco, 1994). Though much progress has occurred in recent years in the development of anger management and anger reduction treatment, such interventions are still not fully developed (Novaco, 1997).

Emotional Dysregulation. Emotional dysregulation refers to the inability to control or modulate the subjective experience and expression of certain emotions, particularly negative emotions such as anger, panic, or dysphoria. Emotional dysregulation is theorized to have three dimensions: (1) a low threshold, or high sensitivity to emotional stimuli; (2) a high amplitude of emotional response; and (3) a slow return to emotional baseline (Linehan, 1993). In other words, these individuals are very sensitive emotionally; they can become easily overwhelmed with emotion and then have a hard time settling down. Emotional dysregulation is generally thought to result from a combination of two things— genetic susceptibility and learned responses to affectively laden early experiences. Over time, such individuals often develop maladaptive ways to deal with their intense emotional experiences, and this sometimes includes violent behavior toward self or others.

Substantial clinical literature supports the notion that violence toward self, for example, self-mutilation, can serve an emotionally self-regulating function in some individuals (Linehan, 1993). As clinicians, we know that self-injurious behavior can be associated with relief from overwhelming negative feelings because our clients tell us this. What happens is that the emotions "fire" under certain kinds of emotional provocation, and the self-destructive behavior that follows, although not planned and intentional, serves a clear function in the pattern of the disorder (M. Linehan, personal communication, 1997). The client feels better afterward. It is also possible that violent behavior toward others may serve a similar function—as a mechanism to regulate emotion by bringing the feeling of being emotionally overwhelmed to temporary closure, although, to date, this is still under investigation (Newhill & Mulvey, 2002).

Impulsivity. Clinicians take impulsivity very seriously when they are assessing the risk of violence both to self and to others. The association between perceived level of impulsivity and perception of dangerousness, in fact, has validity based on what we know about both impulsive and violent behaviors (Cleckley, 1976; Shapiro, 1965), in particular the cognitive style associated with impulsivity and how that style shapes behavior (Barratt, 1994; Lion, 1972; Webster, Douglas, Eaves, & Hart, 1997). Impulsive individuals commonly show a genetic predisposition to impulsivity (probably related to low levels of the neurotransmitter serotonin), difficulty in making planned choices, difficulty anticipating consequences, a tendency to act without thinking, and an inability to control their behavior even if they intend to do so (Barratt, 1994). Impulsiveness thus is directly related to an individual's capacity to control his or her thoughts and behavior (Barratt, 1972).

The "impulsive style" of functioning is one of four so-called neurotic styles, as conceptualized by Shapiro (1965). Although the impulsive style does not completely coincide with any one diagnostic category, impulsivity is a common characteristic in a variety of disorders, including delirium, dementia, some mental disorders due to a general medical condition, substance use and abuse disorders, bipolar disorder, dissociative disorders, some paraphilic disorders, disorders of impulse control not otherwise specified, adjustment disorder with disturbance of conduct, and certain personality disorders. In children and adolescents, one sees impulsivity in attention-deficit/hyperactivity disorder, conduct disorder, and oppositional defiant disorder.

The distinctive quality of the subjective experience of an individual who is impulsive revolves around an impairment of normal feelings of choice, deliberateness, and intention (Shapiro, 1965). An impulsive style, however, does not consist only of overt physical action. Passivity in the extreme can also be a manifestation of impulsivity in some individuals and is characterized by a "suggestibility to action" or a "giving in" to external pressure or temptation (Shapiro, 1965). An example is the passive person who is easily persuaded to participate in an activity with another person, for example, a group assault, about which he or she feels regretful or ashamed later. The persuasion of others pushes the individual into an activity that he or she would not engage in otherwise.

Clinical cases involving individuals in whom the impulsive style is chronic (a trait) are particularly difficult and anxiety provoking for clinicians to assess and manage. It is virtually impossible to predict, with absolute certainty, the future behavior of such individuals. When an impulsive client assures the clinician that he can control his behavior and then, immediately subsequent to the interview, becomes violent, he probably did not lie about his intentions at the time of the questioning. The move to action from impulse is so immediate that formulation of either a motive or a deterrent is short-circuited, or "left out." The process of normal integration from whim to active planned choice is essentially missing. The main objective is satisfaction of the immediate urge. If the immediate urge is to express rage, then hitting someone is a quick means to satisfaction. If the clinician points out to a client who has a problem with impulsivity that her actions have hurt other people and that what she does produces negative consequences for herself, the client may not disagree with the clinician, but she may have great difficulty in integrating the clinician's feedback in a way that would modify her future behavior.

Impulsive individuals are also characterized by a low tolerance for frustration or tension. Nonimpulsive people are able to tolerate frustration because it is experienced within the context of long-term goals and interests. These other priorities keep the immediate tension within a perspective that limits its subjective power and significance; this perspective then serves to control the individual's behavior. For an impulsive person who is unable to sustain long-range goals, immediate frustration gains in significance because he or she lacks a wider perspective. Impulsive individuals also typically have problems with poor judgment, and their decisions are often perceived by others as risk taking and reckless. The impulsive person is impaired in the ability to evaluate the consequences of his or her own behavior beyond the immediate reaction of whether the impulse was satisfied. This helps explain why an impulsive person will often minimize past problematic behavior. It is not only that she may want to hide the past behavior, but also, and perhaps more commonly, that what has happened in the past simply does not seem very significant anymore. Often, impulsive people are genuinely puzzled as to why everyone else remains so upset over something they did. For example:

Jack, a 28-year-old twice-divorced white male, was brought to the emergency room by the police. The police relay the following story: Jack was about to go to work when one of his buddies stopped by with a case of beer. The buddy talked Jack into having a beer with him, and before long both were drunk. Jack knew he couldn't go to work drunk, so he just kept drinking, never calling his employer. After having drunk half a case, the two men went out to get something to eat. They spied a red sports car parked at the curb, and Jack suddenly wanted to steal the car to go joyriding. They broke in, jimmied the wiring, and took off. Driving at high speed, they almost sideswiped another car. The driver of the other car gave Jack the finger, whereupon Jack became enraged and forced the other driver off the road. Both got out and, after swearing at each other, got into a fist fight. Jack was furious that the other guy would fight with him, and so he pulled out a knife "to show him who was the man." Someone who observed the situation from the road called the police. When the police arrived, Jack said something about suicide, so they brought him to the emergency room instead of jail. Upon evaluation, Jack said, "So what's the big deal, man? So I got drunk—the other guy threatened me. It's not my fault" (Newhill, 1995b).

In this example, Jack had originally planned to go to work. The unexpected visit from his buddy led to an escalating sequence of events, each involving impulsive action supported by poor judgment and recklessness to the point at which the police eventually became involved. Jack's reaction to the events was to justify his behavior by externalizing blame, and, in a sense, he was reflecting the reality that he did not engage in each event with active planned choice. Whether this translates into absolution of fault is another issue.

A significant proportion of the clients seen by clinicians in psychiatric emergency rooms exhibit an impulsive style of functioning, either as a trait or as one part of a crisis state. Impulsive behavior frequently results in voluntary or involuntary psychiatric emergency evaluation or the intervention of law enforcement. Understanding the dynamics of impulsivity and acquiring skill in evaluating the potential of such individuals for violent or other dangerous behavior is essential for the clinician, both in terms of personal safety and the general potential for violence. The impulsive individual who also has problems managing and regulating anger, as illustrated in the preceding vignette, is a special case of the impulsive style that has a potential for aggression.

Personality Disorders and Violence

About 10–13% of the general population in the United States meet the criteria for a personality disorder at some point in their lifetimes, and such individuals represent a disproportionate number of those seen in inpatient and outpatient clinical settings (Widiger & Trull, 1993). Individuals with personality disorders tend to exhibit four characteristics that cut across subtypes and form the foundation from which their difficulties emerge: an inflexible and maladaptive response to stress; serious and pervasive problems in getting along with other people, both in terms of working and achieving intimacy; elicitation of symptoms in response to interpersonal conflict; and, finally, a peculiar capacity to "get under the skin" of others (Vaillant & Perry, 1985). These are individuals who are often significantly disabled in their capacity to manage life, and debate continues as to whether a severe personality disorder should be classified as a severe and persistent mental illness. David Adler (1990), for example, argues that individuals with a personality disorder have a nonpsychotic chronic mental illness and that failure to recognize this prevents an appreciation of their significant impairment in functioning socially, occupationally, and interpersonally, thus creating an obstacle to their receiving sufficient and appropriate care and treatment.

Nine subtypes of personality disorder are identified in the DSM-IV-TR (American Psychiatric Association, 2000), and violence is not common to all of them. Although considerable debate exists about the best approach to diagnosing these disorders (Loranger, 1999), it is generally recognized that erratic, emotional, impulsive behavior is most characteristic of four of the personality disorder subtypes: borderline, antisocial, histrionic, and narcissistic personality disorders. Violent behavior, in particular, is seen most often in individuals with borderline personality disorder (Grosz, Lipschitz, Eldar, & Finkelstein, 1994; Snyder, Pitts, & Pokorny, 1986; M. H. Stone, 1990) and antisocial personality disorder (Eronen, Tiihonen, & Hakola, 1997; Robins, Tipp, & Przybeck, 1991).

Substance Abuse and Violence

The link between substance abuse, particularly alcohol abuse, and violence is well established (Teplin, 1994). There are four basic explanations for this link: (1) substance abuse causes violence; (2) violence causes substance abuse; (3) violence and substance abuse form a reciprocal relationship; (4) the relationship between substance abuse and violence is spurious (Parker & Auerhahn, 1998; H. R. White, 1990, 1997). Several direct and indirect levels of interaction are inherent in these different explanations, including the pharmacological effect of drugs or alcohol on aggression-specific brain mechanisms, the possibility that drugs or alcohol promote a social context in which aggression is an acceptable alternative behavior, the creation of a situation in which drugs are a commodity in an drug-trafficking economy enforced by violence, and the possibility of a set of social interactions in which violence simply serves as a means to maintain a drug or alcohol habit (P. J. Goldstein, 1985; Miczek et al., 1994; Virkkunen & Linnoila, 1993).

Examinations of the link between alcohol use and interpersonal violence indicate that intoxication appears to contribute directly to the violence, especially in individuals who are inherently aggressive (Chermack, Fuller, & Blow, 2000; Collins, 1989; Lang, 1993; Pernanen, 1991). For example:

> I had to see a client who had a long history of violence and had been in and out of jail. He had been in our psych hospital once, but it was clear that his basic problem was his antisocial personality and extensive drug abuse. The police brought him to the state hospital because he had threatened to kill his wife. When I saw him, he was clearly intoxicated and in a rage. When I told the police that we wouldn't hospitalize him, and to take him to jail instead, he made a threat to kill me. It was the alcohol talking, but he was also a pretty scary guy (Newhill, 1995b).

Individual characteristics, such as gender, social class, hostility level, and approval of violence affect the relationship of alcohol and violence, as does situational context, although it is still unclear to what extent environmental factors shape the connection (Leonard, 1993; Moss & Tarter, 1993). Furthermore, acute episodes of excessive drinking seem more likely to be associated with violence than is chronic alcohol use (Fagan, 1993). The role of alcohol in the escalation of violence in specific social contexts, however, is one area in need of further research (White, 1997).

The relationship between nonalcohol drug use and violence is murkier. No significant evidence suggests that illicit drug intoxication or dependence is directly associated with violence (Parker & Auerhahn, 1998). Illicit drug-related violence mostly results from illegal activities to obtain money to buy drugs and from efforts to control the drug market (Fagan & Chin, 1990; P. J. Goldstein, 1985). Whether reduction of the drug economy would substantially reduce violence, however, remains an open question, with some experts arguing that those violent individuals associated with the drug market would simply move on to other kinds of violence, such as robbery (Bureau of Justice Statistics, 1992; Osgood, 1994).

Individuals with both a mental illness and a substance abuse problem face special challenges. Today, comorbidity is a clinical expectation, rather than an exception, and the best treatment principles emphasize an integrated treatment model in which each disorder receives appropriate diagnosis-specific care (Minkoff, 2000). Both alcohol and illicit drug use have been shown, in epidemiological research, to be associated with a heightened risk for violence among people with mental illness, across the range of mental disorders (Steadman et al., 1998; Swanson, 1994). Similarly, there is some evidence that drug and alcohol use and symptomatology may have a synergistic effect related to violence, particularly if the individual is noncompliant with prescribed psychotropic medication (Mulvey, 1994; Swartz et al., 1998). How the interaction of substance use and mental illness sets the stage for violent incidents is well illustrated in the following composite case example:

> Janie, a 22-year-old woman, was brought to the emergency room by two friends at 3:00 A.M. They relayed the following story: Janie, her boyfriend, and the two friends were "partying" the evening before and admitted all had been drinking heavily. The two friends eventually went home, and Janie and her boyfriend began to drink vodka. They got into an argument, and the boyfriend told Janie that he wanted to go home, adding that he felt they were spending too much time together and he needed "some space." Janie began to cry, begging him not to leave her. As he started out the door she threatened to kill herself and ran into the bathroom, locking the door. The boyfriend tried to get her to come out, and when she wouldn't, he broke down the door. Janie was sitting on the edge of the bathtub, holding a razor, and her wrists were covered with blood. The boyfriend told her he wanted to take her to the hospital and tried to take the razor from her, whereupon Janie bit her boyfriend severely on the arm, actually biting out a large piece of his flesh. Scared, Janie called her friends to ask them to take her and her boyfriend to the emergency room. According to the friends, the boyfriend told Janie he was "sick of her behavior" and called one of his friends to come and take him to a different emergency room for treatment of his bitten arm (Newhill, 1995b).

Janie was diagnosed as having borderline personality disorder and major depression. She functioned fairly well most of the time, but the combination of alcohol, failure to take her prescribed antidepressant medication, and the perceived abandonment by her boyfriend was enough to set off intense dysregulated emotions, which led to suicidal behavior and to violent behavior toward her boyfriend. It is very important that clinicians always ask their clients about substance abuse. Because of the negative stigma associated with use of drugs, clients often do not volunteer such information, even though it may be a major problem in their lives.

Biological Risk Factors

Low Intelligence Quotient

Level of intelligence can function as either a risk factor or a protective factor for violence. A number of studies have shown that criminal dangerousness can be predicted from the combination of low IQ with antisocial personality (DeWolf & Ryan, 1984; Heilbrun, 1990). Low IQ operates as a risk factor because it contributes to the development of a concrete present-oriented cognitive style and impedes the development of abstract problem-solving abilities and the capacity to generate a range of coping alternatives when difficulties arise (Wilson & Hernstein, 1985). Individuals with low IQ are also less likely to be highly skilled verbally and thus more likely to resort to physical action in response to provocation. In contrast, high IQ can serve as a protective factor against engaging in violent behavior because bright individuals are more likely to have an abstract cognitive style that supports the ability to generate a range of response alternatives to problems and provocations without needing to utilize violence (Kandel et al., 1988; J. L. White, Moffitt, & Silva, 1989). Also, a high IQ can serve to protect a child or adolescent from falling into delinquent behavior by enhancing the probability of academic success and thus encouraging attachment to the school environment and teachers, which provides a source of positive socialization (J. L. White et al., 1989). The exception to this is the association of high intelligence with the type of violent behavior that requires the ability to engage in anticipatory planning and execution of complex activities, such as that involved in a kidnapping (Meloy, 1994). In such cases, high intelligence operates as a risk factor for violence rather than a protective factor.

Neurological Impairment

Although social workers cannot directly evaluate neurological impairment in clients, it is important for social workers to know what kinds of impairment are associated with violence. Information about whether a client has had any kind of neurological problems can often be elicited as part of the biopsychosocial history. A referral for medical evaluation can then be initiated if appropriate. Family input is often critically important in this regard, particularly if a neurological problem has impaired the client's ability to provide a good history.

The types of neurological impairment that have shown some association with violent behavior include dementia, head trauma, temporal lobe epilepsy, and stroke. Aggression in older clients who have dementia is usually reactive to some kind of provocation and is unplanned. Often such incidents occur during normal care by nursing home staff, such as during bathing, dressing, or redirecting a client who is confused (Bridges-Parlet, Knopman, & Thompson, 1994).

As evidenced by the colloquialism "having a fit of rage," popular opinion tends to associate epilepsy with violent behavior. Substantial investigation has been conducted on the association between seizure disorder, particularly temporal lobe epilepsy, and violent behavior (Volavka, 1995), which has shown that the violence usually occurs either during or immediately following a seizure. "The aggressive behavior . . . is usually trivial, appears purposeless, may reflect confusion, and is probably increased or even induced by attempts to restrain the patient" (Volavka, 1995, p. 103).

Head trauma may or may not be associated with violence, depending on the type of injury sustained. Individuals who suffer head traumas, particularly as a result of accidents, often have other risk factors for violence, including substance abuse and impulsivity (Crowner, 2000). Clients with frontal ventromedial lesions are at particular risk for aggressive behavior because such damage affects the ability of individuals to interact appropriately in social situations (Grafman et al., 1996). When provoked, they are unable to control themselves and, instead, may react aggressively (Lau & Pihl, 1995).

Finally, patients who have suffered strokes often become irritable, easily provoked, impulsive, and angry toward others (Paradiso, Robinson, & Arndt, 1996). Essentially, they evidence a biologically based emotional dysregulation, or what Kim, Choi, Kwon, and Seo (2002) refer to as "emotional incontinence" (p. 1106). In a study of 145 patients who were examined 3 to 12 months after suffering a stroke, 32% evidenced an inability to control anger and aggression (Kim et al., 2002).

HISTORICAL RISK FACTORS

History of Violence

The most powerful single factor that predicts future violence is past violence, particularly a history of repetitive criminal violence (Monahan, 1981); and the more frequently and recently that violence has occurred, the greater is the likelihood that violence will occur in the future. Thus, a past history of violence is affected by both the frequency effect and the recency effect (Meloy, 1994). To determine this, one must gather information about any self-reported history of violence toward others, any past arrests and incarcerations, and any self-reported history of violence toward the self. Sometimes clients are forthright in providing such information, but some clients, especially if they are on probation or parole, may be guarded about providing full and accurate information. It is critical to inform clients about confidentiality protections and limitations up front and to emphasize that information about violence is data that will help the clinician to help the client better. It is also useful to supplement client self-reports with official reports covering past arrests and incarcerations. Family members or other collaterals can also be helpful in providing information. In Chapter 6, I address in detail how to compile an accurate historical violence assessment.

Social and Family History

In 1966, Hellman and Blackman reported the triad of enuresis, fire setting, and cruelty to animals in childhood as predictive of adult criminal behavior. Although the association of enuresis and fire setting with violence has not been consistently replicated in subsequent studies, cruelty to animals appears to be more significant. Several authors report a positive association of childhood cruelty to animals, particularly toward pet dogs and cats, with adult aggression against people (Felthous, 1980, 1981; Felthous & Kellert, 1986). Much depends on what kind of animals are involved. Pulling the wings off a fly is not the same as setting a cat on fire. The more socially valuable the animal is, the more significant the cruelty is in terms of the deviance it represents. It is important to talk to family members about this issue, as clients may deny engaging in any animal abuse, even if they have such a history.

There are four family history factors that social workers must ask about when taking a psychosocial history, because these factors can potentiate the development of a pattern of interpersonal violence. The first factor is *remorseless physical brutality, excessive punishment, or abuse by caretakers toward the child, or witnessing intrafamilial violence toward others* (Corder, Ball, Haizlip, Rollins, & Beaumont, 1976; Duncan & Duncan, 1971; Jaffe, Wolfe, & Wilson, 1986). When children are exposed to actual violence in the home, they can become filled with feelings of rage, fear, mistrust, and helplessness, and, in effect, they are taught that violence is an acceptable way to solve problems (Meloy, 1994). Via the process of modeling, such children, especially boys, may develop a propensity for aggressive and assaultive behavior. Although most individuals who were abused or who witnessed violence as children do not grow up to be violent, studies consistently show that being victimized as a child increases the risk of victimizing as an adult (Meloy, 1994).

The second family risk factor is *parental loss, deprivation, neglect, ambivalence, or rejection.* Such experiences can lead to either of two re-actions in the child. Either the continuous frustration of rejection causes the child to withdraw and become submissive and depressed, or the rejection results in the child rebelling and reacting aggressively, which can evolve into a pattern of hostile behavior (Newhill, 1992). The third factor that can lead to interpersonal violence in children is the *presence of mental illness or drug abuse in one or both parents.* Violent psychiat-ric patients and those arrested for violent crimes frequently report histo-ries of parental alcohol or other drug abuse and the parental neglect or abuse that is often associated with it (Lewis, Shanok, & Pincus, 1983). Parental mental illness can negatively affect the parent's ability to meet the child's needs; the parent may be absent off and on due to psychiatric hospitalization; and, when one or both parents are mentally ill, there is a greater risk for mental illness to develop in the child due to both biologi-cal and environmental risk factors.

The *attitude of the family of origin about violence* (Meloy, 1994), especially tacit parental approval of cruelty to animals or people or a lack of consistent cultural taboos against killing or abusing animals or people, is the fourth factor. Margaret Mead (1968) notes how a cycle of violence can develop in children if certain cultural restrictions regarding the treatment of animals are absent. She emphasizes that in every culture children are taught which creatures they may or may not kill and how, which creatures are to be protected or loved, and which should be sim-ply left alone. Neglect of such cultural parameters can result in the child not being exposed to modeling of empathy, care, and respect toward other living creatures. Finally, other high-risk childhood behaviors asso-ciated with violent behavior in adulthood include repetitive fighting, temper tantrums (beyond the age when it is developmentally appropri-ate), uncontrollable rage episodes, bullying, ongoing severe school problems and truancy, interpersonal difficulties, and stealing (Carson, Butcher, & Mineka, 1998).

Work History

Whether an individual is employed, how stable that employment is, and what the individual's perceptions are about work are important factors to assess when considering risk of violence (Steadman et al., 1994). We know that unemployment or economic instability increases the probability of failure on probation or parole, as well as the risk of violence (Meloy, 1994). For example, Catalano and colleagues (1993) examined whether being laid off from work increases the likelihood of violence. They examined data from 4,049 participants from the National Institute of Mental Health Epidemiologic Catchment Area survey. Controlling for concurrent psychiatric disorder, the researchers found that the risk of violent behavior for those who were laid off was nearly six times as great as the rate for their employed counterparts (Catalano et al., 1993).

Furthermore, there is case evidence that economic instability, in combination with paranoid, narcissistic, and antisocial personality traits, may be the primary ingredient in multiple or mass homicides. Levin and Fox (1985) have noted that the profiles of individuals who engage in mass murders are different demographically from those of average homicide perpetrators. "The mass killer typically is a white, middle-aged male who can look like anybody" (p. 60). What triggers the killing? Unfortunately, many individuals who commit multiple murders also commit suicide, either by killing themselves or by engineering a gun battle with police that may be motivated by a wish to die. Consequently, those who study this phenomenon have found few perpetrators left alive to interview regarding motives (M. H. Stone, 1998). However, retrospectively, it is notable that such perpetrators often have had a history of experiencing losses that represent humiliating blows to self-esteem immediately preceding the murders. A job loss or other economic loss often figures prominently, such as being laid off, fired, reprimanded, or other work-related difficulties:

> On July 29, 1999, 44-year-old securities day trader, Mark O. Barton, killed nine people and wounded 12 others in a shooting rampage in two office buildings in the glitzy financial district of downtown Atlanta, Georgia. Barton is also suspected of killing his wife and two children. According to witnesses, Barton walked into the All-Tech Investment Group building and without warning or provocation began firing two guns at employees and customers. He moved from room to room, continuing to fire and then went to the second building. Barton escaped in his van but was located several hours later driving along the street. As police closed in, Barton shot and killed himself. A computer-generated letter and three notes were found near the bodies of his slain family. No motive was immediately apparent, but it was speculated that a Barton's recent marital separation and stock losses from his job as a trader may have played a role. (Sack, 1999)

Social workers often see individuals who have suffered job losses in a variety of settings, including public assistance or unemployment offices or mental health services. However, economic instability is often overlooked by mental health professionals as a factor that can influence both mental health status and risk for violent behavior. Unfortunately, those of us who have good jobs and stable incomes may sometimes not recognize or appreciate the anger, fear, and envy of those who do not (Meloy, 1994). If an individual perceives his job as the primary source of self-esteem and self-worth and that job is lost, and if other risk factors for violence are present, then the probability that a violent incident may occur increases.

ENVIRONMENTAL/CONTEXTUAL RISK FACTORS

Level and Quality of Social Support

In general, good social support seems to play a preventive role in risk of violence (Klassen & O'Connor, 1988). Individuals who live with others who are supportive have a buffer in place that can help them cope with adversity. Supportive others can also help in problem solving and developing nonviolent alternatives to problems. Just because an individual lives with other people, however, does not mean that he or she has good social support. Living with others who are unsupportive, hostile, or unavailable can actually potentiate violence. Thus one must look at the level and quality of social support—not just the presence or absence of cohabitants—and how the individual perceives that support, especially during times of crisis (Duenwald, 2002).

Peer Pressure

When an individual's peer group endorses violence, the risk of engaging in violence for that individual increases. Forty years ago, Wolfgang (1958) coined the term "subculture of violence," and, at its essence, he was referring to the influence of peer pressure. In such a situation, the individual believes that he or she must behave violently to be accepted and respected by the group. Human beings are social animals, and most humans want and need to feel affiliation with other humans. James Gilligan (1996) argues that the logic behind a lot of violent behavior is avoidance of feelings of shame and the desire for respect from others. Feelings of shame provoke humiliation, fear, anger, and paranoia, and those feelings, in turn, can lead to violence. The violence, then, serves to conceal these painful feelings and replace them with feelings of power and competence. When endorsed and reinforced by the peer group, the "logic of shame" becomes even more powerful. Gilligan, who is a forensic psychiatrist, notes that the prison inmates with whom he works comment repeatedly that the reason they assaulted someone was because the person "disrespected" the inmate. Inmates would often state that the event that gave them the greatest respect and feelings of competence was when they pointed a gun at somebody else (Gilligan, 1996, p. 109). Thus avoidance of shame, along with the fact that, for some individuals, violence results in feelings of respect toward self and from others, become primary motivators and reinforcers for violent behavior.

Influence of Popular Culture

We all live in the midst of this variable, and, of course, we are not all violent. So what is the influence of popular culture on violent behavior? Research has consistently shown a small but significant effect of media violence on actual violent behavior. However, important mediating variables determine whether exposure to media violence enhances risk. These variables include the individual's family history, the individual's temperament, the extent to which the individual believes in the reality of TV or movie fiction, the extent to which the individual can distinguish between fiction and reality, whether the individual identifies with an aggressive media character, how prolonged the exposure to violence is, and the nature of the violence the individual is exposed to (Meloy, 1994). We often think that it is the blood and gore that makes media violence so toxic, and, certainly, the level of blood and gore plays a role. However, the negative influence of violence in the media is more complicated than that. Many experts believe that it is the modeling of brutal antisocial behavior, the modeling of cruel sadistic behavior without consequences for the perpetrator, and the minimization of victim suffering that makes such depictions particularly damaging. Action movies, "gangsta rap" music, and violent video games are filled with so-called antiheroes who demonstrate repetitive antisocial violent behavior with little demonstration of empathy or caring for the suffering of others. It is this that distinguishes the horror slasher movie from a movie such as *Saving Private Ryan*, and it is this, I believe, that is most damaging. Finally, the common depiction in popular culture of violence as comedy (for example, the movie *Scream*) and mixing violence with sex (for example, the movie *American Psycho*) communicates a pathological message to viewers, that is, that violence is funny and violence is sexy.

In July 2000, four national health organizations—the American Medical Association, the American Academy of Pediatrics, the American Psychological Association, and the American Academy of Child and Adolescent Psychiatry—issued a statement addressed to Congress during a public health summit on entertainment violence in Washington, DC. The joint statement of the four associations cited 30 years of research supporting a direct link between prolonged exposure to violence in television, music, video games, and movies and increasing violence, aggression, and a desensitization toward violence in real life among children (Associated Press, 2000). Senator Sam Brownback (R-Kansas) compared the statement to earlier claims by the medical community that cigarettes can cause cancer, stating, "I think this is an important turning point. There's no longer any doubt about this" (p. A12).

This "turning point," however, has been long in coming. Concerns about the effects of violent media on children did not begin with violent video games, the Internet, and today's so-called action movies. As far back as 1948, the psychiatrist Fredric Wertham wrote about the brutalizing effect of violent comic book dialogue on children (Boxer, 1999), observing that many juvenile delinquents consumed a lot of crime and horror comic books. Wertham stated that an attitude of brutality was consistently observed in such comics, noting that there must be a connection between prolonged consumption of such material and delinquent behavior. Wertham also fought against racism and sexism in comics and was one of the first psychiatrists to suggest that we must look at the culture in which children are raised, not just their individual characteristics. Wertham's book, *Seduction of the Innocent* (1954), led to a series of congressional hearings that essentially "killed off horror comics [and] crippled crime comics" (Boxer, 1999, p. A19). Restricted by the First Amendment mandates, the federal government did not intervene; rather, the comic book publishing industry decided to police itself in order to save their business. Echoes of the concerns in 1954 are still apparent today, although we know now that violence is multifactorial and that exposure to media violence is but one of several critical factors influencing the expression of violent behavior. Japan, for example, produces comics that are far more violent than American comics, yet Japan's murder rate is much lower than that in the United States.

Means for Violence: Access to Lethal Weapons and Knowledge of How to Use Them

Assessing access to weapons and training is often neglected by mental health professionals, but it is an area that is a critical part of any violence risk assessment. In the United States, lethal weapons are readily accessible to individuals without training or licensing. Every year in this country, an average of 30,000 people are killed by firearms. Only car accidents surpass shootings as the leading cause of injury-induced fatalities; thus assessing ownership of and experience with weapons is critical. One structured assessment instrument, developed by Meloy (1994), is the Weapons History Assessment Method (WHAM). The screening form of the WHAM includes the following questions:

1. Have you ever owned or possessed a weapon?
2. Have you been trained in the use of weapons?

3. Do you continue to practice your skills with weapons?
4. Do you own or possess a weapon now?
5. Do you like to do things associated with weapons?

"Associated with weapons" includes such things as whether the individual likes to go to gun shows, to visit gun shops, to read military or gun magazines, or to see violent movies that feature certain weapons. These questions are intended to assess what Meloy refers to as "approach behavior," defined as an action associated with weapons that creates feelings of narcissistic empowerment or reduces paranoia. This behavior directly relates to the comments made previously regarding the role of shame and desire for respect in the expression of violent behavior. The respect that someone feels when pointing a gun at another person is really the feeling of narcissistic enhancement that the possession of the gun creates for the person holding the gun. The gun directly represents a mechanism for gaining self-respect by having power and control over another person.

Accessibility of Potential Victims

Although the bulk of this chapter has focused on risk factors for violence related to the perpetrator, aspects related to the victim are critical to consider. The larger and more available the pool of potential victims, the greater is the risk that victimization can occur (Meloy, 1994). Factors to consider in defining the potential victim pool include whether an emotional relationship is present, the geographical proximity of the potential victim(s), and how mobile the perpetrator is. Emotional connections between perpetrator and victim relate to motive, and geographical proximity and mobility relate to access. Looking at these factors, it is clear why friends and family, members are, categorically, those most likely to be targeted. One is more likely to have an emotional connection with friends and family, and contact time is likely to be greater than it is with strangers. Clients also have emotional connections with their social workers, and this emotional connection can play a role in some cases of client violence toward social workers. When calculating an individual's risk for violence, inquiring about potential victims—for example, asking whom he or she is angry with or wants to harm—is an important consideration for determining the appropriate focus of intervention. For example, if a paranoid patient indicates that he has a delusion that his mother is trying to poison him and has specific fantasies of killing her, it would not be prudent to send him to his mother's home to stay. Arranging for an alternative living arrangement would be much wiser and would reduce both geographic proximity and access.

CONCLUSION

Identification of the risk factors associated with violent behavior is rooted in a large body of research that has examined correlates of violence in an effort to improve the assessment and prediction of violence and the development of effective interventions for clients. These risk factors may be organized into three major domains: individual and clinical risk factors, historical risk factors, and environmental and contextual risk factors. All of these domains must be considered when conducting a risk assessment or providing treatment to violent clients. The strength or weight of each risk factor varies with each individual client, and thus one must examine the client's situation ecologically on a case-by-case basis when determining risk status. Furthermore, identification of risk factors must be paired with identification of protective factors that can mitigate against violence. For example, a young unemployed man who abuses drugs and has a borderline personality disorder has several risk factors for violence, but if he also has a strong social support network, he may be able to withstand the vicissitudes of his life and be able to manage any violent thoughts or impulses without harming others or himself.

Returning to the case of "Bob," presented at the beginning of the chapter, let's identify factors in the case description that elevate his risk for violence. First, Bob has several individual and clinical risk factors for violence. He is young and male and was diagnosed with ADHD and conduct disorder as a child. Having conduct disorder puts him at risk for developing antisocial personality disorder as an adult. He is also paranoid, he has made two recent threats (one to hit his mother, the other to kill his uncle), he is angry, and he is probably using alcohol and drugs (based on what was found in his room). On the positive side, he has not yet acted on the current threats. In terms of biological risk factors, he has a history of traumatic brain injury that has affected his school achievement and, perhaps, his ability to control his emotions and behavior. He has an arrest history for assault and associates with peers who seem to endorse criminal behavior. He has access to weapons (the rifles and ammunition found under his bed) and has targeted his aggression toward a readily available victim, his uncle, with whom he has a strong emotional attachment. Finally, he is attracted to violence-laden media— heavy metal music and the violent video game "Doom." The main protective factor that Bob has is the positive social support from his family, and this may significantly mediate his risk. His family clearly cares about Bob and has sought help for him. Although Bob says he doesn't want help, their support may eventually change that. There is no question,

TABLE 5.1. Summary of Risk Factors Associated with Interpersonal Violence

Individual/clinical risk factors

- Demographic risk factors
  Young age (although not always)
  Male gender (although not always)
  Low socioeconomic status (although not always)

- Clinical risk factors
  Mental disorder
  High-risk psychiatric symptoms (delusions, hallucinations, and violent fantasies)
  Personality features (anger, emotional dysregulation, impulsivity)
  Personality disorder (antisocial, borderline)
  Substance abuse (particularly alcohol)

- Biological risk factors
  Low intelligence quotient (IQ)
  Neurological impairment

Historical risk factors

- History of violence (recency and frequency of self-reports of violence toward others, arrests, incarcerations, and reports of violence toward self)
- Social and family history (early exposure to violence)
- Work history (economic instability, unemployment)
- History of psychiatric treatment and hospitalization

Environmental/contextual risk factors

- Level and quality of social support
- Peer pressure
- Influence of popular culture
- Means for violence (access to lethal weapons and knowledge of how to use them)
- Accessibility of potential victims

however, that Bob is at high risk for violence, and emergency intervention, such as hospitalization, may be appropriate. Table 5.1 summarizes the risk factors that have been covered in this chapter.

SKILL DEVELOPMENT EXERCISES

Case Analysis Exercise

Using Table 5.1 as an outline, read the following vignettes and, for each one, try to identify and outline all the risk factors that the client's situation presents. Think about what might be an appropriate disposition for the client, given the client's risk factor profile. Finally, see if you can identify any strengths in the clients' situations.

Vignette 1

The client, "John," is a 25-year-old divorced white male who asked for an appointment with a counselor because he wants help with his temper. He is an explosive man with a long history of antisocial acts, including assault and numerous incidents of property damage, always secondary to getting into a fight with another person. As an adolescent he was in and out of juvenile hall and was diagnosed with conduct disorder at that time. Recently, John lost his forklift business and blames the local police for that. Currently he is living with his mother but says he hates her and recently beat her with a shovel, almost killing her. He is asking for Valium but admits to drinking alcohol daily and using other assorted drugs—"whatever I can get hold of." Currently unemployed, John spends most of his time watching TV, smoking cigarettes, and drinking. Upon evaluation by the social worker, John looks furtively around the room and says, "You better help me or someone's going to get hurt, and it just may be you, pal" (Newhill, 1995b).

Vignette 2

"Jorge" is a 32-year-old single Hispanic male who has been diagnosed with paranoid schizophrenia and borderline personality disorder. He has never developed any insight, won't comply with medication, and needs ongoing structure and supervision. Even when on medication, he constantly hears voices but is cagey about telling clinicians what the voices say. According to hearsay, he and his sister attempted to murder their parents by burning down their house, but this was never officially substantiated. His father is now in prison, and his mother works as a prostitute. Jorge never finished school because he "just couldn't learn"and has been on disability since age 21. Jorge is asking for hospitalization and tells the evaluating social worker that he will kill him if the social worker doesn't comply with his request. He is angry and paces in the interview office, refusing to sit down (Newhill, 1995b).

Part III

The Instructional Package

Chapter 6

The Risk Assessment of Violent Clients

The previous chapters show that safety from violence is not just a perceived issue, but a real issue for many, if not most, practicing social workers. So, how do we protect ourselves, our colleagues, and our clients? I would argue that the first stage of protection is knowledge, that is, knowledge about violent behavior in terms of dynamics and risk and protective factors, how to effectively assess a client for violence risk, what interventions are feasible and effective, and what prevention strategies are useful. Chapter 5 addressed the first area. This section of the book addresses the other three areas in the form of an "instructional package" consisting of seven connected chapters.

Chapter 6 discusses the risk assessment of violent clients and provides guidelines to assist you in planning, organizing, and conducting the assessment. Chapter 7 addresses specific skills for approaching and engaging violent clients. Chapter 8 focuses on intervention modalities for treating the violent client. Chapter 9 presents strategies to prevent client violence in office settings and during home or field visits. Chapter 10 presents 12 general strategies for the prevention of violence. Chapter 11 discusses the impact of experiencing client violence on social workers personally; how colleagues, agencies, and victimized social workers can respond constructively in the aftermath of an incident; and how experiencing violence changes social workers' feelings about their profession and how they conduct their practice. Finally, Chapter 12 addresses future directions in the area of client violence and social work safety.

ENCOUNTERING A VIOLENT CLIENT

For most clinicians, the first encounter with a violent client is usually in the agency, for example, the emergency room or the inpatient unit, or in a field visit during which the client has said or done something threatening or violent. The client may have made a verbal or nonverbal threat, or thrown an object, or assaulted someone, and *you*, the social worker, are expected to handle the situation. You may have been part of the situation from the beginning, or you may have been called in after the violent incident occurred to provide intervention. There may be other people around the client—other staff members, police, other clients, or family members—and you may feel very intimidated and overwhelmed. This is a normal reaction. Effective risk management requires foresight, careful thoughtful preparation, the ability to systematically gather a lot of information quickly and in an organized fashion, and the ability to see both the forest and the trees simultaneously. The key to being able to intervene appropriately and effectively is having the right knowledge and skills training. Then, in spite of the stress of the immediate situation, *you will know what to do*, and that will give you the confidence to use the ability you have to help the client and protect your safety and the safety of others.

In conducting a risk assessment, you are essentially engaging in making a short-term prediction of the client's potential for violence. Although the prediction of violence remains controversial, and although some experts maintain that mental health professionals have no greater expertise in predicting violence than the intelligent layperson, the public and the courts continue to believe that clinicians can and should be able to predict whether a client will do harm to others (Beck, 1985; Newhill, 1992; Tardiff, 1996). Although this expectation may appear to put mental health professionals in a bind, Tardiff maintains that clinicians "should be able to predict a patient's short-term violence potential using assessment techniques analogous to the short-term predictors of suicide potential" (Tardiff, 1989, p. 3). "Short-term" is defined as a period ranging from a few hours to a few days, until the client is seen again for a reevaluation. Indeed, a more optimistic "second generation" of prediction research has developed that is based on short-term prediction, specific clinical criteria, statistical approaches, and quantified outcome measures (Monahan, 1984; Mulvey & Lidz, 1998). Making consistent *long-term* predictions, however, is nearly impossible because of the high probability that new factors will intervene and significantly alter the client's risk status: for example, the assaultive individual who is assaultive only when under the influence of alcohol and who, after a period of sobriety, resumes drinking, thus enhancing the risk for engaging in future violence (Tardiff, 1996).

An effective comprehensive risk assessment involves clinically examining a number of overlapping areas. Some of these areas should be addressed, if possible, prior to interviewing the client; some are relevant to the interviewing process itself; and some involve people, places, and events that make up the client's environment and the context of the client's current problems. Throughout the assessment of these overlapping areas, you should note the presence of any of the risk and protective factors reviewed in Chapter 5, which include *individual and clinical risk factors* (i.e., demographic risk factors, personality risk factors, psychiatric disorder, psychiatric symptoms, and biological risk factors), *historical risk factors* (i.e., family history, work history, history of psychiatric treatment, and history of crime and violence), and *environmental and situational risk factors* (i.e., anything relevant to the client's environmental context, including the level and quality of social support and available means for engaging in violence).

ASPECTS TO BE CONSIDERED WHEN MAKING A RISK ASSESSMENT

This section addresses each area to be considered when making a risk assessment and concludes with a summary table.

Background Information

The first sphere of inquiry is background information relevant to the client's immediate situation, including details of the events leading up to the current evaluation. It is a mistake to plunge into the assessment interview before reviewing whatever background data are available. Background data can provide a framework for what is happening currently and can alert the clinician to warning flags that may influence how the client is approached and which topics should be investigated in the assessment interview. For example, the client's clinical record may contain information about whether and under what circumstances the client has been violent in the past. We know that past violence is the best predictor of future violence, so knowing about such a history is important. Sometimes clinicians will argue that they do not want background information because they believe such information could unfairly bias their evaluations. However, having an uninformed, ill-prepared clinician evaluating him or her is certainly unfair to the client, and I would argue that one can have background knowledge and also maintain an open, unbiased mind toward the client's current situation.

Sources for background information include: the client's clinical records, particularly information about past hospitalizations, medication orders, other kinds of treatment, and the client's adherence and compliance with each treatment; information from collaterals, that is, family, friends, neighbors, clergy, other staff, police, and so forth; and other community records, including arrest records and other legal proceedings. Arrest records and other legal proceedings can often be obtained via the local or state police with a legitimate request. As you review records and talk with collateral individuals, pay attention to the following:

- Any history of violent or other antisocial behavior from childhood to the present (and the recency and frequency of the behavior), including fighting, cruelty to pet animals or other people, or the presence of any criminal behavior, particularly violent criminal behavior.
- The target(s) and triggers of past violence toward others, the degree of injury inflicted in such incidents, and the "circumstances and patterns of escalation of violence toward others" for all reported incidents (Tardiff, 1996, p. 128).
- Reports of any history of reckless, destructive, or impulsive behaviors (e.g., suicide attempts, destruction of property, reckless driving, unsafe sexual behavior, significant neglect of one's health).
- Any evidence that the client has experienced severe abuse or witnessed abuse or violence toward significant others, particularly family, as a child or as an adult.
- Whether any past violent behavior led to an arrest, incarceration, or hospitalization.

The importance of input from collaterals, especially those who know the client well, cannot be overemphasized. Such collaterals may include friends, family members, neighbors, coworkers, police, other staff, other clients, and anyone else who has observed your client, particularly in his or her natural community environment, over time. How the client behaves in your interview with him or her may be very different from how he or she behaves in the community. If your plan is to release the client back to the community, you must have an accurate picture of what that community is like and how the client interacts with and manages his or her environment and the people within it.

Under certain circumstances, you may not be able to obtain all the background information that is needed and available. For example, you may be working the night shift in the emergency room when other agencies are closed, charts are locked up, and staff members are not available. Or the computers may be down. (Although computerized records can be fast, accessible, and convenient, they are dependent, unlike a paper record, on the integrity of the computer system.) Finally, there is the issue of confidentiality. Other agencies may be unwilling or unable to provide information without a signed release from the client. Even if the client is willing to sign a release, there has to be time for the agency personnel to receive and process it. Facsimile machines are ideal here, provided that the receipt can be kept confidential. A fax machine located in a public place in the agency can be a problem because anyone might see the release with the client's name on it. Sometimes, particularly in an emergency situation, you cannot wait for all background information to come in. The rule of thumb, therefore, is to gather as much background material as you can in the time available and then proceed from there.

Clinical Status of the Client

Physical Appearance and Behavior

A good risk assessor is a good observer. The first aspect of evaluating the clinical status of your client is to observe how the client appears both physically and behaviorally, for example, facial expressions, speech pattern, and gestures. Note anything significant about the client's physical appearance, such as scars suggesting evidence of injuries from fighting or tattoos suggesting possible gang affiliation (Newhill, 1992). When I worked at a psychiatric emergency service in central California, I learned that a tattooed teardrop in the corner of a young person's eye meant that he or she had spent 1 year incarcerated in a California Youth Authority juvenile detention center. Seeing several tattooed teardrops was an indicator that a kid had spent some serious time in juvenile hall. Interestingly, many kids were very proud of their teardrops and saw them as a kind of honorable battle scar.

Does the client appear angry or agitated? A client who is simply anxious may be agitated but will not appear angry or be verbally abusive. A client who may escalate to violence usually demonstrates anger or hostility along with the agitation and usually expresses this in a verbally abusive manner. An assault without any prior expression of anger, hostility, or threat is rare. The exception to this is the extremely quiet but guarded client who is not overtly hostile but, in fact, may have violent ideation (Tardiff, 1992). Such clients often appear tense, as if they are barely maintaining control. In such cases, the clinician must carefully probe the client to determine whether he or she is experiencing such thoughts and what the content is. How to go about doing this is discussed later in this chapter and in Chapter 8.

The extent to which the client is compliant with routine requests and procedures is another indicator of the client's ability to control his or her behavior. If you ask the client to sit down in the interview room, is he or she able to do so or does he or she pace the room? Pacing behavior can be a precursor to violence (Dubin & Lurie, 1982). Does the client comply in providing basic information? A refusal to give his or her name, age, and other basic data may be an indicator that the client is guarded, suspicious, or paranoid. If the client appears to be paranoid, giving him or her choices as much as possible during the interview process can be helpful. For example, giving the client a choice of interview rooms to enter or chairs to sit in can help the client feel safe and in control, which may serve to encourage cooperativeness.

Does the client appear to be under the influence of drugs or alcohol? We know that drugs have a disinhibiting effect on behavior and thus can represent a risk factor for violence. Of particular concern is abuse of alcohol, cocaine, amphetamines, and hallucinogens (Slaby, 1990). People who are intoxicated with alcohol or drugs often show belligerence, disorganized behavior, lability of mood, hallucinations, and cognitive impairment, including impaired judgment. Other observable indicators of intoxication include tremors, an unsteady gait, and dilated pupils. Use your nose. Do you smell alcohol or marijuana on the client's breath? Being a good observer means using all of your senses, including your sense of smell.

How is the client dressed? Is he or she dressed appropriately for the weather? Is the manner in which the client is dressed within normal limits, or is it bizarre? Admittedly, given variations in dress stemming from differences in culture, ethnicity, and age group, this assessment can be difficult. However, some forms of dress can be clearly categorized as bizarre. For example, I once interviewed a client who was wearing three coats, four baseball caps, and two pairs of sunglasses simultaneously. That's unusual. As it turned out, the client was delusional and believed that without all the layers, radiation from outer space would invade his body and kill him. Thus bizarre dress can be an indicator of underlying problems.

What is the quality of the client's hygiene? Has the client bathed recently if he or she had the resources to do so? Again, use your nose! Deteriorating hygiene can be symptomatic of a range of psychiatric or medical problems, including schizophrenia, depression, and dementia. It also can be an indicator that the client is living marginally on the street without much support or resources. Many times clinicians are uncomfortable asking about hygiene for fear that the client will be offended. However, if the inquiry is posed in an empathic manner and is worded in a way that will be perceived by the client as caring concern, embarrassment can be minimized. In summary, you want to observe how the client appears and how he or she behaves and interacts with you. Talking with collaterals, that is, friends and family, regarding whether the client has changed recently in terms of appearance and behavior can also be very helpful in supplementing your own observations.

Assessment of Biological Risk Factors

An accurate and thorough assessment of biological risk factors must be completed by someone knowledgeable in psychobiology and its measurement. However, social workers must also be knowledgeable enough about such factors to detect evidence suggesting that a referral is needed and to know how and where to make such a referral. There are certain red flags to look for that, if present, suggest the need for a neurological or other medical evaluation. If, for example, the individual's history of violence is sudden, raging, explosive, and lacking in obvious purpose, followed by remorse, a neurological evaluation may be warranted.

Two biological risk factors to look for are the following:

1. *A history of central nervous system trauma,* such as head injuries and periods of loss of consciousness. One can begin the assessment by simply asking if the individual has experienced a recent head trauma, such as a serious fall or other accident. Family members can often be very helpful in providing this type of historical information if the individual him- or herself is unable or unwilling to do so.

2. *Current indicators suggesting possible neurological problems.* Nonmedical professionals can inquire about the so-called neurological "soft signs," including: recurrent dizziness, blackouts, memory lapses, severe headaches with nausea, visual hallucinations, experiences of déjà vu, automatic behaviors, dream-like states, or auras.

If you receive affirmative answers to inquiries about these two categories of risk factors, then referral for a medical evaluation is probably indicated. Meloy (1994) notes, however, that with certain individuals, one should watch out for the possibility of malingering, particularly if the result could affect criminal charges or monetary awards. Self-reports should always be corroborated with medical records or a thorough medical evaluation.

DIAGNOSTIC ASSESSMENT

After taking note of how the client appears and behaves, you should conduct a brief diagnostic assessment. The twofold purpose of a diagnosis is, first, to communicate a large amount of information succinctly and, second, to guide treatment, and thus a basic diagnostic evaluation will give you direction on where to go in terms of intervention (Fauman,

1994). If you are in an emergency situation, in which the primary objective is risk assessment for violence, you will not have time for a lengthy diagnostic workup, but there is much that you can still do in a relatively short period of time.

One handy tool helpful in accomplishing this is the mental status exam. The purpose of the mental status exam is to elicit specific standardized information about the mental condition of the client, which, in combination with the client's history and other assessment data, can suggest a diagnosis and the most appropriate initial treatment. The six main elements in the mental status exam are summarized in Table 6.1. (For a detailed description of the mental status exam, see Kaplan & Sadock, 1989.)

Based on the findings of the mental status exam and your own observations of the client's appearance and behavior, it can be helpful next to try to make a quick differential diagnosis, categorizing the client into one of four groups:

1. A mental disorder due to a general medical condition or a substance-induced disorder.
2. A psychotic disorder not due to a physical disorder, drugs, or alcohol.
3. A nonpsychotic mental disorder not based on a physical or substance use condition.
4. No disorder.

Depending on which category is the "best fit" for your client, certain considerations should be kept in mind.

Mental Disorder Due to a General Medical Condition or a Substance-Induced Disorder

Clients who have a mental disorder due to a general medical condition or a substance-induced disorder are often almost impossible to intervene with effectively through verbal means alone. With many such clients, your intervention must wait until the client is treated for the underlying general medical condition or has completed detoxification from the substance. Relying on medication to control the client's behavior without identifying the underlying cause first is not wise, because you do not know what is really going on with the client and thus will not be able to provide the most effective treatment. If the etiology is unknown and violence has been committed or is imminent, it is often the wisest move to have the client physically restrained or safely secluded until the nature of the problem can be determined. You may be able to achieve some prog-

TABLE 6.1. Elements of the Formal Mental Status Examination

1. *General appearance of the client.* Make an observation of the client's general appearance, demeanor, behavior, manner of dress, grooming, facial expressions, and motor activity.

2. *Speech and stream of thought or thought form.* Includes the rate and rhythm of speech and speech abnormalities, such as neologisms, pressured or slowed speech, blocking, circumstantiality, mutism, mumbling, incoherence, and problems with associations, for example, loose, tangential, or circumstantial associations.

3. *Mood, feelings, and affect.* Includes assessment of affect or feeling tone; assessment of mood, which refers to the sustained feeling tone expressed by the client; and range of mood—is the client's affect appropriate or is it inappropriate, labile, expansive, constricted, flat, or blunted?

4. *Perceptual disturbances.* Includes the client's general perception of world, such as friendly versus hostile; the client's level of reality testing; presence of hallucinations, which can be auditory, visual, olfactory, or tactile; presence of illusions; and reports of depersonalization or derealization.

5. *Thought content.* Includes relevancy of thought content; paucity or abundance of thought; abstract versus concrete thinking; the nature and content of any delusions, which can be categorized as persecutory, grandiose, erotomanic, jealous, or somatic; ideas of reference or influence; and, finally, phobias, fantasies, and dreams.

6. *Cognition.* Includes evaluating the client's consciousness, for example, clear versus clouded; orientation to time, place, and person; assessment of recent and remote memory capacities; findings on various intellectual tasks to test information and intelligence; and, finally, assessment of judgment and insight.

ress in helping the client by at least interviewing the client's family or friends, along with collecting whatever background information is available, while you are waiting for the client to be medically stabilized or cleared.

An important caution here is that psychiatric *symptoms* do not automatically mean that the client has a psychiatric *disorder*. Many general medical conditions produce psychiatric symptoms, and thus the possibility of a coexisting medical condition must always be considered. Background history is often very helpful in determining whether the client's life course suggests a psychiatric disorder or whether it is more likely that there is some other problem. For example, a 50-year-old client who comes to the emergency room agitated, psychotic, and combative and has no psychiatric history should raise concerns, because a first episode of psychotic illness usually occurs at a much earlier age.

General medical conditions in psychiatric clients are often overlooked. Inexperienced nonmedical clinicians, in particular, tend to underestimate the significance of physical disorders in clients with mental disorders. For example, research on risk factors for major depression and schizophrenia have shown that the occurrence of physical injury or illness in the year preceding the initial onset of the psychiatric disorder is a strong precipitating risk factor. Many physical problems have implications for clinical management of the psychiatric illness (e.g., drug therapy), and, in general, it is better to err on side of *over*inclusiveness rather than *under*inclusiveness. Individuals who have both a psychiatric and a medical disorder often have longer hospital stays than those with only medical illnesses (Hall & Frankel, 1996). Physical illness is particularly common in dually diagnosed clients, that is, individuals with major mental illness plus a substance abuse problem. Let's look at a clinical example:

> John, a 40-year-old homeless man who has suffered from schizophrenia for the past 20 years, came to the emergency room very agitated, complaining that the city's water system had poisoned his blood. He told the emergency room resident that he wanted all of his own blood removed and replaced with new blood, "and if you don't do this, somebody will pay." The resident concluded that John was psychotic and was about to prescribe a high-potency antipsychotic medication when he noticed the smell of alcohol on John's breath. Looking more closely, he noticed that the whites of John's eyes were yellow, suggesting jaundice. John admitted that he drank about a pint of vodka and a half gallon of "rot gut" wine per day and smoked marijuana "whenever I can get it." Suspecting alcoholism, the resident asked for a medical evaluation of liver enzymes, which revealed cirrhosis of the liver. Because of John's chronic mental illness, the first order of treatment would have been antipsychotic medication. Antipsychotic medication for people with liver disease, however, can be dangerous (Fauman, 1994), and therefore John's medical condition had serious implications for management of his mental illness (Newhill, 1995b).

As illustrated in the case vignette, substance abuse is a very common problem with violent clients. Furthermore, many clients these days, rather than using only one drug of choice, present as polysubstance abusers, particularly those who are dually diagnosed as having both a mental illness and a substance abuse problem. Although hospitalization is often the preferable means of sorting out such complicated clinical pictures, managed care and changing therapeutic philosophies may favor avoidance of hospitalization, and thus a careful outpatient plan with close monitoring may have to suffice.

When assessing substance abuse, it is important to determine *why* the individual is using substances. For those with coexisting mental illness, substance use may serve to medicate the psychiatric symptoms. Other clients may face peer pressure for continued use. For clients who may be socially isolated and lonely, drug use provides social support. Finally, of course, like most non-mentally-ill substance abusers, the mentally ill substance abusing client may just want to get high. Other issues that further complicate the picture are that clients can be intoxicated and withdrawing simultaneously, and that some substances cause medical complications, for example, heart attacks secondary to cocaine use, or HIV and hepatitis as a result of intravenous drug use (Slaby, 1990).

Psychotic Disorder Not Due to a General Medical or Substance Use Condition

Violent clients in this category usually have schizophrenia or mania and, again, are difficult to work with effectively using verbal means alone (Tardiff, 1989), although there are some approaches that can help. These approaches are addressed in Chapter 8. The typical initial treatment of choice with such clients prior to conducting a risk assessment is what is called "rapid tranquilization." Rapid tranquilization treatment means that a high-potency antipsychotic medication, for example, haloperidol (trade name Haldol), is administered and that an interview assessment can be attempted after a half hour or so (Dubin & Lurie, 1982; Slaby, 1990). To reduce side effects, a benzodiazepine, such as Valium, or a medication specifically for side effects, such as Benadryl, Artane, or Cogentin, may also be given. If the client cannot take antipsychotic medication (e.g., if he or she has evidenced neuroleptic malignant syndrome in the past or has a medical condition that precludes the use of antipsychotics), a barbiturate can be substituted, such as chloral hydrate. In some cases, to avoid the possibility of violence, the client should be restrained or secluded until the medication takes effect. Rapid tranquilization can provide clients with relief from agitation and partial relief from psychotic symptoms, thus enabling them to focus and participate more comfortably in a verbal interview.

Because this book addresses social work practice, it should be noted that social workers cannot prescribe medications and thus cannot institute a procedure such as rapid tranquilization independently. Because of this, it is incumbent on the social work clinician to anticipate that medication may be a necessary adjunct of clinical work and to plan ahead by identifying who he or she can contact for a medication evaluation and dispersal. For example, if the social worker is seeing clients in an outpatient clinic, psychiatrist backup should be arranged ahead of time. You do not want to be in the position of seeing a client who needs medication without a doctor being available. If you are in private practice, a cooperative arrangement with a psychiatrist should be arranged ahead of time so that you have someone to call on when needed.

Nonpsychotic Mental Disorder Not Based on a General Medical or Substance Use Condition

Violent clients in this group include individuals with personality disorders, most commonly antisocial, borderline, or paranoid personality disorders, who are often amenable to verbal intervention and usually do not require seclusion, restraint, or medication. In some cases, medication may be an appropriate course of treatment, depending on symptoms; for example, the transient psychotic symptoms of the borderline client may respond well to a low dose of an antipsychotic medication. Other individuals, who do not have personality disorders, may be violent in reaction to severe trauma or stress, such as experiencing a violent sexual assault or losing a loved one in a car accident. The following is a good example of this kind of situation:

> Mrs. L., a 76-year-old widowed grandmother, was brought to the crisis service by her son following an episode in which she had become very upset and thrown some china plates. The son was puzzled as to why his mother had become violent, because she had no history of violence and was typically very genteel and restrained in her behavior. Mrs. L. told the receptionist at the clinic that she would be willing to talk to someone, but only if it was a woman. Upon evaluation, Mrs. L. told the female social worker that she didn't know why she became upset but that she had been feeling very nervous over the past couple of days. During a detailed psychosocial history, however, Mrs. L. revealed that she had been sexually assaulted 1 year previously by an elderly widower whom she had known for many years and trusted. Although she was not seriously injured physically and did not see her doctor for treatment, she felt intense shame and emotional shock following the incident. She had told no one about it and had thought she had put it behind her. However, close to the 1-year anniversary of the incident, she had became very distressed over recurrent intrusive recollections of the assault and had difficulty sleeping and eating. Finally, when her son pressed her about calling a tree service to cut down a dead tree, she

became very angry and threw the plates. The social worker concluded that Mrs. L. was suffering from posttraumatic stress disorder with delayed onset and would probably benefit from some counseling and a short-term course of medication (Newhill, 1995b).

No Disorder

Finally, one has to consider the possibility that the client has no disorder. Violent behavior does not automatically mean that there is a mental disorder. All people have the capacity for violence, given the right (or wrong) conditions. For example, the most peace-loving nonviolent individual may resort to violence if he or she believes it is necessary to protect his or her child. Most individuals will fight to protect their own lives and may resort to violence in self-defense. Given the constantly increasing number and range of identified mental disorders, per the DSM-IV-TR (American Psychiatric Association, 2000), it is easy to make the mistake of labeling someone as mentally ill when, in fact, he or she may not be ill at all but may simply be angry, frustrated, or frightened. Anger, frustration, and fear are normal human emotions and are not necessarily indicative of pathology. Finally, some argue that there is merit in the so-called "evil theory" (Freud, 1930/1962), that is, that there are some individuals who are just evil and who prey on other people for their own narcissistically driven pleasure and gain but who do not have a mental illness per se. Fortunately, such individuals are still relatively rare.

THE ASSESSMENT INTERVIEW

After careful observation of the client's appearance and a diagnostic assessment, you should interview the client about his or her capacity for violence. Question the client directly in an empathically neutral manner about his or her potential for violence, including any violent thoughts or fantasies, obsessions or ruminations with violent content, and violent impulses (Newhill, 1992). You should note whether the client is currently making any threats, whether he or she has made threats in the recent past, and the degree to which the threat is planned and details of subsequent action worked out—that is, are the current threats well planned and feasible? In inquiring about violence, it is important to balance the questioning with calm, sincere, affectively neutral empathic support. Because clients may feel ashamed about their thoughts or actions, it is important that they believe you are willing and able to hear what they have to say.

During the interview, be actively aware of any changes in the client that suggest that he or she is becoming provoked by the interview. In such cases, it is best to stop the questioning and immediately provide calm support. If that fails, the option of imposing external controls—for example, restraint or seclusion—should be considered. Slaby (1990) notes that allowing a client to become violent harms the client because, from that point on, he or she will be labeled violent, and his or her care will be modified. Other people will avoid treating him or her, and certain services will be closed to the client. Thus preventing violence from occurring is one of the most therapeutic things you can do for your client.

If the client admits that he or she has thoughts of wanting to harm others or fears that he or she might harm others, even without wanting to, then you must ask about the circumstances. Does he or she have a specific plan? A specific plan would include details about *who* he or she may harm, *why* he or she may harm the person, and *how* and *when* he or she may harm the person. The more specific and lethal the plan, the greater the risk. Then you should ask the client if he or she will act on those plans and determine whether he or she has the available means for inflicting serious injury, such as any lethal weapons. For example, if the client has a fantasy of killing his mother with a gun, find out if he owns a gun. If so, does he have easy access to his mother? Finally, you should investigate the client's perception of his or her ability to control his or her behavior. Clients are often amazingly candid about this, and the client's own perception about her ability to control her behavior is a very important piece of data. Clients often feel tremendous relief in having the opportunity to share their thoughts and fears with someone who is willing and able to hear them in the context of helping them. Most people do not want to hurt others, and if alternatives are presented to them, they often are receptive to them.

You must also ask the client if he or she has ever thought of harming him- or herself and if he or she has ever attempted suicide or engaged in self-injurious behavior (Slaby, 1990). Violent individuals are significantly more likely to have a history of suicide attempts than nonviolent individuals (Tardiff, 1984; Tardiff & Sweillam, 1980). Why this is so is not entirely clear, although basic research has suggested that the mechanisms in the brain that produce impulsive actions may influence both violent and suicidal behavior (Brown, Goodwin, Ballenger, Goyer, & Major, 1979). After inquiring about violence to self and others, you must be prepared to deal with the answer (Slaby, 1990). The following is a dialogue based on a composite of several of my former clients that illustrates how inquiry about violence can be framed in an actual interview situation:

Case Example

The client, Joe Gonzales, was a 26-year-old Mexican American male who was brought to the emergency room by the police. Joe's mother called the police after Joe got into a fight with his brother and threatened to cut his brother with an axe. The police said that Joe did not resist going to the hospital with them, but Joe's brother didn't want to press charges, and the police officers were concerned about letting Joe go home. Joe had never been seen for a psychiatric evaluation prior to this one and, according to the family, had no history of mental illness.

SOCIAL WORKER: Mr. Gonzales, my name is Christina Newhill and I'm a social worker with County Mental Health Services. The police asked me to see you because they're concerned about what has been going on with you today. Do you know why they brought you to the hospital?

JOE: Look, call me Joe. I don't know . . . my mom called them, I guess. I just want to go home.

SOCIAL WORKER: I understand that you want to get out of here—I appreciate that—but first I want to talk with you a little bit, is that okay?

JOE: Yeah . . . okay (*reluctantly*).

SOCIAL WORKER: Joe, do you know why your mother called the police?

JOE: Well, uh . . . I got into it with my brother.

SOCIAL WORKER: Got into it?

JOE: Yeah, well, we got into a fight . . . over a girl . . . it was stupid.

SOCIAL WORKER: What happened exactly?

JOE: See, I broke up with my girlfriend a couple weeks ago and then I found out that my brother went out with her. I was pissed, you know, so we got into a fight.

SOCIAL WORKER: That must have really hurt, knowing your brother went out with your girlfriend. I can understand your being upset. What happened in the fight?

JOE: We were arguing about something . . . I can't remember what . . . then he threw it up in my face about my girlfriend and him . . . I called him a charro . . . so he tried to punch me and I got mad.

SOCIAL WORKER: What happened when you got mad?

JOE: I wanted to hurt him.

SOCIAL WORKER: Hurt him?

JOE: Yeah.

SOCIAL WORKER: Did you want to hurt him physically?

JOE: Sort of.

SOCIAL WORKER: Can you tell me what you did specifically?

JOE: Yeah . . . well . . . I got my dad's axe.

SOCIAL WORKER: And what did you do with the axe?

JOE: Tried to hit my brother with it. No . . . I don't know . . . I really didn't want to hurt him . . . just scare him a little. Him and my girl-friend . . . they hurt me, you know. I wanted him to hurt like I was hurt.

SOCIAL WORKER: How are you feeling about all this now? Do you still want to hurt your brother?

JOE: I'm okay. I wouldn't hurt him. I'm over it.

SOCIAL WORKER: Have you ever hurt your brother or anyone else in the past?

JOE: No, I've never done anything like this before. I'm not a violent per-son.

SOCIAL WORKER: Have you ever threatened to hurt anyone?

JOE: No, uh-uh.

SOCIAL WORKER: Joe, sometimes when folks feel like hurting others, they also feel like hurting themselves. Do you ever have any thoughts about wanting to harm yourself or feelings that life just is-n't worth living?

JOE: Nah, I don't think that kind of shit. Suicide's a sin, man. I was just mad at my brother.

SOCIAL WORKER: Are you eating and sleeping okay?

JOE: Yeah.

SOCIAL WORKER: Do you work at a job?

JOE: Yeah, I have a good job . . . I work construction . . . hey, they're not going to find out about this, are they?

SOCIAL WORKER: No, absolutely not. This conversation is completely confidential and since your brother isn't pressing charges, there won't be a criminal justice record. The police were called out so they have to make a report, but that's all.

JOE: Oh, okay. I just felt kind of scared you know. I mean, I like my job.

SOCIAL WORKER: Sure, I understand . . . now, let's imagine something for a minute. Let's say that you leave here and go back home. And you're sitting in the living room and in comes your ex-girlfriend with your brother. How would you feel?

JOE: It'd bother me.

SOCIAL WORKER: What would you do about that?

JOE: I don't know.

SOCIAL WORKER: Imagine how you'd feel if that happened. Would you feel like hurting your brother again?

JOE: I might. I don't know . . . I don't want to see him. If I don't see him, I'll be okay.

SOCIAL WORKER: It sounds to me like it would not be safe for you to go home where you might run into your brother. Is there any other place you could stay tonight?

JOE: I could stay with my uncle. He lives on the other side of town.

SOCIAL WORKER: If you stayed with your uncle, would you still want to hurt your brother?

JOE: No, I'd be okay. I wouldn't go looking for him or anything. I wouldn't hurt him. Look, I feel real stupid about the whole thing.

SOCIAL WORKER: Let me ask you this. Do you own any guns or other weapons?

JOE: No. Just my dad's axe—my mom took it when the police came and locked it up, though.

SOCIAL WORKER: What about your uncle? Does he own any guns or axes or other weapons?

JOE: No. I don't think so—I've never seen anything at his house.

SOCIAL WORKER: Okay, I have a phone here. Why don't you give your uncle a call right now with me here, tell him what happened, and see if he'd be willing to let you stay with him. If he is, will you stay with him and come back to the hospital to see me tomorrow?

JOE: Okay—that'd be fine. I could come by and see you on my lunch hour from work.

SOCIAL WORKER: Do you have a way to get here?

JOE: I could take the bus over.

SOCIAL WORKER: And, if you have any thoughts of wanting to harm your brother, or if you just feel like talking to someone between now and then, I can give you our number and you can call us anytime. Can you promise to call if you have any feelings of wanting to harm your brother or anyone else tonight?

JOE: Yeah, I can promise.

SOCIAL WORKER: Great. Before we call your uncle, I want you to talk with the crisis clinic doctor. . . .

JOE: (*interrupts*) Why?

SOCIAL WORKER: I just want to get another opinion about whether it's okay for you to go and stay with your uncle. We work as a team here at the clinic and when we see someone we're concerned about, as I am with you, it can be helpful to have more than one person see the individual. If the doctor agrees with my opinion, then you and I can call your uncle, talk with the police officers, tell them our plan, and you can go on your way.

JOE: Okay—but, like, how am I going to get to my uncle's? I don't have any money with me for the bus.

SOCIAL WORKER: Let's see if your uncle can come and pick you up. If not, perhaps the police would be willing to give you a ride.

JOE: Okay.

This case example depicts a client who has engaged in an act of violence and is brought to the clinic by the police, a common type of scenario. He is young and male—two demographics that place him in a high-risk group. However, he denies any history of violence, which is a protective factor. The social worker begins by telling the client who she is and where she is from and calls him "Mr. Gonzales" to convey respect, although the client subsequently asks her to call him by his first name. The social worker empathizes with the client's desire to go home but says she wants to talk with him. She then proceeds to investigate the incident that led to the police bringing him in. The client, in bits and pieces, reveals that he threatened his brother because he was hurt after learning that his brother dated his former girlfriend. The incident is particularly difficult for this client because, in Mexican culture, this type of situation is experienced as an exceptionally painful humiliation to his masculine pride. Recent humiliation is a common dynamic in violent behavior generally.

Next, the social worker explores whether the client intended to physically harm the brother and what circumstances might lead to a re-occurrence. The client indicates that he wanted to scare his brother rather than hurt him and says clearly that, as long as he doesn't see his brother, he can control himself and that he isn't going to go looking for him. The social worker then does a "rehearsal" with the client by asking him to imagine seeing his brother again with the ex-girlfriend and anticipating what he would feel and do. This emphasizes to the client the importance of staying away from his brother to avoid further violence, and the client agrees to ask his uncle if he can stay with him. The social worker ends by contracting with the client not to harm himself or others, inviting him to call the crisis line if needed, and setting up a specific follow-up appointment for reevaluation within the next 24 hours. Finally, the social worker arranges for the client to see the crisis doctor.

Getting consultation and second opinions from colleagues is a very important aspect of competent risk assessment. Others may see things you have missed, or the client may, for whatever reason, reveal information to the second person that he or she did not to you. A second opinion is also important in terms of liability. Having two people agree on the assessment decisions strengthens the position of both. Finally, it is extremely important that you have written documentation that the preceding information has been obtained and weighed, that the decision as to whether the client poses a potential for violence has been based on that information, and that a follow-up plan for reevaluation of violence potential has been implemented. The preceding dialogue is a condensed version of what would actually go on in a risk assessment interview, but it illustrates a number of the factors one should address.

Inquiring about Violence with Quiet, Guarded Clients

The loud, angry, agitated client raises obvious red flags, suggesting that a risk assessment for violence would be appropriate. These are the clients that get our attention because their behavior is overt. In contrast, the quiet, guarded client who may be equally at risk for violence is more likely to be bypassed because the indicators of violence potential are subtle or even intentionally hidden from superficial clinical observation.

Such clients are often paranoid and should be approached somewhat differently as a result. One must always bear in mind that paranoid clients see the world as a hostile place populated by numerous persecutors and potential persecutors, and thus they believe that they must be constantly on guard and hypervigilant to avoid harm. They project their own hostile, angry feelings onto others and may attribute malicious intent to the most innocuous actions by others. These are clients who engage in excessive faultfinding, are hypersensitive to criticism, and vigilantly collect perceived personal injustices.

Strict honesty, with genuine concern for the client's rights, is critical when assessing a paranoid client, along with maintaining a formal concerned distance rather than a warm empathic approach (Perry &

Vaillant, 1989). Being overly friendly or even too empathic may be met with suspiciousness. Assuming a stance of "consultation with an expert" with the client rather than one of providing treatment can also help in the process of conducting a risk assessment with guarded clients (Perry & Vaillant, 1989).

A central question in any client assessment is always, "What precipitated the current clinical contact?" If the paranoid client shows up on his or her own to the clinic, you can assume that he or she is there for a reason. Neutrally inquiring as to how you can be of help can begin the conversation. Sticking to gathering facts can be less threatening than attempting to discuss personal feelings. The key initial goal is establishing some modicum of rapport, and once this is accomplished, you can proceed as described previously. Quiet, guarded clients may require more time to connect with and elicit information from, but the same issues must be addressed. The following example is a good illustration:

> Mr. A., a 34-year-old married white male, came to the county mental health walk-in clinic asking to see someone "for advice." He sat quietly in a corner of the waiting room clutching a large grocery sack full of papers. When seen by the social worker, Mr. A. stated that he needed legal advice. When informed that he was at a mental health clinic, not a legal firm, Mr. A. stared at the social worker and again stated he needed advice. At that point he proceeded to reach into his sack and pull out papers and photographs, which he arranged on the worker's desk. "Do you see what I am up against?" he asked. The worker was puzzled and asked Mr. A. to tell her a little more about the papers. Mr. A. revealed that he believed that the papers were evidence that his wife was having an affair and later admitted that he had thoughts of wanting to harm her. He was very paranoid and had delusions of jealousy about his wife. The process of getting to this point took about an hour, but by that time, the social worker had established a fragile initial rapport and proceeded to conduct a formal risk assessment for violence. Although the client threatened to leave several times and often refused to answer questions, he didn't actually walk out, suggesting that on some level he recognized his need for help.

ENVIRONMENTAL ASSESSMENT OF THE CLIENT'S SITUATION

Now that you have collected background and collateral information and assessed the clinical status of the client, you must conduct the next phase of the risk assessment, which is an environmental assessment. Taking an ecological approach to risk assessment is the most effective in ensuring safety, and that means assessing the client within the context of his or her environment (Silver et al., 1999). Thus you must conduct an *environmental assessment*, which addresses factors related to the client's personal environment that the clinician should consider when assessing the client's individual risk for violence in the community.

The keystone to the social work practice perspective is viewing individuals, families, and groups within the context of their environment, sometimes referred to as the "ecological approach" (Hepworth et al., 1997). What this means is that the social worker takes into account the client's environment as a critical sphere to assess and understand as part of the helping process. In today's era of managed care, services that control the client's environment, such as 24-hour residential services, are being severely curtailed in favor of outpatient or ambulatory care services. This means that most clients are receiving help while living in their own environment and thus the nature of that environment and how it supports or hinders the client's functioning is important to consider. We know that where people live affects individuals, families, peer groups, and social networks (Silver et al., 1999). Consequently, when conducting a risk assessment for violence, you must assess whether returning the client to his or her environment will support safety or increase risk.

Issues related to the environment are also pertinent to clients living in 24-hour residential services, such as inpatient units, residential treatment, and therapeutic board-and-care homes. Just because the living environment is part of treatment does not mean that it is therapeutic and safe for your particular client. For example, the match between the client's needs and the residential service approach may not be a good one. A client who functions best in a highly structured environment would have difficulty adapting to a board-and-care facility that is open and has a hands-off supervisory style. Thus environmental assessment must always been conducted regardless of where the client lives.

The first area to assess, therefore, is the nature and quality of the client's social support system. In general, good social support seems to play a preventive role in risk of violence (Klassen & O'Connor, 1988). When assessing social support, you should look at the client's situation in terms of the following areas:

- *The client's living arrangements*: Does the client live alone or with others? If with others, are those relationships positive and supportive, or are they hostile and unsupportive?
- *The client's activities of daily living*: Does the client engage in activities involving positive interpersonal contact?
- *The client's perception of his or her social support*: Does the cli-

ent perceive him- or herself as having friends and positive social support, or does he or she perceive those individuals as not supportive?

- *What is the nature and quality of the individual's social networks?* Whether an individual perceives and experiences his or her social network as supportive and positive is extremely important (Estroff & Zimmer, 1994).

It is important to remember that, although someone may live with other people, the environment is not necessarily positive and supportive. Individuals who live and interact with others who are hostile, unsupportive, and provocative are more at risk for violence than those who live with others who are supportive and caring. For example, Hafner and Boker (1973a) emphasize the effect of strained family relations on the potential of a psychotic person to become assaultive. Furthermore, if the client suffers from chronic psychotic symptoms with systematized delusions that focus on his or her relationships with significant others, acts of violence are often committed against these very individuals. Violence is more likely to occur between individuals who have an emotional connection than it is between strangers.

Another important area to assess is the nature of the individual's neighborhood. Silver and colleagues (1999) examined the extent to which individual client characteristics related to violent behavior are conditioned by the context of the neighborhood in which they live following hospital discharge. That is, to what extent do the factors in the individual's home neighborhood serve as a source of or protection from risk for violence? They found that concentrated neighborhood poverty was a more powerful predictor of individual client violence than any of the individual risk factors, concluding that taking neighborhood context into consideration in risk assessment is critical (Silver et al., 1999).

Sampson, Raudenbush, and Earles (1997) found that the level of "collective efficacy" in a neighborhood is another factor that plays a significant role in determining how much violence occurs. An example of collective efficacy would be the extent to which neighborhood residents are willing to intervene in neighborhood activities to promote positive social order. Promotion of positive social order would represent a protective factor. In fact, several surveys of police departments in the United States have shown that 80% of the average police officer's time is spent on calls involving the promotion of positive social order, or what is referred to as *order maintenance* (Goldstein, Monti, Sardino, & Green, 1979). Police officers know that such work is important to the community because it directly relates to reducing subsequent crime. In certain neighborhoods, such as poor inner-city areas, this work is an ongoing challenge, because violence is part of the "code of the streets" and an expected and tolerated means to resolving conflict (Anderson, 1997). Such aggressive environments heighten the risk not only that the client may be violent but also that clients who cannot fight back will be bullied and victimized by the aggression of others (Estroff & Zimmer, 1994). Thus, when assessing the client's environment, you should consider the following:

- What is the quality of the client's social support in the environment? Is it supportive, absent, or hostile?
- What is the socioeconomic status of the neighborhood? Is the neighborhood characterized by concentrated poverty? Is it a stable community or a transient one? Transient neighborhoods high in poverty typically have low levels of social cohesion, which influences the extent to which neighbors can influence and control each other's behavior, such as aggression (Sampson et al., 1997).
- Will the client have easy access to the resources he or she will need day to day, for example, public transportation, grocery stores, laundromats, churches, and so forth? Are these resources welcoming toward individuals like your client?
- What is the culture of the neighborhood? Is it characterized by collective efficacy, or is there a street code that tolerates and encourages violence to solve problems and control resources? For example, will your client be accosted by drug dealers who attempt to extort money in exchange for safety in crossing the street?

Answering these questions can give you a summary picture of whether the neighborhood context will be a protective factor in the client's life or a factor that will increase risk for violence. This, then, has implications for intervention. Table 6.2 summarizes the main points of risk assessment that have been discussed in this chapter.

CONCLUSION

This chapter has addressed the risk assessment of violent and potentially violent clients and has provided guidelines to assist you in planning, organizing, and conducting the assessment. In conducting a risk assessment, you are essentially engaging in making a short-term prediction of the client's potential for violence by examining a number of overlapping areas, including:

- Background information relevant to the client's immediate situation that incorporates details of the events leading up to the current evaluation.
- Input from collaterals.
- The clinical and diagnostic status of your client.
- The client's potential for violence toward others and self, includ-

TABLE 6.1. Summary of the Guidelines for Risk Assessment of the Violent Client

Background and collateral information

- Review available official documents: clinical records, including past hospitalizations, medication orders, other treatment; criminal justice records, such as arrests and incarcerations.
- Determine whether there is any past history of violence toward self or others or any history of abuse, either as perpetrator or victim. If there is a history, determine triggers, targets, and circumstances.

Clinical assessment of the client

- Note anything significant about the client's physical appearance that suggests risk for violence, including scars, tattoos, or certain dress patterns.
- Note whether the client is angry, hostile, agitated, threatening, or verbally abusive.
- Note the extent to which the client complies with routine requests and procedures as an indicator of the client's ability to control his or her behavior.
- Conduct a diagnostic assessment to determine the presence of any psychiatric or medical risk factors, including any evidence of substance abuse.
- Inquire about the client's potential for violence toward others, including who, why, how, and when he or she may harm another individual.
- Inquire about the client's potential for violence toward self.
- Following your evaluation, obtain consultation from colleagues. Provide written documentation that sufficient risk assessment information has been obtained and evaluated, that the decision as to whether the client poses a potential for violence has been based on that information, and that a follow-up plan for reevaluation of violence potential has been implemented.

Environmental assessment of the client's situation

- What is the quality of the client's social support in the environment? Is it supportive, absent, or hostile?
- What is the socioeconomic status of the neighborhood? Is the neighborhood characterized by concentrated poverty? Is it a stable community or a transient one?
- Will the client have easy access to the resources he or she will need day to day?
- What is the culture of the neighborhood? Is it characterized by collective efficacy, or is there a street code that tolerates and encourages violence to solve problems and control resources?

ing any violent thoughts, violent fantasies, obsessions with or ruminations about violent content, and violent impulses.

- An environmental assessment.

Some of these areas should be addressed, if possible, prior to interviewing the client, some are relevant to the interviewing process itself, and
some involve people, places, and events that make up the client's environment and the context of the client's current problems. The completed
risk assessment will then guide the choice of interventions. Bear in mind,
however, that interventions must be provided as needed and some—for
example, rapid tranquilization with medication—may be appropriate
during the process of assessment to enable its completion. Chapter 7 addresses intervention approaches with violent clients.

SKILL DEVELOPMENT EXERCISES

Case Analysis Exercise and Role Play

This two-part exercise presents a case of a client who has made a threat
to kill a social worker, a doctor, and a nurse. First, read the case and discuss the case analysis questions. Next, follow the instructions for the
risk-assessment role play. Both parts of the exercise can be done together
or either part alone.

The Vignette

Mr. A. is a 58-year-old divorced Vietnam War veteran who was escorted to the psychiatric emergency clinic by police for evaluation.
Mr. A. has been using an electronically powered wheelchair ever
since he lost both legs in the war in 1968. He is on full veteran's disability and has been treated several times at the nearest Veterans
Administration medical center for alcoholism and posttraumatic
stress disorder. One month ago he again requested admission to the
alcohol inpatient unit, but this time was refused entry. Staff told
him that until he was willing to follow up with outpatient treatment
and involvement in AA, they would not consider another admission. This made Mr. A. extremely angry. He immediately returned
home, got drunk, and then called the alcohol unit and threatened to
kill the admitting physician, the head nurse, and his former social
worker. The staff member who answered his initial phone call hung
up on him, which angered him further, and he continued to make
threatening phone calls until staff members finally called the police.
The police went to Mr. A.'s home, and when he refused to answer
the door, they broke it down. They claim that they found Mr. A. sitting in his wheelchair holding a bottle of sleeping pills and a bottle

of vodka. They interpreted this as an indication that he was sui-cidal, and, based on that and the threats, they brought him to the local community mental health center. Upon arrival, police stated to the evaluating social worker that "nobody really takes his threats seriously because he's in a wheelchair, and so what could he really do?" (Newhill, 1995b).

Case Analysis Questions

1. How is this client being responded to by others? Would others' responses be the same if he were not paraplegic? Do you detect any prejudices, stereotypes, or insensitivities displayed by the various professionals in contact with him?
2. The client is angry and has made threats to kill three people. What are the obvious sources or triggers of his anger? What unmet needs or wants are reflected in his anger? What interventions might be employed to respond to his anger appropriately and constructively?
3. What helping systems are involved in the situation? What systems should be involved that are not?
4. Briefly outline the first five steps you would take in interviewing this client and dealing with his threats.

Risk-Assessment Role Play

This exercise is a role play between two people using the preceding vignette. One person plays the client portrayed in the vignette, and the other person plays the social worker. A third person could also be included as an observer. Using the Summary of the Guidelines for Risk Assessment of the Violent Client in Table 6.2 as a framework, the person playing the social worker interviews the person playing the client and attempts to gather as much information as possible about all the facets in the risk assessment summary guidelines.

At the end, the "social worker" summarizes his or her assessment of the "client" and his situation. The "client" then gives the "social worker" constructive feedback about the assessment interview process. Did the "client" feel empathized with? Did the "client" feel understood by the "social worker"? Did the "social worker" miss any important information? What were the perceived strengths of the interview? Could anything have been done differently to enhance the effectiveness of the interview?

Chapter 7

Approaching and Engaging the Violent Client

This chapter addresses the various approaches that are effective in engaging and interviewing clients who have problems with violent behavior. First, I discuss how to prepare to intervene with an aggressive client, including anticipating your role in the relationship and the kinds of countertransference reactions that may occur. Next, I discuss how to choose a safe interviewing environment and how to verbally connect with an aggressive client, including clients who may be psychotic or involuntarily hospitalized, using empathy, communication skills, and the strengths approach. These engagement skills can be used both in the office and during home visits. More detail regarding special considerations for home visits is provided in Chapter 9.

PREPARING FOR THE INTERVENTION

The Role of the Social Worker

Violence is a relationship between the person who perpetrates the violence and the person who is the target of the violence. A social worker who is the target of a client's violent behavior often plays a critical role in the precipitation and escalation of the violence. This is not to imply that the social worker should be blamed; rather, the point is that the victim is always part of the relationship in some way. In 26% of 588 homicides reported by Wolfgang (1958), the victim was the first to show or use a lethal weapon or to use physical violence. Also, words, looks, and attitude can be as provocative as physical blows. A sarcastic remark, an

147

angry look, a belittling statement can be very powerful in provoking a threat or in serving to move a threat toward violent action. Clinicians' countertransference reactions, for example, projecting rage onto or rejecting a client, may also provoke violence, and these feelings may not be fully conscious. As previously mentioned, it is important to bear in mind when analyzing client violence that such violence does not occur in a vacuum. To make a threat, one needs someone else to threaten. The dynamics of the relationship between the one who makes the threat and the one who is threatened can provide clues to motive and, subsequently, to the focus and goals of preventive action, as the following composite case from the CV Study illustrates:

> "I was seeing a very clingy, demanding client that I had known for about 6 months. I didn't want to see him that day, and I guess I wasn't as empathic as I usually tried to be with him. It was late on Friday afternoon, and I wanted to finish up and go home. Suddenly he accused me of not caring about him and then threatened to smash my head against the wall. I immediately confronted the threat, apologized for not being supportive, told him I wasn't feeling well, and asked him to not take my mood personally. Eventually I managed to get the client to calm down. I know now that the next time I feel angry toward a client, I need to get a grip or talk to a colleague or even reschedule the client rather than risk setting the client off because of how I'm feeling."

In this case, the social worker did not deliberately provoke the client, but his attitude toward the client was one of resentment and lack of empathy. The client immediately picked up on the worker's mood, felt rejected, and then became enraged. Fortunately, the worker was able to engage in immediate self-reflection and recognize his role in provoking the client—including an understanding of how perceived rejection can lead to rage—and was then able to neutralize the rage by providing empathic support. Because the worker's action was immediate, the threat was reduced, and physical violence was avoided.

Which Social Workers Are Most at Risk?

When I conduct workshops on risk assessment and intervention with violent clients, I am invariably asked the following question: "Which social workers are most at risk of being victimized?" We know that some worker characteristics do seem to elevate risk in practice. The CV Study found that male social workers were significantly more likely to be targets of client violence than female social workers and that they experienced higher rates of violence than female workers (Newhill, 1996). Explanations for this finding may lie in gender differences related to practice setting and the greater willingness of male social workers to work with violent clients. Paradoxically, male workers *perceived* themselves to be *less* at risk than females did. One could speculate that this factor may play a role in male workers being more willing to place themselves, or in being asked by others to place themselves, in high-risk situations, thus leading to a higher probability of experiencing violent incidents. Anecdotally, many male respondents in the CV Study stated that they were frequently called in to intervene with violent clients, particularly when the client's worker was female; thus case assignment practices by supervisors may play a role in male workers' elevated risk (Newhill, 1996).

These findings on gender raise some important questions. Is it more culturally acceptable to express violence toward males than toward females? Is it more acceptable to place males in risky situations than to place females in risky situations? Do males self-select high-risk positions, or are cultural forces in operation? Do some male workers incite violence somehow by their practice approaches? For example, some investigators have reported that clinicians who are more authoritarian are more likely to experience client violence (Kronberg, 1983; Ray & Subich, 1998). If we want to ensure safety for all workers, males and females, we need to look for answers to these questions.

CHOOSING A SAFE INTERVIEWING ENVIRONMENT

Facing an agitated, angry, verbally threatening, and abusive client is very intimidating, particularly if the client is unfamiliar to the clinician. Violent clients are often brought involuntarily to the agency. They are not asking for a social worker's help and may be forced to see you against their will by other interested parties, such as family, friends, the police, or the court system. Under such therapeutically adverse circumstances, how do you successfully engage the client? Here you must balance two considerations: (1) safety and (2) choosing the approach that will best serve to empathically connect with the client and provide compassionate care.

Safety is important not only because you want to protect yourself but also because any feelings of nervousness, apprehension, or fear will interfere with the effectiveness of any interventions you apply and may result in escalation of the violence and increase the risk of subsequent physical injury. Thus, when you decide how and where to interview the client, you must be sure that your decision supports feeling safe and being safe with the client.

There are a range of choices in terms of interviewing environments, from most restrictive to least restrictive. Most social workers believe strongly in the importance of employing the least restrictive alternative when working with clients. This is an ideal, however; and although one might value it, reality may dictate a more restrictive alternative in order to fulfill the goal of safety. Because the level of restrictiveness can change as your work with the client progresses, your initial choice of a more conservative approach to restrictiveness can be changed if you judge such change to be prudent and therapeutic. Tardiff (1996) identifies five interview options, graded from least to most restrictive, as follows:

- Interviewing the client alone in the office with the door closed.
- Interviewing the client alone in the office with the door open.
- Interviewing the client alone in the office with the door open and staff members present outside the door.
- Interviewing the client with staff members present inside the office.
- Interviewing the client while the client is in physical restraints.

The least restrictive and most private option is to be alone with the client in the interview room with the door closed. Being alone with the client means that you do not have immediate visible access to other people who may be a source of protection, but there is still much that you can do to promote your personal safety. For example, the usual recommendation is that the clinician should sit between the client and the office door. If the client becomes violent, you will be the closest to the door and can easily escape. Some have made the argument that allowing the client to sit by the door decreases the risk that the client will feel trapped, which serves to reduce the potential for violence. The problem with this argument is that such a seating arrangement traps *you*, and you will have more difficulty escaping. The best design for an interview office is to have two doors so that both you and the client can sit by an exit. Many clients will choose escape before they choose violence. For example:

> "I was interviewing a client who had been brought in by the police because he was trying to direct traffic in a busy intersection downtown and had almost been hit by a car. I had seen this client twice before, so we at least had an acquaintance. As I began to inquire about what had happened to cause the police to bring him in, the client became very agitated and then threatened to punch me. Fortunately, the interview room had two exits—I was sitting by one and the client was sitting by the other. The client stood up and

balled up his fist as if to try to hit me but then he saw the door next to him, opened it, and ran out of the room and out of the clinic. The police caught him and brought him back, this time keeping hand-cuffs on, along with sitting unobtrusively in the interview room with me" (Newhill, 1995b).

In the CV Study, 8% of the clients who engaged in attempted or actual physical attacks were trying to escape from some kind of confining situation, usually a locked inpatient unit, and attacked the social worker simply because he or she was in the way or because the worker was perceived as the main obstacle between the client and escape.

To recap, the most private option, albeit the least protective of safety, is to be alone with the client in the office with the door closed. If you do not feel safe with the client under these circumstances, the next option is to interview the client alone in the office with the door open. If you do not know the client, or the immediate history is one of violence and unpredictability, or the client appears agitated and threatening, this option is preferable to the first. This option preserves some privacy and enhances safety, because the open door increases the probability that staff members will hear any calls for help. Safety is further enhanced if staff members stand by right outside the open office door. In this case, however, privacy is further decreased because the staff members can hear clearly what is going on in the interview.

What do you do if the client asks you to close the door? Remember, safety is one of the main priorities, and you must respect your assessment and gut feelings and not feel obligated to abide by the client's request. However, it is important to be sensitive to the issue of privacy, and the client is entitled to an explanation as to why you prefer the door to remain open. For example, you could say the following: "I understand that you would prefer that I close the door, however, I am more comfortable with the door open for now until we've had a chance to talk some more. Could you tell me more about what was happening when your mother called the police?" If the client still insists that he or she wants complete privacy, you can then say: "I understand that you want privacy, but I'm concerned about what your family has told me about what happened today, and you still seem pretty upset. For everyone's safety, I would prefer that the door remain open until we've sorted out what is going on and how we can help you." In this statement, the clinician is frank about the safety issue but is not blaming the client. Furthermore, the safety issue is combined with the message that the clinician wants to learn the facts of the situation objectively and, most important, wants to help the client.

The fourth option is to interview the client with staff members present inside the interview room. This option is the best alternative if the client is not in restraints but is highly agitated, unpredictable, or threatening. Intoxicated clients usually fall within this category. It is also a good alternative in cases in which, although the client may appear in control when you see him or her, a reliable witness has reported serious threats or violent behavior just prior to the evaluation. Even with staff members present in the room, violence can still occur. For example, Newhill (1995a) reports the case of a social worker who was interviewing a psychotic client who had been brought to the hospital by two sheriff's deputies after he was found walking naked down the middle of a highway. Although the social worker interviewed the client with the deputies present in the room during the interview, the client was still able to leap across the room and try to strangle the social worker. However, because the deputies were present and were able to act quickly, the social worker suffered only minor injuries.

The final, and most restrictive, interviewing option is to interview the client while the client is in physical restraints. Other clinicians and researchers have written extensively about the proper use of restraint and seclusion (see, e.g., Bernay & Elverson, 2000; Tardiff, 1996), addressing indications and contraindications, proper procedures, methods of containment, and proper documentation; thus these issues are not addressed here beyond briefly noting the primary indications. Restraint and seclusion are two different interventions with different purposes. Restraint is indicated under three conditions (Tardiff, 1996): (1) to prevent imminent harm to the client or others when less restrictive means are not effective; (2) to prevent significant disruption of the treatment program or serious damage to the physical environment; (3) as an appropriate consequence in a behavioral treatment program. In contrast, the purpose of seclusion is to reduce the stimulation a client is exposed to, either by recommendation of staff or at the client's request. Psychotic and manic clients, for example, are often highly sensitive to any kind of sensory stimulation, and seclusion can help reduce stimulation, which can have a beneficial effect on the client's symptoms and the client's response to medication.

Attempting to physically control a client can be a high-risk activity for staff members, and many studies report that a significant proportion of staff injuries occur during containment procedures (see, e.g., Fisher, 1994). To be physically restrained by someone else can be a dehumanizing and humiliating experience for the client (Bernay & Elverson, 2000), and thus it is usually viewed as a treatment of last resort. To ease the client's fear and humiliation, it is extremely important to explain to the client clearly why he or she is being restrained or secluded and what will happen to him or her in the immediate future, even if the client is grossly psychotic or manic and may not appear to follow what you are saying. On some level, he or she will hear you, and such understanding will be a significant comfort for the client. As a former client once commented to me: "I know I was really out of it and you probably didn't think I heard you but I did, and knowing why the cuffs were on and that they'd be taken off once I felt better helped me feel less scared in the hospital" (personal communication, 1983).

When making a decision about restrictiveness, rely on your clinical judgment, based on your gut feelings related to safety combined with a thorough risk assessment of the client. In addition, you should pay self-reflective attention to any negative countertransference reactions, such as anger or denial, on your part that might interfere with effective intervention with the client. If you realize, for example, that you are feeling resentful about seeing the client, give yourself a time-out before you begin the interview or make any decisions about restrictiveness. Talk it over with a trusted colleague, take a few minutes by yourself to sort out your feelings, or consider the possibility that perhaps you should refer the client to a coworker if you are too angry, upset, or resentful to provide effective intervention. Even in high-pressure settings such as emergency rooms, you can always take a few minutes to reflect and collect your wits. In addition to countertransference reactions, we all have bad days, and things can happen in our personal lives that can temporarily affect our clinical abilities. You must be able to recognize when this happens and be willing to make decisions accordingly, with the client's best interest in mind.

ENGAGING AND TALKING WITH THE VIOLENT CLIENT

Once you have decided where you will interview the client, the next question is: How do you approach the client? First, you should speak in a normal tone of voice, not loudly or too softly, in a nonprovocative, nonjudgmental manner and begin by commenting in a neutral, concrete way about an overt aspect of how the client appears and behaves (Tardiff, 1996). For example, you could say to an angry client, "You look angry," or to a visibly anxious client, "You seem to be very anxious." This opens the conversation with an clear concrete message that you are attempting to understand what the client is experiencing. You want to avoid any negative or belittling comments, because such comments are provocative and may result in goading the client into aggression. You want to appear both in control and nonthreatening.

Second, you want to be sure that there is adequate space between you and the client. You should both be on the same level, either both sitting or both standing, preferably sitting. You want to avoid being physically above or below the client, because such differences symbolize differences in power and control. You don't want to be literally "looking down on" or "looking up to" the client. If the client is on a gurney in physical restraints, rather than standing by the gurney, sit down so that, although the client is lying down, you can still be at eye level with him or her. You don't want to present yourself in an intimidating way, because you want to avoid putting the client in the position of feeling powerless and having to defend him- or herself. Respect for the client must be consistently conveyed, both in your verbal and nonverbal messages.

Third, you should try to avoid continued direct eye contact with the client, because it may be interpreted as a challenge that could provoke violence. Communicating a challenge via direct eye contact is an aggressive behavior demonstrated by most animals, including humans. Two wolves, for example, who are preparing to fight over territory will circle each other and stare at each other's eyes until one of them makes the first aggressive move. You also don't want to appear to be avoiding eye contact. A good way to handle this is to look at the client at a point between his or her eyes. This way you are looking at the client and communicating interest and involvement, but you are also avoiding direct eye contact.

What do you do when the client begins to talk? When the client begins to talk, you should listen and appear empathic, concerned, and uncritical, which should be natural for most social workers. It is important that you do not interrupt the client and that you let him or her have his or her say. Often clients who are violent or threatening have difficulty in expressing themselves verbally, and so your role at this stage is to support and encourage their verbal expression without interrupting them with premature advice. If you do not do this, you may provoke the client:

> "I was interviewing a client who had been brought in by the police after threatening to kill himself and his child. The client had great difficulty in expressing himself, and I was feeling really anxious about the situation and wanted to get it resolved. As he was slowly telling me about how his life was unraveling, I stupidly jumped in and finished a sentence for him. He became very angry and then wouldn't talk to me anymore. I had to call in a colleague to finish the interview. The best thing I learned from that experience was the importance of being quiet" (Newhill, 1995b).

The goal is to try to obtain the client's view of the situation and what led up to the violent incident. Once this information has been elicited, then you can gently begin to state your perception of the situation and work on correcting any misunderstandings or misperceptions held by the client. Finally, as you proceed with the interview, avoid making any premature promises (Tardiff, 1996), for example, promising not to admit the client to the hospital before your evaluation is complete or promising a resource that may not be available. The reason for this precaution is straightforward: You may not be able to keep that promise, and not keeping a promise can rupture the fragile trust built between you and the client. Say to the client honestly, "I don't know yet if you will be hospitalized or not. I need to complete my evaluation first, and a decision will be made."

Engaging Violent Clients Who Have Delusions and Hallucinations

As noted in Chapter 5, violence in psychotic individuals usually occurs when the psychotic symptoms, such as paranoid delusions or command hallucinations, make the individual feel personally threatened (Link & Stueve, 1994). You should not try to argue the client out of a delusion, nor should you collaborate in the delusion. The job of the clinician, when intervening with such an individual, is to understand the nature of the symptoms and then take whatever action is needed to help the client feel safe. Helping the client feel safe is the best antidote to preventing violence in such cases.

Taylor and colleagues (1994) also suggest that certain qualities of the delusional beliefs carry a greater risk of violence. For example, the strength of the individual's delusional belief and the nature of the content of the belief—for example, the extent to which the individual believes that an outside agency has spiritual or physical control of him or her—has a significant association with subsequent violent behavior. Thus clinicians should do more than simply note whether a delusion is present or not. Rather, adequate evaluation of the potential of the delusional belief itself to influence violence is critical. Such an evaluation involves assessing the content and fixity of the delusion, along with exploring the client's perception of the impact of the delusion. Does the client feel safe? If not, what does the client believe needs to be done to achieve safety, and does such action involve violence? Some clients are very guarded about revealing the content of their delusions, and others are not. However, if the client believes that the clinician's motive in gathering information about his or her delusion is to ensure his or her safety and welfare, and if the clinician empathizes with the client's fear and anxiety, then enough trust may be achieved for the client to reveal the information needed. At that point, the clinician can engage in problem solving with the client, with the goal of identifying alternatives that avoid violence. The following composite case provides an example of how this approach works:

> The client was a young woman who had been diagnosed with paranoid schizophrenia. She was compliant with her medication but still had an unshakable delusion that workers at a certain fast-food restaurant were controlling her mind. In the town where she lived, there were several restaurants in this chain, and she had to pass by one of them to get to the day treatment program at the mental health center. She was becoming very anxious and revealed that she was thinking of doing something violent to the personnel of that particular restaurant to force them to close. I discussed with her the risks of doing this and asked if we could talk about some alternatives that would help her to feel safe. She agreed to work on this, and we identified an alternate route to the mental health center that would allow her to avoid passing by the restaurant. The plan included identifying alternative public bus stops so she could easily make the trip, whether she walked or rode the bus. She tried this and it worked well for her. The delusion remained, but she felt safe and didn't have any more thoughts of violence (Newhill, 1995b).

Clients who experience command hallucinations telling them to harm others are more than twice as likely to be violent as those who do not have such hallucinations (McNeil et al., 2000). Thus, when evaluating violent or threatening clients who are psychotic, it is important to investigate whether the client is experiencing command hallucinations and, if so, what the content of the hallucinations is and whether the client thinks he or she can ignore the hallucinations or whether he or she must comply with them. The individual's actual and perceived ability to cope nonviolently with hallucinations is a critical variable when assessing violence risk and determining the most appropriate treatment. The following composite case example illustrates this:

> The client was a 23-year-old man with paranoid schizophrenia who came to the hospital emergency room asking for admission. He had been seen at the psychiatric emergency clinic every other day in an effort to get treatment to control his severe auditory hallucinations but hadn't had much relief. Up until that day, the voices had been loud but benign. At this point, he said he was hearing command hallucinations telling him to kill other people, particularly family

members. With an impending holiday, his family was having various gatherings. The anticipation of having so many people around was making the client more anxious and fearful about losing control. He stated he could not ignore the voices any longer and was afraid he would get a gun or knife and kill someone that night if he was not admitted. He was very agitated, preoccupied, appeared to be responding to internal stimuli, and was irritable. In spite of close outpatient follow-up and compliance with his medication, he had not stabilized, and, therefore, it was decided to admit him to the hospital. When he was told of the admission decision, the client said he felt relieved and began to cry (Newhill, 1995b).

Although evidence from numerous studies over the past decade have shown a positive relationship between command hallucinations and violence, this association may be related to a number of moderating variables (McNeil, 1994). For example, the nature and course of the disorder causing the hallucinations is relevant (Monahan, 1988). During acute episodes of psychosis, there is a stronger relationship between command hallucinations and violence than there is during periods in which the individual is stabilized with treatment, even if he or she is still experiencing hallucinations. Medication seems to help not only in controlling the hallucinations but also in enabling the individual to better handle the hallucinations that remain. As a client once commented to me: "When I had to go to the hospital I couldn't handle the voices—they were too loud and I just lost it [meaning that he had became violent]. Now after being in the hospital and taking my medicine, I still hear voices, but I can ignore them" (personal communication, 1985).

The individual's environment is another critical variable that affects whether or not the hallucinations will lead to violence. Studies have shown that individuals with paranoid schizophrenia are more likely to be violent outside the hospital, in the community, than they are when stabilized within a structured hospital setting (Krakowski, Volavka, & Brizer, 1986). McNeil (1994) suggests that the reason for this may relate to a variety of factors, including differences in how a client responds to medication in the community versus in the hospital, different responses related to the structure provided by an inpatient unit versus the openness of the community setting, greater compliance with treatment on inpatient settings, and the greater likelihood that the client will encounter individuals in the community about whom he or she has delusions. In sum, the best treatment for psychotic symptoms to prevent violence is medication and positive, structured social support. If that fails, hospitalization should be considered.

Engaging Involuntarily Admitted Violent Clients

Many violent individuals come to clinical attention involuntarily, and thus it is important to know the strategies that can be effective in engaging and intervening with such clients. The *legally involuntary* client is under some kind of judicial mandate that requires social work intervention, whereas the *socially involuntary* client is not under legal mandate but is under strong social pressure to participate in treatment—for example, the husband whose wife tells him to get counseling or she will file for divorce. Being involuntary means that the client has lost some valued freedoms, and this loss can precipitate a range of responses, including hostility and aggression, obstinacy, and refusal to cooperate or participate in treatment. To reduce these responses and increase the probability of engaging the client, the clinician can use a number of useful strategies, including the following (Murdach, 1980; Rooney, 1992):

- Approach the client with respect and present yourself in an authentic and genuine manner.
- Support client self-determination by increasing the client's choice of alternatives as much as possible.
- When using confrontation, combine it with empathy. You can empathize with the client's feelings, such as anger and resentment, but remain firm about mandates and behavior limits.
- Explore two or more sides to questions and decisions.
- Avoid overemphasizing suggestions for behavior change.
- When identifying areas in which the client must change, be highly specific, identify areas in which the client doesn't have to change, and emphasize that the clinician–client contract will focus on the eventual restoration of freedom.
- Use bargaining and negotiating as a strategy for treatment contracting and goal setting and set feasible goals that support clients's strengths.

As you can see, these strategies emphasize the use of empathy and drawing on client strengths. These are two very critical areas when working with violent clients.

THE ROLE OF EMPATHY AND COMMUNICATION SKILLS IN WORKING WITH VIOLENT CLIENTS

Along with presenting yourself in an authentic and genuine way, empathy and good communication skills play crucial roles in working with violent clients. Empathy involves communicating an understanding of the other person's feelings without taking that person's position, thus retaining one's separateness and objectivity. There are several ways in which empathy can be used to connect with violent aggressive clients (Hepworth et al., 1997).

First, empathy helps to establish initial rapport with the client. Violent clients are often clients who have not experienced much empathy from others. In spite of the fact that the client may be experiencing painful feelings, the violence he or she has engaged in has usually served to elicit angry punitive responses from others rather than support and understanding. Connecting with someone who is willing to empathize with whatever feelings are behind the violence can be very beneficial. This does not mean that you condone the violent behavior; rather, you attempt to understand what the client is experiencing and feeling.

Second, empathy enables you to stay in touch with the client as you are interviewing him or her so that you can sense any subtle shifts in mood and behavior that may be precursors to violence. This can serve to promote safety because you will detect minute changes indicating escalation of anxiety, agitation, or aggression. Third, empathy assists in gathering data from the client. Many violent clients are guarded about answering questions and providing information, but empathy can serve to build trust. Fourth, empathy can help in correcting clients' misunderstandings, confusion, fears, or anxiety and can help in managing anger and aggression. Violent clients often report feeling angry, hurt, and frustrated about their conflicts with other people and their inability to resolve such conflicts without violence. Empathic responding can help clients work through such feelings by ventilating, by encouraging them to think through their conflicts, and by clarifying and relinquishing painful feelings until they feel more in control and can begin to make some rational decisions about their situation and develop nonviolent alternatives to solving their problems.

Fifth, and finally, empathy is helpful in maintaining your safety if the client becomes angry with you, because it can help you to avoid a defensive reaction and will support efforts to understand the client and tune in to his or her frustration and feelings of helplessness. For example, clients may expect you to make the police disappear or the criminal charges go away, or they may have other unrealistic expectations of what you can do to help them. When faced with the reality of their situation, they may lash out at you. Being clear about limits but at the same time empathizing with their feelings of frustration can help de-escalate the client's anger and prevent any violent action.

Client violence and aggression, however, come in all forms, and sometimes clients have committed behaviors that you find repellent and difficult to understand—for example, the husband who is brought to the clinic on charges of domestic violence and then indignantly complains to you that his wife won't obey him even when he beats her. Or the mother who is referred to you from jail on charges that she shook her 2-week-old baby, causing brain hemorrhaging, because the baby wouldn't stop crying. Conflicts can occur between your personal and professional values and your client's expressed values or behavior that can negatively affect your ability to empathize. How can one empathize with someone who has committed a heinous act? How can we as social workers remain helpful and nonjudgmental toward someone whose behavior upsets or even disgusts us?

One approach that can be useful is to try to separate the *person* from the *behavior*. In this way, you can affirm the client's worth and dignity *without* condoning behavior that may be destructive or harmful to the client and other people. It is important to realize that in order for the client to be willing to look at alternative ways of handling his or her life, he or she must feel understood and respected by you.

Although it may be tempting, you should avoid moralizing with clients, particularly with clients who have problems with aggressive behavior. Moralizing can induce shame and humiliation, and these are individuals who often already harbor such feelings. You should give the client an opportunity to save face, and moralizing will only reinforce the shame that the client is already experiencing (Gilligan, 1996). Avoiding this, however, requires that you are clear about where you stand in terms of values so that you can separate your values from the values and needs of the client. Then you will be better equipped to approach clients who are behaving in ways you would never personally condone in an empathic and nonjudgmental manner. This will give you a better chance to help the client change his or her destructive behavior into positive behavior.

ROLE OF THE STRENGTHS PERSPECTIVE

Another important component in working effectively with violent clients is using a strengths perspective. The strengths perspective is an important ingredient when working with violent clients because, rather than immediately focusing on what may be wrong with the client, it capitalizes on the client's strong points, positive qualities, current coping abilities, and overall potential for resolving his or her problems and controlling his or her behavior. In contrast, the violent client is usually focused on his or her own weaknesses, limitations, or past mistakes and often feels powerless and ashamed. The strengths perspective can be helpful for clients who have problems with violence because it engenders hope and encouragement and enhances motivation rather than simply punishing them for their behavior. The following is an example of a dialogue between a social worker and a client that illustrates both the use of empathy and the strengths perspective.

Case Example

The client was a 26-year-old single African American man who was brought to the emergency room by the police. The client had been drinking and got into an argument with his father. When the father took his bottle of whiskey away, the client assaulted him with a broom. The client came willingly into the social worker's office but kept his head down and wouldn't make eye contact.

SOCIAL WORKER: My name is John Smith and I'm a social worker here in the emergency room. The doctor asked me to see you because he thought I might be able to help you with what is going on tonight. Could you tell me why the police brought you in to see us?

CLIENT: I don't know. What difference does it make?

SOCIAL WORKER: Well, the police usually don't bring someone in unless something happened. Who called them out?

CLIENT: My mom.

SOCIAL WORKER: Do you know why your mom called them?

CLIENT: I'm just a piece of crap . . . (*begins crying and doesn't say anything else for a couple of minutes*) . . . oh man, I was just drunk. Look, just get out of my face. I don't need some social worker poking into my life.

SOCIAL WORKER: Sounds like things aren't going so well and you're feeling pretty upset. I really want to help you, but I'd like to hear your side of things. I don't want to just go on what the police have told me. Or what your mom says. Could you tell me a little about yourself? Are you living with your parents?

CLIENT: Yeah.

SOCIAL WORKER: Are you working?

CLIENT: Yeah, I work. I have a good job. Look, I know I have a drinking problem, you know. And I went to rehab and got sober—I've been sober for six months and I'm just living with my folks 'til I can save up enough money to get an apartment. But my girlfriend left me and I bombed out—starting drinking again—my dad tried to take the bottle away and so I hit him and I feel like crap about it . . . (*sobs*) . . . my folks have been good to me. Are they going to put me in jail?

SOCIAL WORKER: I don't think you're going to jail—my understanding is that your folks aren't pressing charges—they just want you to get some help. From what you're telling me, you've been doing great until today. You've been sober for several months—that's a tough thing to do—and you've got a job and plans for the future. Part of recovery is realizing that everyone can relapse, and most folks do, particularly when there's a crisis, but the key is to get back into recovery and you can do that—you did it before. You haven't lost all you've accomplished.

CLIENT: Yeah, I guess . . . I have an AA sponsor and he's an okay guy.

SOCIAL WORKER: Good. You can give him a call from here if you want after we finish talking. I can understand that you're feeling really bad right now, but you've got a lot going for you and I think your folks know that. Tell me a little more about what happened with your girlfriend. . . .

This excerpt illustrates how the strengths perspective can be interwoven into the clinical interview. Here we have a client who has been doing well with his substance abuse problem, but a crisis sent him into a relapse and an incident of violence. What the social worker does is to validate and empathize with his painful feelings and also give him positive feedback about the areas in which he has significant strengths. These strengths represent resources that can be tapped to help the client resolve the current problem. If you view your clients positively, with a sincere belief that they can work out their problems, they will usually adopt the same attitude eventually, if not immediately. They will leave your conversation feeling realistically hopeful that they have the capacity to solve their problems.

CONCLUSION

Approaching and successfully engaging a violent client is a challenging task, particularly if the client comes involuntarily and has not sought help on his or her own. This challenge is compounded if the client is suffering from serious psychiatric symptoms, such as psychosis, that can impede his or her ability to trust and connect with the clinician. This chapter has addressed how to prepare for interviewing the violent client, both clinically and in terms of the interviewing environment, and how to use empathy, communication skills, and the strengths approach to do this successfully. One must always remember that violence is a relationship, and thus establishing an empathic, trusting relationship with the client is one of the best strategies to prevent violence toward you, the clinician. Chapter 8 focuses on reviewing a range of suggested treatments for work with violent clients, with emphasis on the indications and contraindications for each type of intervention.

SKILL DEVELOPMENT EXERCISES

Engaging Violent Clients Role-Play Exercise

Following are five client situations in which the clients are violent and either legally involuntary, socially involuntary, resistant, or a combination thereof. Role-play participants should be divided into pairs—one plays the role of the client, the other plays the role of the social worker. A third participant may be added in the role of observer to give feedback to the role-play participants. In the role play, the social worker should interview and engage the client and try to accomplish the following goals:

- Directly address the violence expressed by the client
- Establish initial contact and rapport
- Express appropriate empathy
- Identify, communicate, and draw on the client's strengths
- Monitor his or her own feelings throughout the role play
- Provide appropriate confrontation
- Establish the beginning of an intervention plan

Client Situation 1

The client is a white male, age 18, on probation for motor vehicle theft and reckless driving. His probation officer has sent him for counseling because she is concerned about the client's inability to control his temper; thus counseling has been made a condition of probation. Failure to comply will result in jail time. The client has been given a dual diagnosis of personality disorder and chemical dependence. Before he can even be called into the social worker's office, he barges in and kicks over a chair.

CLIENT: Look, man, I don't need no social worker. I've got to find me a job and a place to crash—the courts have messed me over enough already. I don't have nothing to talk about.

Client Situation 2

The client is a Hispanic male, age 36, who had been ordered to counseling by the court because he was convicted of a second driving under the influence (DUI) charge. When arrested, he got into a fight with the police officer and punched him. Failure to comply with treatment will result in jail time. He looks angry, slouches in his chair, and glares at the social worker:

CLIENT: I don't know why I have to talk to you. So I had a couple of beers one night? So what? I don't have a drinking problem—I can stop any time I want to. My only problem is having to see you. Get out of my face or I'll fix you like I did that cop.

Client Situation 3

The client is a 28-year-old African American female who has been accused of neglecting her baby. The child protection social worker makes a home visit. When she introduces herself, the client slaps the social worker across the face and tells her to leave. The client's family then restrains the client and asks the social worker to please stay and talk with them. According to the family, the patient suffered a head injury six months ago after a car accident and has been unpredictable since then. They say that they have tried to help her care for the baby but she refuses their help.

CLIENT: (*Doesn't say anything and just cries*)

Client Situation 4

The client is a white female, age 21, ordered to counseling by the court and child protection services after she left her two children, ages 5 months and 6 years, home alone for 2 days. The court claims she was out copping dope with her boyfriend; she also has a history of bipolar disorder. To get her children back, she must comply with treatment. She sits sullenly in the chair and digs out a crumpled yellow paper from her purse and throws it at the social worker.

CLIENT: Here's the damn court paper. Do what you have to do and let me get out of here.

Client Situation 5

The client is a Japanese American male, age 21, seen in the jail infirmary after trying to hang himself in his cell. The jail has requested that you evaluate him for a possible psychiatric commitment. He was jailed on a charge of assault with a deadly weapon and has been diagnosed with antisocial personality. As the social worker enters the room, the client throws a wastebasket toward him, although it doesn't end up hitting him.

CLIENT: You don't give a shit about me—it's just your job. You think I should live? Well, just give me one good reason. Don't have one, huh? Get out of here and leave me alone.

Chapter 8

Intervention Modalities for Treating the Violent Client

This chapter reviews the range of suggested treatments for working with violent clients and emphasizes the indications and contraindications of each. Several treatment modalities can be appropriate, including medication, hospitalization, restraint and seclusion, psychotherapy, and behavior therapy. I consider how to intervene when a client makes a threat, with a special emphasis on the duty to protect potential victims from client violence. The chapter concludes with a report of findings from the CV Study regarding the types of interventions that social workers actually use when faced with an incident of client violence and the outcomes for the clients involved.

MEDICATION

There is no such thing as an antiviolence drug per se, but, depending on the etiology of the violent behavior, medications may be helpful. There are five main classes of psychotropic medications: antipsychotic or neuroleptic drugs, side-effect medications, antidepressants, mood stabilizers and antianxiety medications. Within each class are several different types. For example, the antidepressant class includes four types: SSRIs (selective serotonin reuptake inhibitors), the tricyclic antidepressants, the MAOIs (monoamine oxidase inhibitors), and the so-called atypical antidepressants (Diamond, 1998).

If the client's violence is related to psychotic or manic conditions, antipsychotic medication is usually appropriate. There are two classifications of antipsychotic drugs: (1) the traditional or older antipsychotic drugs (e.g., haloperidol and fluphenazine), and (2) the atypical newer antipsychotic drugs (e.g., clozapine, risperidone, and olanzapine). The newer atypicals are often preferable because they cause fewer acute and chronic extrapyramidal side effects. Clozapine, in particular, is effective in treating aggression because it affects both the serotonin neurotransmitter receptors and the dopamine D2 receptors (Tardiff, 1996; Weiden, Scheifler, Diamond, & Ross, 1999). However, the traditional antipsychotics, particularly haloperidol and fluphenazine, have the advantage of being effective for both rapid tranquilization and long-acting depot use. Depot atypical antipsychotics are currently in development.

Social workers' main responsibilities in the area of medication use include helping to educate the client about his or her medications; intervening in identifying and removing obstacles to appropriate medication treatment, such as cost or accessibility; and promoting compliance when medication is necessary. There are a number of obstacles to compliance. First is the client's feelings about taking medication. Medication may be perceived symbolically as a crutch and a reminder that the client has a psychiatric disorder. Second, dependence on medication can reinforce feelings of helplessness and hopelessness and runs counter to Western values of being tough, independent, and self-sufficient. Third, aspects related to the psychiatric difficulties of some clients may affect medication compliance. Violent clients who are paranoid are often noncompliant with prescribed medication. Medication is intrusive and produces chemical changes in the body. Clients who have ideas of reference or influence may resist taking medications under the belief that the medication is poisoning their body or influencing their thoughts. Finally, clients may have subjective responses to side effects of the drugs that can differ from individual to individual. Some clients are particularly uncomfortable with anticholinergic effects or self-conscious about obvious extrapyramidal symptoms. Weight gain, acne, and sexual dysfunction may also prompt clients to stop taking prescribed medication. As your clients' social worker, you can help by encouraging your clients to talk about their feelings about medication, by helping them sort out realistic and unrealistic concerns, and by joining the client is seeking alternatives to noncompliance. Possible alternatives include raising or lowering the dosage prescribed, introducing antiparkinsonian medications, changing the type of drug, using a new or adjunctive medication, or trying a drug holiday.

Clients can also assist in helping their peers understand and adjust to taking medication. Medication compliance groups composed of clients treated with similar types of medication can be very helpful in educating clients about medication, encouraging compliance, and providing positive social support. As a former client once commented to me:

"I wish there was a program in which those of us who have been in the hospital and are on medication could talk to people coming into the hospital to give them support and help. I know how scary it is to be in the hospital, and I know how awful it is to have to take medication, and you think it won't help and the side effects are terrible but it's not your fault and it will help in time—you just have to stick it out. And so many times professionals—well, they have no bedside manner. They don't understand what it's like but I do because I've been there."

THERAPEUTIC USE OF FOOD OR DRINKS

Giving someone a cup of coffee, a sandwich, or an apple can be one of the most nurturing things one can do for someone in crisis. In my practice, I have found that food or drinks have enormous therapeutic value because they are a concrete, tangible, immediate demonstration of caring. It's what I call the "chicken soup effect." Violent clients often come to clinical attention after having been through some kind of upsetting crisis. Contact with you may be the latest in a series of contacts with other people that so far have not proved to be very helpful. Asking someone if they are hungry and if they want food or drink shows the person that you care. And although this runs counter to health advice, I always kept a couple of packs of cigarettes in my desk drawer. Many an aggressive client relaxed and was willing to talk with me after being offered a granola bar or a cigarette. Even liquid medication given in juice is often preferred by clients over pills because the juice itself is soothing and thus has therapeutic value, in addition to the pharmacological impact of the medication (Dubin & Lurie, 1982).

WHEN TO HOSPITALIZE

Hospitalization is clinically appropriate if the client is imminently suicidal or homicidal, grossly psychotic with an unsupportive community environment, or unable to care for his or her basic necessities because of mental illness. It can also enable 24-hour observation for diagnostic evaluation in complex puzzling cases (Slaby, 1990). Although hospitalization is often seen as the treatment of last resort in today's environment of managed care and scarce resources, it is still an essential component of community care.

In all 50 states, clients may be involuntarily committed to psychiatric hospitals through civil procedures. The state has assumed the authority to do this via two historic roles: (1) the role of parent, or *parens patriae*, in which the state assumes a benevolent position acting in the best interest of the client, and (2) through the role of a *police power* to protect the public from danger, in which the state's focus is on the best interest of the community. Thus the legal foundation for involuntary management of the violent client attempts to achieve a difficult balance between individual rights and public protection (Fellin, 1996).

Although the content of commitment statutes varies somewhat from state to state, most recognize three universal criteria that apply to cases of civil commitment:

1. Mental illness must be present, as demonstrated by a diagnosis of mental disorder.
2. Individuals must be judged to be dangerous to themselves or others based on specific evidence (usually the presence of suicidal or homicidal acts). Regardless of the behavior, the dangerousness must be related to the mental illness.
3. The client has demonstrated an inability to provide for his or her basic necessities (i.e., food, clothing, and shelter), often termed "grave disability."

Clinical social workers employed in emergency or other community mental health services often participate in involuntary commitment procedures. Most typically, social workers do the initial screening of the client to determine if the client meets the criteria for hospitalization and whether it is clinically warranted. A physician may do the actual admitting, although some states give social workers the authority to admit. In any case, social workers often play significant roles in influencing the admission decision and facilitating the admission process. Although executing a civil commitment action runs counter to the social work profession's belief in the importance of supporting client self-determination, such action is justified if the client clearly meets the criteria of danger to self or others or (in some states) grave disability. The safe survival of the client and others must take precedence over the principle of self-determination (Loewenberg & Dolgoff, 1985). It is a serious ethical issue, however, and commitment decisions must always be made with utmost care and consideration for client rights and dignity. The outcome of your risk assessment will help determine whether hospitalization is indicated or whether a less restrictive modality of care will suffice.

One less restrictive option is called "involuntary outpatient commitment," which is a growing practice in community mental health services. With this procedure, clients are involuntarily committed to a community outpatient treatment center instead of to a hospital, and community tenure is contingent on compliance with treatment, such as medication and other prescribed aftercare. This is a good alternative for chronically aggressive clients who tend to be noncompliant with treatment but for whom treatment is beneficial in reducing violence and the need for hospitalization.

If you are in the position of making a decision about involuntary hospitalization, it is critical that you make the process as painless as possible for the client. First, even though civil commitment is an involuntary paternalistic action that temporarily suspends certain civil liberties, *clients do not relinquish all rights*, and there are many areas in which even involuntary clients can exercise self-determination. As the client's social worker, you have an ethical responsibility to make sure that the client understands his or her rights. For example, in the hospital, the client has the right to receive mail, have visitors, make telephone calls, and refuse certain treatments. Clients also have the right to be served with informed consent, which, in short, requires that the clinician provide the client with information about treatment benefits and risks and allow the client to choose whether or not to consent to participate. Informed consent, however, is not required in an emergency or in cases in which the client is judged to be incompetent. The latter means that the client is not capable of understanding information provided to him or her about treatment and is unable to make a rational decision about accepting or refusing treatment due to symptoms of mental illness (Lidz, Meisel, & Zerubavel, 1984).

Second, it is important that the client be informed as to why he or she is being hospitalized. Furthermore, particularly with violent clients, you should not waffle about your decision. Explain clearly to the client what the decision is, what will happen next, and what factors led to the decision. For example:

> "Mr. Smith, I have decided that for your safety and the safety of others, it would be best for you to be admitted to the hospital. Because you and the police told me that you hit your father with a baseball bat because the voices told you to, and because you are still hearing voices and are telling me that you don't think you can control yourself, I am admitting you involuntarily on the basis of danger to others. This commitment is for 72 hours. You will receive treatment that will help you with your problems, and prior to the end of that period, the doctor will reevaluate you and discuss with you what the next step should be. Are you willing to walk with me to the inpatient unit?"

In this example, the social worker tells the client what she is going to do, the evidence that forms the basis for her decision, what will happen during and at the end of the commitment period, and ends with a request to walk to the unit. Sometimes clients will refuse to be admitted, saying, "You can't make me go." In such cases, you tell the client that there is no choice about admission but that he or she has a choice in how that admission is executed:

Choice 1: You can walk voluntarily to the unit with me.
Choice 2: I can call security to take you to the unit. The choice is yours.

Most clients, if they are able, will opt for Choice 1.

PSYCHOTHERAPY WITH VIOLENT CLIENTS

Three modes of psychotherapy are appropriate for working with violent clients: crisis intervention, short-term treatment, and long-term psychotherapy, with each modality tailored to the specific needs of violent clients. Crisis intervention always involves a risk assessment evaluation and the creation of a short-term (defined as 24 hours to 2–3 days) crisis intervention follow-up plan for risk management. Treatment usually involves crisis counseling, environmental manipulation, and medication, if needed. The case of Joe Gonzales presented in Chapter 6 is a good example of the use of crisis intervention.

Short-term treatment (6–10 outpatient sessions; 3–5 days inpatient treatment) with violent clients attempts to solve the immediate problems and to resolve conflicts that are serving to trigger the violent behavior. Such treatment can be helpful to begin to teach the client strategies for avoiding provocative situations. However, short-term treatment may not provide enough time to establish a strong working alliance with violent clients, who are often guarded and develop trust slowly. Furthermore, in-depth examination of the dynamics of violence for a particular client and how those dynamics interact with their families and environments takes time. However, short-term treatment can be beneficial for clients who are not chronically aggressive. For those who are, a series of short-term efforts can often help, for example, a 5-day inpatient stay followed by six sessions of outpatient treatment.

Long-term treatment of violent clients usually occurs on an outpatient basis or in a forensic unit and may involve individual, family, or group modalities. As stated earlier, violence is a relationship between the individual and his or her environment. Most interpersonal violence occurs between friends and family members; thus treating the client within his or her family context and social environment is critical.

Assaultive behavior is usually reported to occur less frequently in outpatient settings than in inpatient settings, and outpatient clients are usually in a more stable state and able to participate more meaningfully in psychotherapy than are inpatient clients, for whom behavior control and medication stabilization is often a major focus. Most violent clients treated on an outpatient basis have personality disorders, substance abuse problems, or both. The best candidates for psychotherapy are those individuals who are episodically rather than chronically violent and who express remorse following the violence and a desire to change their behavior (Tardiff, 1996).

Group treatment with peers who also have problems with impulse control and violence can be very effective in reducing aggression. Such change will not happen overnight, but change is often facilitated when the client hears feedback about his or her behavior from peers in a collaborative sharing method of assistance. It is amazing how clients will "hear" the same thing from equals more readily than from those perceived as superiors (Perry & Vaillant, 1989).

Group therapy that is formatted to set limits and provide structure is the best method, because structure helps clients to avoid maladaptive behavior, such as violence, and helps them to reflect and anticipate consequences. Setting limits can produce anxiety and depression, but these are affects that can be treated. It is not unusual to find that violent clients are depressed and anxious underneath their behavior problems. Group support can help immensely in the process of working through depressed and anxious feelings, and effective social support is the best protective factor for avoiding violence. Encouraging the client to help his or her peers in group treatment also enhances clients' self-esteem and can replace narcissistic defenses with altruism. Confronting problem behavior empathically and helping the client think through the consequences of his or her actions in a Socratic fashion can be very useful. Violent clients often report that their move from impulse to action is instantaneous and out of their conscious control, and thus learning how to anticipate consequences and short-circuit that pattern is critical. Following are five main treatment goals for outpatient psychotherapy with violent clients (Tardiff, 1996):

- *Evaluate the client's motivation and reasons for entering treatment.* Does the client express a desire to change his or her behavior, or does he or she simply want to avoid some kind of negative consequence, such as jail time?
- *Facilitate verbal expression of problems and concerns in an empathic and nonjudgmental manner.* Violent clients often have difficulty in expressing feelings and conflicts verbally, and the development of such skills may serve as an alternative to resorting to violence.

- *Help the client to develop self-control.* This requires teaching the client how to handle impulses and make choices. Violent clients often describe their behavior as being out of their control and thus claim that they are not responsible for the harm they may cause to others.
- *Monitor both transference and countertransference feelings on an ongoing basis.* It is normal to feel anxiety about working with violent clients and to fear that the client may hurt someone, including the clinician. These feelings are normal, but you must take responsibility to monitor them and work them through, preferably with a trusted supervisor or colleague, so that they do not adversely affect the client's treatment. Working with violent clients is very stressful, and support and consultation from colleagues is critical for treatment success.
- *Teach the client how to anticipate the consequences of the choices he or she makes and to understand how those consequences will affect his or her life.* Anticipating consequences can be an effective deterrent to violent behavior. Knowing that if you assault someone you'll end up in jail and lose valued freedoms can be a good cautionary measure for preventing future violence.

BEHAVIOR THERAPY WITH VIOLENT CLIENTS

Behavior therapy can be an effective approach to treating violent behavior, and formal behavioral treatment programs are often used in controlled highly structured settings, such as correctional, medical, or forensic settings. Describing all of the elements of intensive behavioral treatment is beyond the parameters of this book, but the reader can access such material by looking at some recommended sources (see, e.g., Liberman & Bedell, 1989; Liberman & Wong, 1984; Quinsey, Harris, Rice, & Cormier, 1998; Wong et al., 1988). The role of the behavioral approach called "social skills training," however, is addressed briefly because social skills training can be used in a variety of treatment settings, both inpatient and outpatient, and with both forensic and nonforensic populations.

As has been noted previously, clients who have persistent problems with violent behavior often have poor social skills, with particular difficulty in verbally expressing their needs and wants and getting those needs and wants met without coercing others. Improving social skills, therefore, has the potential to reduce or prevent violence (Bell & Fink, 2000). Social skills training is a highly structured group behavioral treatment that can be used with adults, adolescents, and children and that has explicit goals and planned sessions that emphasize *in vivo* practice and homework assignments to develop good social skills (Liberman &

Mueser, 1989). Violent clients often have difficulty forming and maintaining positive interpersonal relationships and resolving everyday conflicts in a constructive, nonviolent manner. The development of good social skills also promotes the development of positive social support, which serves as a protective factor for violence. Individuals who have good social skills are also less likely to provoke or be provoked into violent action because they can accurately "read" the social cues from others.

Social skills training uses role playing as the primary vehicle to assess the client's pretreatment competence and to work on targeted behavioral excesses or deficits during treatment. Aggressive provocative behavior is a behavioral excess, whereas the inability to express empathy toward others is a behavioral deficit. The role-play scenarios are determined by the particular individual's difficulties, along with the general difficulties this population usually demonstrates. Social skills training provides each participant with both direct and vicarious learning opportunities via observations of other clients' behavior and reinforcement from peers. As with group psychotherapy, clients will often respond more readily to peer feedback than to feedback from the clinician. The essential ingredient of social skills training is the specific, instrumental, and goal-oriented nature of the behaviors targeted for change.

INTERVENTION STRATEGIES WHEN A CLIENT MAKES A THREAT

Because threats are the most common type of client violence toward social workers, this section specifically addresses intervention strategies that can be used when threats occur. Threats may be spoken, written, or behavioral, for example, stalking. They may be communicated in person, over the telephone, by letter, or by computer. In the case of threats, the usual interventions for treating violence may not be feasible or possible. For example, the threat may come from someone unknown to the clinician, or it may be anonymous. The police or judicial system may not have a mechanism with which to intervene.

Using an Understanding of the Client's Motive to Shape the Intervention Approach

Threats are not random events (Lion, 1995); rather, they occur within an interpersonal context, and an examination of this context can sometimes provide clues to motive that can serve to suggest target goals for intervention. Common motives include rage stemming from loss or rejection, anger over limit setting, an out-of-control transference, frustration stemming from an inability to obtain resources to meet pressing needs, or an effort to extort compliance in a request. Sometimes the threat stems from the client's frustration over being in a stressful situation and denial of basic needs, such as not being able to make a phone call following admission to a hospital:

> She was a new client, just admitted to the psychiatric unit in our hospital. She was very frustrated because she had no money for the phone, was angry with the nursing staff because they had become impatient with her, and just frustrated about everything. When I inquired how I could help, she threatened to knock my "goddam head off." I took her to the admissions office and helped her put the call through on the office phone. One of the nursing staff stayed by the door in case of trouble. When the call was unsuccessful, the client just sat in the chair and cried (Newhill, in press).

In this case, the social worker recognized the immediate source of the client's frustration and attempted to help her. Although the client was unable to complete her phone call, rather than continuing to threaten the worker, the client perceived the worker's genuine desire to help and this time responded to her feelings of frustration by crying rather than threatening violence. At this point the worker was able to provide support:

> Although she was belligerent, she calmed down once I had gotten her away from the rising confrontation. I did not really expect her to hit me—but I did leave the office door open and was careful not to provoke her (Newhill, in press).

For many clients, the threat serves as a vehicle for expressing fear, loss, and panic over situations they cannot control. Threats are messages and, as such, deserve a response (Lion, 1995). Understanding this can help us to empathize with the client's feelings and shape our responses in a manner that encourages the client to share his or her feelings and move from seeing us as adversaries to seeing us as allies and advocates who will help him or her as much as possible. Sometimes, however, in the heat of the moment, the client cannot see beyond the rage, and in such situations, ensuring safety should be the first priority:

> I was working for a community hospital emergency room, and the police brought in a young man who was planning to jump off a bridge. I do not think he intended to be found on the bridge (it was 2:00 A.M.), and he was angry that someone had called the police

and that his suicide attempt had been thwarted. His life was falling apart, and he saw no other options for himself. I told him I had no choice but to hospitalize him, and hearing that, he became enraged. He threatened to kill me once he was out of the hospital, telling me that if he couldn't get to me, he'd find someone who would. After he was discharged, whenever he saw me in the clinic, he would threaten me. Quite frankly, I was scared, and so I filed for an order of protection. Eventually, I learned he had moved away to another part of the state (Newhill, 1995b).

Countertransference Reactions to Threats

The most common psychological response by a threatened person appears to be denial (Lion & Pasternak, 1973, 1995; McCarthy, 1991). This denial may serve to protect the target of the threat from feeling fear or anxiety, but it also enables both individuals—the one making the threat and the one being threatened—to avoid dealing with the underlying issues motivating the threat, thus eliminating the opportunity to take preventive action. Threats do not always predict future violent action, but sometimes they do. They should always be taken seriously and not cavalierly brushed off (Tardiff, 1996). A physical assault not preceded by a threat is rare.

Lion (1995) observed that when he was asked to intervene in a situation in which a patient had made a threat, he often found that the threat had gone on for weeks with little attempt to deal with it. Why was little or no action taken? Lion suggested that, in an agency setting, often strong group forces mitigate against mobilizing definitive intervention. Such group forces can include a sense of group helplessness ("There's nothing we can do"), group resignation ("It's just part of the job; it goes with the territory"), group machismo ("If it's too hot, get out of the kitchen"), group minimization ("The patient is just posturing—he doesn't really mean it"), and group myths ("People who threaten never take action"). Threats that have occurred and been ignored numerous times over months or years tend to lose their impact, but the potential for danger does not necessarily diminish, particularly if no effort to intervene has occurred (MacDonald, 1967).

Following are some steps that can help prevent threats from occurring and aid in intervening when they do occur:

• Clients who are at risk of becoming threatening, for instance, individuals with borderline or antisocial personality disorders or paranoid and paranoid psychotic disorders, should be seen with other staff members around both for protection and because "the institutional ambience serves to dilute what otherwise might be a threatening experience" (Lion, 1995, p. 47).

• Monitor both the transference and the countertransference in treatment carefully and continually. Any concerns should be addressed immediately with the client or through consultation with a skilled colleague. Tell the client that the threats are frightening to you and that they will not be tolerated, and inquire about how the client is feeling. Threats are often used by clients to establish control or reject the therapist, and if they are acknowledged as such, they may stop. If you give the client the message that the threat has no effect by ignoring it, the threats may escalate and lead to violence (Lion, 1995).

• If you are unsure of what to do, obtain consultation from an expert in threat management who can assist in developing a management plan, including mechanisms to ensure safety. Such an individual should be identified ahead of time by you or your agency so that staff members know who to contact when a threat occurs (Berg, Bell, & Tupin, 2000).

• Immediately document and report even minor threatening exchanges with a client. It is not uncommon for serious threats to evolve from relatively minor but hostile interactions. File copies of all communications related to the threat. If judicial action is taken, you will need these materials.

• Do not allow your desire to be empathic, patient, and understanding toward clients to prevent you from taking decisive protective action when a client is threatening or becoming volatile (Lion, 1995). Recognize when external controls, such as inpatient care, are needed, and then take immediate action. Preventing a threat or assault from occurring is the kindest thing you can do for your client.

• Evaluate the need and advisability of obtaining a restraining order (Berg et al., 2000). Restraining orders can be effective in some cases; however, sometimes they only serve to provoke actual violence or are simply ignored by the perpetrator.

• Discuss and debrief with all staff members involved after the threat has been contained.

The Duty to Protect

Sometimes a threat made by a client is not toward you but toward someone else. The landmark 1976 court ruling, *Tarasoff v. Regents of the University of California*, along with a number of subsequent court cases involving similar legal and clinical situations, laid out the obligation of mental health professionals who have a professional relationship with a client to protect intended victims of violence from the client (Beck, 1985). The length or depth of the relationship does not matter.

Evaluating a client for the first time in an emergency room constitutes a professional relationship. Because such a duty is usually activated by a threat that the client makes toward or about the intended victim, discussion of this issue is included here. For those not familiar with the case that led to the *Tarasoff* legal decision, a summary of the case follows:

> Prosenjit Poddar, a graduate student who was receiving psychotherapy at the University of California Student Health Service in Berkeley, told his therapist that he intended to kill Tatiana Tarasoff, a female student who had rejected his romantic overtures. A friend of Poddar's also told the therapist that Poddar had purchased a gun. The therapist and his supervisor decided that Poddar was dangerous and should be hospitalized. They asked the university police to go to Poddar's apartment, find him, and initiate an involuntary commitment. The police investigated the matter and were assured by Poddar that nothing would happen. The police left, and nothing further was done. At that time, Tatiana Tarasoff was on vacation and out of the country. When she returned, Poddar went to her apartment, and Tarasoff, not knowing she was in potential danger, let him in, whereupon Poddar killed her.

Tatiana Tarasoff's family sued the therapist, the campus police, and the University of California, arguing that Poddar should have been confined and that Tatiana should have been warned she was in danger. An initial 1974 ruling by the California Supreme Court stated that the therapist and police could be liable for failing to *warn* intended victims of patient threats. In the aftermath of the 1974 Tarasoff ruling, mental health professionals voiced a number of concerns regarding the impact of the duty-to-warn mandate on clinical practice, which is still of concern today:

- Duty-to-warn is incompatible with an effective therapeutic relationship and would deter clients from seeking treatment (Beigler, 1984; Meyers, 1984; Wise, 1978).
- Duty-to-warn would deter therapists from treating dangerous patients (Huber, Roth, Appelbaum, & Ore, 1982; Shah, 1978).
- Duty-to-warn is a serious breach of confidentiality and forces a shift from the therapist's alliance with the welfare of the client to an alliance with the welfare of the public (Beigler, 1984; Meyers, 1984).
- Duty-to-warn will increase the number of civil commitments (Steadman, 1980; A. Stone, 1976; Wise, 1978).

- Considering the inaccuracy of clinical predictions of dangerousness, duty-to-warn would only produce more false positives, because the evidence supports the conclusion that therapists tend to overpredict rather than underpredict dangerousness (Cocozza & Steadman, 1978; Gordon, 1977; Kozol, 1982; Steadman, 1980, 1982).
- Duty-to-warn will result in reluctance on the part of both therapists and patients to probe the topic of violence in treatment (Wise, 1978).

These concerns were taken seriously by the California Supreme Court, and, on appeal, a subsequent 1976 ruling (Tarasoff, 1976) stated that the therapist could be liable if he or she did not "exercise reasonable care" to protect the victim. Most states today do not mandate a duty to warn but, rather, require that the clinician fulfill a duty to protect via the provision of reasonable care. Appelbaum (1985) proposes a three-stage model that, if followed, would fulfill the obligation to provide reasonable care:

- *Stage 1*: The clinician should conduct a thorough risk assessment by gathering all data relevant to making an evaluation of dangerousness and evaluate the patient based on these data. Thorough written documentation, along with consultation with colleagues, is important.
- *Stage 2*: If the conclusion is that the patient poses a threat of violence toward others, the clinician then decides on a course of action designed to reduce the probability of harm. Such action could include any of the following: hospitalization; intensifying treatment via increasing the number of clinic visits, dosage of medication, and so forth; taking steps to increase treatment compliance; involving family or other community supports in reducing risk by, for example, preventing access to weapons; consulting with colleagues to coordinate the plan of action; issuing a warning to the intended victim or, in the absence of an identified victim, warning the police; and continuing to gather risk assessment data.
- *Stage 3*: Implement the plan and follow up by monitoring the outcome of each step.

If the decision is made to actually warn the identified potential victim, it must be done in a manner that is sensitive to the feelings and needs of both the victim and the client. First, because you are breaking confidentiality by issuing a warning, the client must be informed that a warning will be made and why that is necessary. Second, when contacting the potential victim, it is critical that support and counseling be provided in tandem with the actual warning. For example, discuss with the potential victim what kinds of steps he or she can take to ensure safety and offer counseling or other clinical assistance.

SOCIAL WORKERS' IMMEDIATE
RESPONSES TO INCIDENTS OF VIOLENCE

So far I have reviewed the various standard treatment modalities, but how do social workers actually intervene when they are faced with a violent client? The CV Study (Newhill, 1996) suggests that, for the most part, social workers follow recommended interventions in various combinations, with some variation depending on the type of violence involved (property damage, threats, or physical attacks) and the specific circumstances of the individual client, practitioner, and agency.

The most common response by social workers in incidents of property damage was to restrain or seclude the client. Clients who engaged in property damage were usually angry and out of control, and respondents often reported that immediate verbal intervention was not very effective. The priority was to control the client's behavior and then provide counseling. The typical sequence was: (1) control the client's behavior through restraint; (2) wait for the client to calm down; (3) provide counseling. A good example is the following:

> "I worked on a locked substance abuse treatment unit. The client, a young woman, set a fire in another client's room. I called the hospital police, who helped us put out the fire. We then put the client in seclusion for her safety as the other clients were very angry at her, and when she calmed down, I talked with her about why she set the fire."

Some of the incidents of property damage were not directly witnessed by anyone—for instance, the client stole some property or admitted to having sprayed graffiti on the agency walls. In these cases, behavior control was not an issue, but imposing consequences and discussing the incident therapeutically were typical responses.

Threats were handled differently from property damage, because behavior control is often not an immediate issue. A threat implies the possibility of future harm, and thus the interventions primarily addressed preventing future violence. The most common response was to maintain composure and respond calmly and assertively toward the client and the situation. The next most common response was to call the police or security, and, finally, the third most common response was to provide therapeutic intervention. A good example of these three responses in combination is the following:

> "I was working for aging services and my primary client was an elderly man who had dementia. The hospital petitioned the court to choose a guardian other than my client's daughter, whom we suspected was abusing her father at home. The daughter came to take her father home, and I told her she could not. She threatened to get a gun and come back and kill all of us. I immediately hit the silent alarm to call security, and they came quickly. I told the daughter that her threat wouldn't accomplish anything other than getting her arrested, and then tried to empathize with her anger and frustration. I managed to engage her in talking about what it was like caring for her father, and she finally admitted that it was very stressful and that she had hit her father on occasion and knew she needed help."

Finally, in dealing with attempted physical attacks, the most common response was to provide therapeutic intervention, and for actual physical attacks, the most common response was to restrain or seclude the client. When a worker is literally assaulted, with a possibility of physical harm, controlling the client's behavior is paramount. Attempted attacks were attacks that "missed the target." No physical harm occurred; thus the primary consideration could be providing therapeutic help.

The second most common responses to these situations were the opposite: With attempted attacks, the second most common response was to restrain or seclude the client; and with actual attacks, the second most common response was to provide therapeutic help. The next two most common responses were the same for attempted and actual attacks: getting help from other staff members and calling the police. An example of an attempted attack in which these responses were combined is the following:

> "The client was psychotic and believed I was the cause of all his problems. He was in walking restraints, but he managed to break through them and began throwing chairs around—one of the chairs just missed me. Other staff came running and approached the client collectively. He was still very agitated, so nursing staff 'took him down' and put him into four-point restraints."

The following is an example of an actual attack:

> "I was working in residential treatment with a 13-year-old who had just been told that he couldn't have a home visit over the weekend. He became very angry and bit, kicked, and hit me, and then pulled my hair. I managed to escape and called security. They came and put him in seclusion. Later I went to see him, and he had calmed down and we talked about how hurt he had felt when he was told he couldn't go home. He also apologized for assaulting me."

Reviewing the findings on social workers' immediate responses to incidents of violence reveals certain common threads that cut across types of violence. Most commonly, the social workers responded in the following ways: to provide therapeutic intervention, including directly confronting the client about his or her behavior; to restrain or seclude the client; to call the police or security; and to join with other staff members to help control the situation.

CLIENT OUTCOMES FOLLOWING INCIDENTS OF VIOLENCE

The outcome for most of the clients following a physical attack against a social worker was some kind of consequence, usually involving behavior control, and a protective placement setting in the psychiatric, medical, or criminal justice system. The only exception to this was that group of clients who were removed from the premises and not jailed or hospitalized. Some of these clients were temporarily terminated from services with planned follow-up, whereas others were permanently terminated. This decision was, in part, determined by the client's response following the incident. If the client calmed down and apologized, staff members were more likely to tell the client to leave for now but to come back later. If the client did not express remorse, if the aggressive behavior continued, and if the client had a history of repeated aggression, the client was more likely to be permanently terminated.

CONCLUSION

This chapter has addressed intervention approaches for working with violent clients. It has shown that the interventions reported by social workers who have experienced incidents of client violence are right in line with what the clinical literature suggests is effective, that is, behavior control through setting limits and providing structure, therapeutic intervention with counseling and medication, protective placement (e.g., hospitalization), and the use of empathy and the strengths approach. The notion that violence is untreatable is not supported, although such treatment is challenging, and clinicians must be constantly vigilant in monitoring their own feelings about working with this population and must use self-reflection and consultation with trusted colleagues on a regular basis.

SKILL DEVELOPMENT EXERCISES

Use of Medication Role-Play Exercise

Vignette

In this scenario, a 24-year-old Asian American client tells you that he hears auditory hallucinations telling him that you are going to harm him. He is very frightened and agitated and has a history of assault, although he has never, so far, harmed you in any way, and you have had a good relationship with him. He admits that he has stopped taking his medication, clozapine, which has helped him effectively with his problems with aggression since he began taking it a year ago.

With another participant playing the role of the client, do a role play with the goal of helping the client understand the importance of medication, in this case clozapine (which has been shown to reduce aggression), in controlling both his psychotic symptoms and his violent behavior. In the role play, discuss the use of medication, along with your role in helping the client comply with medication, for example, helping to educate him about his medication, intervening in identifying and removing any obstacles to appropriate medication treatment, such as cost or accessibility, and promoting compliance when medication is necessary. Finally, encourage your client to talk about his or her feelings about medication, helping him sort out realistic and unrealistic concerns, discussing problematic side effects (clozapine often causes drowsiness and weight gain), and join the client is seeking alternatives to noncompliance, for example, adjusting the dosage or changing to a different medication.

Hospitalization Case Analysis Exercise

Many times social workers are in the position of being victimized by a client's violence without having the authority to hospitalize the client when it is clinically indicated. In such cases, the social worker has to turn to someone else to make the decision, usually a psychiatrist or other physician. In most cases, the physician will support the social worker's judgment and work collaboratively with him or her, but sometimes that doesn't happen. The following vignette illustrates this kind of dilemma and is followed by some questions about how one might handle such a case.

Vignette

The client is a 26-year-old Caucasian man who has been diagnosed with chronic undifferentiated schizophrenia. No medication has been very effective with him, but when he takes his medication, his behavior is not a problem. However, when he is off meds, he behaves in a very sexually inappropriate way toward women. One day he came into the clinic, and I had to see him as the clinic triage worker. When I called him into my office, he had a peculiar smile on his face. He then shut the door, grabbed me, and tried to kiss me, quite forcefully. I pushed him away, managed to get out of the office, and went to see the psychiatrist down the hall to discuss an evaluation for hospitalization. He brushed off my concern, saying, "Oh well, that's just the way he is. He's much better now than he used to be. Don't get upset about it—he didn't really hurt you." Later, this client was charged with the rape of a fellow client at his board-and-care home.

Case Analysis Questions

1. This client's problem behavior toward females was well known. Should the social worker have refused to see him and insist he see a male clinician?
2. How should the social worker have responded to the doctor's minimization of the client's assault?
3. Are there any other alternatives that the social worker could have pursued in this case?
4. Should the social worker press charges against the client for sexual assault? What are the pros and cons of such an action?

Hospitalization Role-Play Exercise

Three participants are needed for this role play. One participant plays the role of the social worker, one plays the role of the client, and one plays the role of the client's sister.

Vignette

The client is a 30-year-old divorced Haitian woman brought to the admissions unit of the state hospital at 1:30 A.M. by her sister. The client was crying, terrified, complaining of smelling bad odors, felt food and drink were poisoned, had not eaten for a week, and had had no liquids for 5 days. She thought her children were causing all of this, and her family feared for the children's safety because she was caught trying to smother one of them earlier that day. Upon evaluation, the client was agitated and angry. She paced back and forth and gave the evaluating social worker the feeling that she was barely maintaining control.

This is a client who needs to be hospitalized; also, a report must be made to child protective services. With one participant playing the role of the clinician and one playing the role of the client, role play how the hospitalization decision could be presented to the client, and then discuss the child protective services' report with the client and her sister. In the three-way role play, include the following:

- Express empathy and understanding of the client's feelings of fear, anxiety, and panic stemming from the symptoms she is experiencing.
- Clearly inform the client why she is being hospitalized and what will happen next in her treatment in the hospital. Because the client is psychotic, be sure that the explanation is clear, simple, and easily understood.
- Ensure that the client understands her rights and support her right to self-determination as much as is feasible given the circumstances.
- Make sure the client is provided with information about treatment benefits and risks.
- Talk with the client's sister about making a report to child protective services regarding the attempted smothering of the client's child.

Intervention Strategies When a Client Makes a Threat: Case Analysis Exercise

I was working for a community hospital emergency room, and the police brought in a young man who was planning to jump off a bridge. I do not think he intended to be found on the bridge (it was 2:00 A.M.), and he was angry that someone had called the police and that his suicide attempt had been thwarted. His life was falling apart, and he saw no other options for himself. I told him I had no choice but to hospitalize him, and hearing that, he became enraged. He threatened to kill me once he was out of the hospital, telling me that if he couldn't get to me, he'd find someone who would.

Case Analysis Questions

1. How would you feel if you were the social worker in this case?
2. As noted in the chapter, threats often function as a vehicle for expressing fear, loss, and panic over situations the client can't control. In his case, how do you think the client is feeling?
3. Explore the client's underlying feelings and, in that process, begin to explore and identify the underlying motive for the threat.
4. Empathize with the client's feelings.
5. Try to develop the beginning of a therapeutic alliance so that the client moves from seeing you as an adversary to seeing you as an ally.

Discussion Exercise

The last part of Chapter 8 discusses social workers' immediate responses to incidents of client violence and the outcomes for the clients involved. In a small group of 3 or 4 participants, describe any incidents of client violence toward clinicians that the participants have experienced, either as a direct victim or as a witness. Talk about what happened and what the outcome was. Reviewing the treatment modalities discussed in the chapter, discuss any alternative responses to these real-life events that might have been preferable to what actually happened. That is, if such an incident occurred again, what would be the best treatment response to it that would meet both the clinician's needs and the needs of the client?

Chapter 9

Strategies to Prevent Client Violence in Office and Field Settings

Neathery (1992) relates the old story about the town that built a trauma unit below a cliff because people kept driving their cars over the edge. The trauma unit did a good job of caring for those who were injured but did nothing about figuring out how to keep people from driving over the edge in the first place. The same can be said for client violence toward social workers. Up to this point, we have reviewed what we know about the risk factors and dynamics of violent behavior, how to conduct a risk assessment, and what interventions are useful, but now we must begin to address strategies to prevent client violence from occurring in the first place.

To establish a context, this chapter begins by looking at the kinds of practice settings in which social workers are most at risk of encountering client violence and at the level of risk in office settings versus field or community settings. Next I discuss prevention strategies that social workers and agencies can use in the office setting and specific strategies for field visits and other community contacts. I address protective measures for the physical interviewing environment, how to prevent injury from weapons, physical maneuvers that clinicians can use to protect themselves when a client initiates a physical attack, and, finally, the rather controversial issue of pressing charges or prosecuting clients for violent behavior as a measure to deter future violence.

WHICH PRACTICE SETTINGS ARE THE MOST RISKY?

When attempting to answer this question, we have to look at two things: the *type* of practice setting, that is, what kinds of services are provided to which clients, and the *location* of the delivery of services, that is, office based or field based. As it turns out, where we work does affect our risk of encountering client violence. Findings from the CV Study (Newhill, 1996) showed that the settings of highest risk were criminal justice services, drug and alcohol services, and children and youth services. *Seventy-five percent or more* of the respondents in these settings reported at least one incident of client violence. Settings of moderate risk (over 50% of respondents reporting incidents) included mental health services, developmental disability and mental retardation services, school social work, and family services. Medical and health care services and services to the aged were comparatively low risk (less than 50% of the respondents reported incidents; Newhill, 1996).

These findings suggest that client violence toward social workers cuts across types of practice but that there is a *variation in level of risk* shaped by the clientele served and the risk factors associated with each type of clientele. For example, we know from Chapter 5 that a history of violent behavior is the best predictor of future violence. Many clients served by criminal justice services have such a history, and thus the fact that criminal justice is the highest risk setting in the CV Study sample is not surprising. As another example, we know that use of alcohol and certain drugs is a risk factor associated with violent behavior. It is not surprising, then, that an agency providing services to people who have problems with substance abuse would be a high-risk setting.

One piece of "practice wisdom" often heard in social work circles is that the field setting, particularly the client's home, is the most dangerous place for social workers to go. Police officers are well aware of this. Twenty-two percent of police deaths and 40% of police injuries occur in cases in which an officer has gone to someone's home in response to a call about a domestic disturbance (Bard, 1969; McPeak, 1979). Because of this risk, many agencies, particularly those in child welfare and mental health, have taken specific steps to develop safety plans for workers who go out into the field. But do most incidents of client violence actually occur in the field? In the CV Study, respondents were asked specifically where the most serious incident of violence that they experienced occurred. Table 9.1 summarizes their responses across types of violence.

This table shows two things. First, it shows clearly that violence can occur anywhere and that no location is completely risk free. Second, it shows that in this sample, the majority of incidents across types of violence occurred in the agency setting, that is, the social worker's office, a coworker's office, or elsewhere in the agency rather than in the field. How can this be explained? Part of it may be that in many social work jobs, workers no longer go out into the field; thus all violent incidents experienced by such workers would have to be agency based. But could it also be that social workers have learned to

TABLE 9.1. Location of the Incident of Client Violence

	Property damage	Threats	Attempted or actual physical attacks
In the agency (social worker's office, coworker's office, other area of agency)	93%	72%	66%
In the client's home	3%	17%	14%
Elsewhere in the community	4%	11%	20%

be more safety conscious outside the agency and that, therefore, potential incidents are averted, thus leading to a lower incidence? Or, because many agencies have made more of an effort to ensure safety in the field, could it be that these steps are working? Or do we, perhaps, carry with us an "illusion of safety" when we're in an office setting and, therefore, let our guard down and not take the same precautions as we do in the field? We don't know all the answers to these questions, but the data should make us ponder some of our assumptions about where we are safe and where we are not.

The CV Study also found that 24-hour residential agency settings are at particular risk for violence. Residential treatment for adults, residential treatment for adolescents, psychiatric inpatient units, and forensic units accounted for more than one-half of all the incidents reported. There are two possible explanations for this finding. First, *eligibility criteria* for admission to such facilities often includes the requirement of behavior problems of one kind or another, and thus the admission standards select for a treatment population at risk for violence. Second, because such facilities are residential, *time at risk* for the social worker is greater. In other words, there is a difference between seeing a client once a week for a 50-minute outpatient visit and seeing the client off and on for 8 hours 5 days a week during a shift in a residential treatment center. Having direct contact with clients for a lengthier period of time enhances the probability that the social worker will be present when violence occurs.

PREVENTION STRATEGIES FOR OFFICE SETTINGS

Interviewing and the Physical Environment

It is important to consider the physical aspects of the environment in which the client will be interviewed and to eliminate or minimize any factors that may serve to precipitate violence or enhance the probability of serious injury. Steps to take include the following:

1. *Evaluate all of the furnishings in the room.* In the office setting, the furniture chosen should be solid and heavy enough to be difficult to move or throw. I recall an interviewing room in which all of the furniture was literally bolted to the floor. It isn't necessary to go to that extreme, but it is important that the furniture not be accessible as a weapon.

2. *Avoid having heavy objects that can be thrown and used as weapons* (e.g., paperweights, vases, lamps, or ashtrays). One of the most lethal objects, which, fortunately, in today's nonsmoking work environments is less common, is the heavy glass square ashtray. One of my former clients murdered his father by beating him to death with a heavy glass ashtray (Newhill, 1991). Letter openers are very effective as knives and thus are very dangerous to have out in the open. However, soft objects, such as pillows, can be useful as shields in case of attack.

3. *Interview rooms should be in a safe location and designed with safety in mind.* In settings in which there is a high risk for violence, interview rooms should be strategically located where help can be immediately accessed. As noted previously, the ideal design for an interview room or office is to have two doors so that both the clinician and the client have the option of sitting near an exit. Such interview rooms should also be designed in a manner that does not serve to aggravate agitated clients. That is, the room should be quiet, lighting should not be too dim or too bright, and the color scheme should be neutral (Kaplan & Wheeler, 1983). The following story provides an illustration:

> A certain county hospital emergency service was having problems with their restraint and seclusion room. Whenever they used it, the patients seemed to get more agitated. They asked one of the admitting psychiatrists, who had expertise in violence prevention, to look at the room, and she saw that the solution was obvious. Apparently years ago (back in the 1960s) someone had suggested that bright colors were cheery and would help boost staff and patient morale. The only leftover relic from that old color scheme was the seclusion room, which was painted bright bubble-gum pink. This, in combination with the harsh fluorescent lights, created an atmosphere that would be intolerable to most people, especially someone who was psychotic. The psychiatrist suggested to the staff that they re-paint the room blue-gray and replace the fluorescent lights with nonfluorescent ones, and that solved the problem (Newhill, 1995b).

4. *Methods for calling for help should be established and routinely reviewed.* Prearranged methods for the clinician to alert others if he or she is in danger must be established. Such methods can include code

words, panic buttons, or silent alarms. Panic buttons or silent alarms can be strategically located under a desk, on the wall or telephone, or on a pendant that can be worn by the staff member. Developing code words signifying the need for help costs no money and can be very effective. For example, "Please call Dr. Smith" can be a code word for getting security. All staff members should be aware of this code, including support staff, paraprofessionals, and professionals. Another possible prearranged option could be to call the clinic receptionist to say, "Please cancel my appointment for 3:00" as a code phrase to let someone know that you have an agitated or violent client in the office and need help. Both phrases will seem innocuous to the client and will not alarm him or her. Likewise, there should be a way for the clinic receptionist or other person outside the clinician's office to alert the clinician that there is potentially dangerous situation. So, for example, if the receptionist is aware of a volatile person in the waiting room or discovers that a client has a weapon, he or she can alert the clinician or security.

5. *Consider installing a metal detector.* In settings of high risk, a metal detector can be installed at point of entry. If a client is unable to bring a weapon into the clinic with him or her, that alone may be sufficient to ward off a serious violent incident. One concern about metal detectors is that such a device will make the clinic seem prison-like, which would be upsetting to clients. My experience has been that clients generally say that they feel much safer with a metal detector in the clinic. Finally, the presence of security personnel can be very effective in preventing the occurrence of violence. Just the presence of a "uniform" alone can be an effective deterrent for violent clients who are able to make choices about their behavior.

6. *Pay attention to how you are dressed.* When interviewing and working with clients who have been violent or are aggressive, always pay attention to how you are dressed. Do not wear clothing that is provocative, for example, clothing that is too tight or too revealing. Some violent clients have great difficulty with boundaries and appropriate interpretation of social cues. Revealing clothing, for example, might be interpreted as a sexual invitation, regardless of the wearer's intent.

Avoid wearing loose dangling earrings or necklaces. I recall an incident in which an agitated client yanked on a nurse's dangling earrings and ripped them through her earlobes. Keep neckties tucked in or remove them altogether, wear low-heeled shoes so you can run and maneuver, and remove your glasses before commencing the interview (assuming you will still be able to see the client).

7. *Be vigilant about removing any potential weapons from the client.* If the client has been violent and is now placed in seclusion, you should make sure that staff members remove any potentially dangerous

clothing (belts or neckties) and dangerous objects (pens, jewelry, matches, pocket knives, and nail files) from the client. Unfortunately, metal detectors do not pick up items not made of metal, such as plastic knives and pens. Here is an example of what can result from lack of vigilance about weapons:

> "I was a social work student on an inpatient unit, and I recall one time we admitted a man who was very paranoid. He refused to bathe or shower, and his hygiene was poor to begin with. Finally, even the other patients began complaining how bad he smelled, so the nurses insisted that he take a shower. He still refused, so a couple of male staff approached him and told him he would have to bathe. As he was undressing, with the staff's direction, a loaded gun fell out of his pants. We were in shock, and the hospital took immediate action to make sure that never happened again. Thank goodness the gun didn't discharge when it fell out!" (Newhill, 1995b).

Preventing Injury from Weapons

What do you do if the client has a weapon? In spite of the best precautions, sometimes weapons still slip through. Of course, you may encounter weapons while making a home visit. The little research that does exist on the prevalence of client violence with weapons suggests that weapon use is relatively rare due to use of various prevention strategies (Hunter & Love, 1993); however, when it does occur, it can lead to serious injury.

Sometimes, a client's possession of a weapon represents the last step in a deteriorating clinical situation in which there may have been previous threats, unattended- to negative transference, or a failure to set appropriate limits; or the client may be clinically decompensating (Dubin, 1995). In many injury cases, the potential for prevention existed at the beginning but, for whatever reason, was ignored. In other cases, an unknown client who has a weapon may suddenly appear at or be brought in to the clinic for evaluation, or a client may be experiencing an unanticipated life crisis that has made him or her feel desperate.

If the client produces a knife or other cutting instrument, *do not* try to wrestle the knife away. There is a good possibility that you will be cut. Instead, use a shield, such as a chair or clipboard, and verbally try to disarm the client. If this doesn't work, leave the area, and get help immediately. The same precautions apply if the client is trying to harm him- or herself with a knife. Trying to thwart the client's self-destructive behavior can quickly turn the client's violence toward you:

"I was seeing a borderline client who wanted to go into the hospital. When I told her I thought it would be better not to admit her, she reached into her purse and pulled out a razor. She began to cry and lightly nick her skin with it. I told her to put the razor away, she refused, and so I reached over to take it from her. She immediately became furious with me, saying that she wanted to be in the hospital, and if she had to hurt someone, she would, and then she cut my forearm with the razor. I ran out of the room and called security" (Newhill, 1995b).

What if the client has a gun? If a client appears in a treatment setting with a gun, the first priority is to expose as few staff members as possible to the situation by clearing everyone out of the area. For example, if you're aware of such a client in the waiting area, get out and get help rather than singlehandedly trying to intervene with the client in the waiting room. Help should be summoned, and as many people as possible should be removed from the area. These first few minutes are crucial. If you are trapped and cannot escape, you should try to verbally connect with the client, beginning with something obvious, such as, "I see you have a gun" (Tardiff, 1996).

Whitman and colleagues (1976b) emphasize the importance of verbal coping skills as a prevention technique when faced with a client who has a weapon—that is, permitting the client to ventilate, making small talk, being honest and empathic, and communicating that you have the client's best interest at heart. It is important that you appear calm and in control but not threatening in any way—what Dubin (1995) refers to as "minimization of self as a threat." Encourage the client to talk, and then repeat the client's concerns empathically. As with knives, do not try to take the gun from the client or suggest that the client drop the gun, because both situations can result in the gun discharging. Instead, you should calmly suggest that the client put the weapon down on the table or chair.

The most effective prevention technique is to anticipate ahead of time that such incidents may happen and to work out ways of warning others that you or someone else is in danger. Again, silent alarms or code words can be helpful. Using a pretense to enable escape can be very effective in protecting you and getting help, for example, saying to the client: "I can see that you want help—let me call Dr. Jones to come and talk with you." This can enable you to get away and call for help. The best prevention is developing a specific written plan of action worked out beforehand by staff, such as who alerts the police and how, how the area will be cleared of people, who will make "the show of force," and so forth. For example:

The client was a 32-year-old single white male with chronic schizo-phrenia and a personality disorder who came to the hospital seeking admission. In all the years I've known him, he has never developed any insight, won't comply with medication, and needs ongoing structure and supervision. He has a long history of serious violent offenses, including attempting to murder his parents. Both parents are now in prison for violent offenses. I evaluated him and was about to discuss alternatives (I didn't think he needed to be in the hospital) when he pulled out a gun, cocked it, and put it in his lap, stating in a quiet voice, "You better admit me." I told him (not true) that as a social worker, I couldn't directly admit him and I would have to find the doctor. He shrugged and said okay. I left the room and immediately called security to clear the area and then called the local police to come to the admissions unit. The police came quickly and, since the client was on parole, it was back to prison for him (Newhill, 1995b).

If the clinician becomes trapped in a hostage situation, then a pro-fessional hostage negotiator should be summoned; who that person is and how to contact him or her should be established ahead of time. A critical aspect of survival in such a situation is the ability of the clinician who is trapped to establish a rapport with the client. Again, verbal com-munication skills are critical. Hostages who are regarded as people rather than faceless targets are more likely to survive. Turner (1984) makes specific recommendations regarding such situations:

- Do exactly as the hostage taker says and avoid an open display of despair or loss of control, such as crying or begging, because such behavior escalates the hostage taker's panic, anxiety, or fear and thus elevates the risk of violence.
- Be observant and blend in with the other hostages. In cases in which a number of hostages were held, the hostage killed was of-ten the one who behaved in a manner different from the rest. This is not the time to be a nonconformist.
- Don't try to escape or overpower the hostage taker unless abso-lutely certain of success.

If You Suspect You Are Being Stalked or Followed

If you suspect that you are being stalked by a client or if a client has made a threat and you fear that it may be carried out, you must first *document everything* and report exactly what has happened to your su-pervisor or agency administrator and the police. Agencies should provide an escort to your car or bus in such situations. This should be part of the agency's safety plan (discussed in Chapter 10). When driving, vary your route, avoid predictable stops, and change your parking spaces.

Physical Maneuvers by the Clinician

Another important area of training to mention, although it is beyond the parameters of this book to examine in depth, is the use of physical self-defense maneuvers by the clinician. Such moves can prevent injury or death or enable the clinician to escape. There are many groups that provide this kind of training, and such training can be very important for your protection, particularly if you work in a high-risk setting. A workshop in which you physically practice the techniques is ideal (see, e.g., Griffin & Bandas, 1987). Therefore, the following is simply an introduction to some of the physical maneuvers and basic strategies that are taught in such workshops (Thackrey, 1987):

- When standing, do not face the client; rather, turn sideways, preferably with the arms folded, or with one arm across the stomach and the other around the chin. Both stances allow for rapid protective movements with the arms or hands.
- How you respond to an attack depends on the intended target. You want to protect sensitive areas, such as the face, throat, and ears. For example, you can protect your face with your hands, use the palms to fend off a punch, or prevent an injury by tucking the head and covering the ears.
- If the client kicks you, deflect the kick with your legs. Your legs are one of the strongest defensive areas of your body. If you have fallen to the floor, keep your feet toward the client to block kicks. Again, your objective is to protect the more sensitive areas of your body, in this case your groin or abdomen, from injury.
- If the client gets you in a choke hold or headlock, tuck your chin as close to the chest as possible. This protects critical blood and air circulation to avoid loss of consciousness.
- If the client attacks you from the front, raise your arms and use them as leverage to avoid or break physical contact.
- If the client attacks you from the rear, turn, using your arms as leverage to break the hold.
- If the client tries to pull out your hair, the immediate impulse is to pull away. Instead, you should get hold of the client's hand and try to pry his or her fingers loose while verbally telling the client to let go. If that fails, pulling backward on the client's thumb often works to get the client to let go.

- If the client bites you, rather than trying to pull out of the client's mouth, force the bitten part further into the client's mouth while closing off his or her nostrils. This maneuver cuts off the client's breathing. When he or she takes a breath of air, you can escape.

The following is a good composite example of the use of physical maneuvers:

"I was working on an adolescent inpatient unit, and we had been having a wave of kids with bad behavior problems. One teen, in particular, had the knack of stirring everyone up and 'splitting staff' against each other. I had set some behavior limits with her in the morning, and I guess she was still angry with me. She came up behind me and got me in a choke hold, demanding that I let her out of the unit. I used my arms as leverage and managed to twist around and break the hold, but then she grabbed my hair. I pulled back on one of her fingers and she let out a yelp and let go of my hair. Other staff came running and restrained her. I was shaking afterward but so relieved that I wasn't hurt."

Pressing Charges or Prosecuting Clients for Violent Behavior

It may seem odd that a section on pressing charges or prosecuting clients for violent behavior would be included in a chapter on the prevention of client violence. However, we know that setting appropriate limits with clients can prevent violence from occurring, and prosecuting clients for violent behavior is a form of limit setting. This is a controversial area, however. Clinicians who argue for prosecution claim that, under certain circumstances, it can give clients a clear message that violence will not be tolerated and can even serve therapeutic goals. Those who argue against it say that prosecution can harm the therapeutic alliance and even encourage litigation by clients (Gutheil, 1985; Miller & Maier, 1987). Of course, this assumes that there is a therapeutic alliance, which Miller and Maier (1987) argue is increasingly less likely to be present given the clinical characteristics of certain segments of our inpatient population these days (e.g., the increasing proportion of clients with antisocial or psychopathic personalities). Furthermore, the impact of cost containment strategies, such as shorter hospital stays, inherent in the demands of managed care limit opportunities to develop a strong therapeutic alliance (Simon, 1998).

Many authors have noted that since the change from a "need for treatment" standard to the "dangerousness" standard for involuntary commitment, the composition of our public inpatient population has changed, as more severely ill patients with assaultive and criminal histories have been selected for admission (see, e.g., Appelbaum & Appelbaum, 1991; Levinson, Briggs, & Ratner, 1980; Steadman, Cocozza, & Melick, 1978). One dilemma facing providers of care to such patients is that the courts have decreed that even patients who have been committed involuntarily to a psychiatric unit can refuse treatment except under emergency circumstances (Perlman, 1987). What this means in practice is that clinicians cannot prevent violence by administering medication if the patient refuses it; rather, they can dispense medication involuntarily only after an assault has occurred. Notes Perlman (1987), "if involuntary patients are to be considered competent by the courts, then, however absurd it may seem to mental health workers, they should be treated as such by those who bear the burden of their assaults" (p. 673), that is, staff members should be able to press criminal charges against patients who engage in violent acts during the period in which medication cannot be dispensed without a court order or emergency situation.

Another question that remains is, if patients *knew* ahead of time that their violence might result in criminal charges, would that serve as a deterrent for violence and enhance the willingness of staff to work with violent patients (Mills, Phelan, & Ryan, 1985; Phelan, Mills, & Ryan, 1985)? And furthermore, it is ethically defensible? Deciding whether to prosecute or not must be determined on a case-by-case basis. However, in general, the answer might be yes if the patient possesses full capacity to control his or her behavior, make rational choices, and anticipate consequences. In this case, prosecution could serve as a reality-testing consequence for unacceptable behavior. If the patient's violence is clearly driven by psychosis or mania and is not under his or her control, then the answer is probably no. One must also consider the impact of the consequences of pressing charges on the patient's well-being and the well-being of the staff members involved (Miller & Maier, 1987). For example:

> We were having a lot of problems on our adolescent inpatient unit with some of the boys breaking the windows in the unit. This particular unit was located in an old wing of what used to be the state hospital, and they had large windows that formerly had bars to protect them, but now there were no bars and the glass wasn't shatterproof. The staff met on several occasions and began to track which boys were involved in the breakage. In almost all cases the windows were broken by boys who had been diagnosed with conduct disorder and who generally had problems with aggressive behavior. We

decided to try an experiment. We informed all new admissions that nonaccidental property damage would be prosecuted and that the child and his or her family would have to pay for the damage. Over the next 6 months, not a single window was broken. As a consequence, staff were less angry at boys admitted with conduct disorder, and the boys' behavior overall seemed to improve (Newhill, 1995b).

Both clinicians and legal experts need training to help them to learn how to differentiate between behaviors due to a client's mental illness that are not under the client's control and behaviors that are instrumental and driven by choice or character pathology, which are more appropriately dealt with via criminal justice measures (Miller & Maier, 1987). Appelbaum and Appelbaum (1991) offer a model hospital policy on prosecuting clients for presumptively criminal acts and argue that filing a criminal complaint against a client is justified in two prototypic instances: (1) that of a nonpsychotic patient engaging in deliberate criminal activity, and (2) that of a client—psychotic or nonpsychotic—who is judged to be a high risk for seriously injuring another person (p. 1234). The model spells out a 16-step implementation policy that outlines procedural steps supported by fundamental principles of biomedical ethics. Furthermore, the policy guarantees that the hospital or clinic will support a staff member's action as long as the staff member follows the policy's procedures. The policy was implemented at Worcester State Hospital in Massachusetts amid a storm of controversy, primarily from patient advocacy groups. Some argued that it was unfair and too restrictive, and others argued that it was not restrictive enough. However, it represents the first attempt to balance ethics, patients' rights, and staff rights in the area of client violence. As Miller and Maier (1987) state:

> Mental health professionals certainly can, and should, make allowances for the pathological behavior of their patients and should not act out their own negative feelings. However, this principle should not be taken to the extreme of permitting and excusing illegal behavior that patients can control. (p. 53)

In the CV Study, charges were pressed against the client in 10% of the cases involving assaults toward social workers. In a few of the other assault cases, the social workers indicated that they had wanted to press charges but were told by their supervisors or agency administrators that they could not or should not do so. These cases typically involved adolescent clients who committed actual attacks that resulted in injury to the social worker. Arguments against pressing charges included the belief that the charge would not hold up in court, particularly if the client was an adolescent, was mentally ill, or both; that it would be harmful to the client; or that it could result in bad publicity for the agency. This type of situation, however, was often reported to be very demoralizing for the social worker who had been victimized and left most of the respondents feeling as though their well-being was of little concern to the agency.

PREVENTION STRATEGIES FOR HOME VISITS
AND OTHER CONTACTS IN THE FIELD

Home visits are a long-standing part of the traditional social work approach for many reasons. Interviewing clients within their home environment provides a much clearer picture of their lives and environmental situations. One can get a more relaxed and accurate picture of family interactions and a better sense of the nature of the client's life day to day. For clients, having a social worker take the time to come to see them at their home can be a meaningful demonstration of caring and commitment. However, there are disadvantages, too. Clients may view a home visit as intrusive and threatening, and, for social workers, home visits present additional risks in terms of safety.

Prior to this point, I have assumed that you are evaluating the client in an agency setting, such as a crisis clinic, emergency room, outpatient clinic, or inpatient unit. In these settings, the environment is more controlled and controllable than it is in a community setting. In your agency, you know where each room is and what staff resources there are, and, hopefully, you can rely on a range of preventive strategies that have been instituted to minimize the probability of violence occurring. (Preventive strategies for the agency setting are discussed in Chapter 10.) The most important facet, however, is that the agency setting is *your* turf, not the client's, and that gives you a strategic advantage because it is familiar. The community at large, however, is a wide-ranging environment that is not necessarily your home turf, and that fact, without preparation, can be a strategic disadvantage. It may, however, be the client's familiar turf (Harman & Davis, 1997). As a result, you must prepare to enter the community within a risk assessment framework, meaning that you carefully conduct research ahead of time on what the community and the client's home are like in order to identify potential dangers.

Harman and Davis (1997) observe that one of the major obstacles to social workers' safety in general is our strong commitment to helping people. This desire may lead us to minimize danger, overlook existing danger signs, be lax in anticipating danger, and not recognize that some clients cannot be helped and that some clients do not want our help.

Knowing when to back off, when to take a time-out, and when to terminate a client's session or even terminate the helping relationship entirely is critical in managing risk (Lion, 1995). Pushing a client, insisting on change when the client isn't ready to change, or forcing an interview can sometimes provoke violence and increase the risk for future violence. Looking for the best in people and wanting to help can sometimes override normal protective caution. All of this is heightened when making a home visit because you are an outsider to the client's home and family and your visit may be perceived as an invasive intrusion. Whereas the social worker may view the home visit as an explicit demonstration of a desire to help, the client may perceive it as threatening.

The belief that "we social workers are helpful people so no one should want to harm us" is another obstacle to safety. As a social work colleague once commented:

> "When I look back on the kinds of things I did and where I would go alone in my early days as a social worker, it's a wonder I came through it unscathed. I would go into neighborhoods that I would never venture into today, especially alone and at night. But I felt at the time, I think, that I had some kind of a protective bubble around me and nobody would hurt me because my intentions were good. Although the neighborhoods I used to work in are more dangerous today than back then, I'm also more realistic about my safety now. I sometimes wonder, though, that if I hadn't had that protective fantasy, would I have been able to do my work? I think I would have been too scared. It would have immobilized me."

It is true that if we live in constant fear and hypervigilance, we will not be able to do our work and connect with our clients (Weinger, 2001). But fear is also a protective force (De Becker, 1997). The key to safety is to *balance* prudent courage with reasonable caution and to avoid being a victim. The riskiest situation is one in which you do not know the environment you are entering or the people living within it and have not been trained in environmental risk assessment and planning.

Table 9.2 summarizes the guidelines for home and field visit assessment to protect the safety of social workers.

One issue that I have not yet discussed is aggressive dogs. Aggressive dogs can be a problem with home visits, particularly in high-crime neighborhoods. The reality is that in dangerous neighborhoods, people usually take a range of precautions to protect themselves, including possessing firearms and dangerous dogs. Although whether a dog is aggressive or not depends in large part on how the dog is raised and treated,

TABLE 9.2. Summary of the Guidelines for Home/Field Visit Assessment for Social Worker Safety

DO:

- Take a *proactive* rather than a *reactive* approach to safety (Huff, 1999).

- Always remember that you are not on your own turf and that the unexpected can happen at any time.

- Bear in mind that although *you* may view the home visit as an explicit demonstration of your desire to help, the *client* may perceive it as intrusive and threatening.

- Get to know the neighborhood ahead of time. Talk with experienced colleagues and the local police about how dangerous different areas are. If the police have identified a certain neighborhood area as dangerous, then you should go to that neighborhood only during daylight hours with another person as a team, and you should never go out after dark. In cases of clearly identified violence, you should go out only with the backup of law enforcement.

- Plan your route ahead of time so you won't get lost. Do this with consideration of the nature of the neighborhoods you will be driving through.

- Dress appropriately; leave jewelry at home. Wearing a simple wedding band, however, can serve as a deterrent to inappropriate sexual advances. Do not carry your credit cards or checkbook unless you intend to use them. While visiting the home, carry only your identification, not your purse. Wear comfortable shoes that allow you to run, if necessary.

- Before your visit, make sure your car is in good working order, have a fully charged cell phone with you, know how to access emergency help, make sure your gas tank is full, and keep your car locked at all times, including when you are driving. Lock all valuables in the trunk and never leave anything in view inside the car that might be tempting to thieves.

- If you are going to a client's home, find out what potential dangers are in the home and who and what will be there. Call ahead and talk with both the client and another key person who lives in the home, such as the client's spouse, sibling, or parent. Ask if there are any weapons in the house and where they are kept (particularly firearms), who else lives there, and if there are any dangerous animals. Expect the unexpected.

- Use a buddy system when making a home visit to a client who has a history of threats or assaults or who lives in a dangerous neighborhood. A "buddy system" means that you make the visit accompanied by another social worker, trained social service staff person, or law enforcement officer (Newhill & Wexler, 1997; Scalera, 1995).

- Consider your experience with similar client situations in the past. What did you learn from your experiences that could inform your current safety plan? Think not only about the usual sequence of events in similar situations but also the unusual cases (Goldstein et al., 1979).

- Before you leave the office, sign out in a central area and make sure that others know where you are going, when you expect to return, your cell phone number, and the phone number of the client you will be visiting.

(continued)

- As you proceed from your car to the client's home or other field location, walk confidently, and look alert and aware of your environment. Don't act like someone who would be easily victimized. Be aware of your body language and the body language of others that you encounter. Sometime a confident but neutral "hello" and brief eye contact can prevent trouble. Avoid secluded areas or unfamiliar groups of people.
- Know when to back off, when to take a time-out, and when to terminate a home visit.
- Avoid arguments with family members or lengthy, overly emotional conversations. Try to continually maintain structure and boundaries. If your gut feelings tell you that things are getting out of hand, leave immediately.

DON'T:

- Don't allow the desire to help to override prudent caution.
- Don't subscribe to the belief that, because you are committed and helpful to clients, that you will not be harmed (Huff, 1999). Beware of the "protective bubble" fantasy, in which on some level you believe you walk around in a metaphorical "bubble" that will keep you safe and secure, regardless of how dangerous your surroundings may be, because everyone must know that you are a "good person." This can cause you to overlook or minimize danger.
- Don't interview clients in the kitchen. All kitchens have knives, frying pans, hot liquids, and other objects that can be used as weapons. Also, avoid interviewing clients in rooms in which you are boxed in and do not have ready access to an outside exit. Choose the room that has an outside door.

---

certain breeds have the strength and temperament to be more aggressive and defensive than others. Pit bulls, Rottweilers, Akitas, and German shepherds are disproportionately represented in dog-bite cases (Keidan, 2002) and are far more likely to be trained as guard dogs than toy poodles are. Thus it is important to ask not only if there are dogs in the home but also what kinds of dogs and how many. More than two dogs is a pack, and "pack mentality" can kick in if the dogs feel threatened. If the client has a potentially dangerous dog, then you must ask the client to take steps to ensure safety. For example, set up a specific appointment with the client and ask him or her to leash the dog or lock it in another room prior to your arrival. In the CV Study, several social workers reported being attacked or almost attacked by aggressive dogs during home visits. Sometimes this was accidental, but sometimes it was intentional on the part of the client, particularly if the home visit was unannounced:

> "I was working for child welfare and had to investigate an allegation of abuse. I was a new worker and pretty naive, and so I just went on

out to the house alone without calling ahead and without much investigation about the home environment ahead of time. I was walking up to the door when I heard this snarl. I turned around and a huge German shepherd was coming for me. I ran and had to climb a tree to get away from him. The client came out of the house and started asking me what the hell was I doing there, making no effort to call off his dog. I must have been in that tree for an hour. Finally the dog went away behind the house—I got out of the tree fast, jumped in my car, and left. I was incredibly scared, and I never went out again without making arrangements ahead of time and asking about whether there were any dogs in the home."

CONCLUSION

It is clear that client violence toward social workers cuts across types of practice, but there is variation in level of risk shaped by the clientele served and the risk factors associated with each type of clientele. Criminal justice services, drug and alcohol services, and children and youth services carry the most risk, followed by mental health services, developmental disability and mental retardation services, school social work, and family services. With this understanding of risk, a range of prevention strategies for both office-based practice and home visiting were discussed. There is clearly overlap between the two in that some of the same strategies apply to both kinds of settings, although home visiting has some unique challenges for the social work practitioner. Chapter 10 looks at some general strategies for the prevention of violence and includes a model training syllabus, a model incident reporting form, and a model for an agency safety plan.

SKILL DEVELOPMENT EXERCISES

Discussion Questions

This chapter focused on strategies to prevent client violence in office and field settings. Participants in the discussion of the chapter topics should begin by reading Table 9.2 and thinking about their own practice environment in both the office and, if applicable, the field.

1. Based on what we know about which practice settings are the most risky, how risky is your practice setting? What is your risk as an individual practitioner in terms of the types of clients you work with?

2. Evaluate the physical environment of your office or interview setting. Are there any modifications that should be made to reduce your risk?

3. Review the guidelines in Table 9.2 point by point with the discussion group and discuss how each guideline affects the way you conduct your practice and where and how changes need to be made.

Chapter 10

General Strategies for the Prevention of Violence

Up to this point, I have discussed risk assessment, approaching and engaging violent clients, interventions appropriate for treating violent clients, and strategies to prevent client violence in office and field settings. Most of the safety strategies presented so far, however, address steps that individual practitioners can take. Now, we must look at the bigger picture of what agencies and the profession of social work can and should do.

A social worker in an agency has only so much control over how work is conducted and how much he or she can do as a lone individual to reduce risk of exposure to violence. To ensure risk reduction and safety, collective efforts are needed, and, in this case, all staff from top management on down must be invested in the process. Griffin (1995) notes that safety must be a key component of an agency's overall planning process "and included in staff orientation and training, physical plant development, and crisis response and post-victimization and trauma training" (p. 2295). As noted by a former president of the Michigan chapter of NASW, Jeanne McFadden, "Training alone can't protect social workers without the proper institutional support system" (as quoted in Vallianatos, 2001, p. 3).

This chapter discusses several general strategies for the prevention of violence that can serve as a foundation for the development of an agency safety policy. A model for the development of a safety policy is presented, along with a model for a violent incident report form that agencies can use to enable them to track the incidence and prevalence of violence toward staff. Having a mechanism for putting information on client violence in writing can also be an effective strategy in ensuring that incidents of violence do not get swept under the rug and, instead, that constructive action is taken for all involved: the social workers, the agency, and the clients.

> **Strategy 1:** *We as social work professionals must raise our consciousness, recognize, and openly acknowledge that client violence is a realistic and legitimate practice concern.*

We do a disservice to ourselves and our clients by denying or minimizing job-related risks. Raising awareness can combat the three central issues that often undermine staff safety in agencies: inconsistency in application of safety procedures across staff levels, lack of communication about safety between line workers and management, and not including safety as a key issue in administration and planning of agencies (Griffin, 1995). Without open recognition, these problems will persist, the underreporting of incidents of violence will continue, and both workers and clients will continue to be victimized with the kind of negative consequences that have been discussed throughout this book.

> **Strategy 2:** *Agency administrators and supervisors must take the lead in facilitating the development of a safe workplace, which is a fundamental component of the obligation that agencies have toward their social workers and other staff.*

Two steps can accomplish this goal:

1. Agency administrators and supervisors must consistently take workers' concerns seriously and take responsibility for establishing a climate that encourages open discussion of safety issues. Taking workers' concerns seriously means that administrators and supervisors establish safety as an important topic for regular discussion in staff and supervisory meetings and as part of any agency planning process. Workers may not bring the issue up themselves because of stigma and fear of retribution; thus it is incumbent on administrators and supervisors to set the tone for discussion. For example, "staff safety" would be listed as a regular or periodic discussion item on staff meeting agendas, and discussion would be opened by an administrator, who might say something like the following:

> "As you know, staff safety is a high priority at this agency and is part of our overall planning process. I would like to spend the next portion of the meeting discussing any concerns or actual incidents that

have happened over the past week. Remember, this forum is a safe and confidential place for you to bring up whatever you want to bring up, and we've all agreed not to criticize or laugh at any concerns any of you have. Let me start by sharing one of my concerns."

In this opening statement, the administrator reminds staff members of the "ground rules" for airing concerns and takes the first step by sharing one of his or her concerns, which opens the floor for others to participate.

2. Management must take the lead in developing and implementing a safety committee composed of representatives from all staff levels. This committee should also be representative of the staff composition in terms of discipline, race, gender, and age. The charge for the safety committee is to develop the agency's safety policy, a model of which is included at the end of the chapter.

Strategy 3: *Within the agency setting, staff members should be offered regular high-quality in-service safety training that meets workers' self-identified needs, along with agency priorities.*

Line staff participation in designing safety training is critical to ensure that the training is tailored to meet workers' informational and skill needs. Administrators and supervisors who have little direct contact with clients cannot truly understand what workers on the front lines need. Those who are directly in the cross fire of violence must have a voice, and their voice must have influence on decisions made regarding staff training. When we think about who is on the front line, we often forget to include support staff, for example, receptionists or transportation aides, who are equally, if not more, vulnerable in their direct contact with clients. Thus they should be included in safety training efforts as well.

Agencies must be honest about the impact of agency intervention on clients' lives and how such intervention can trigger violence and aggression. Communication and training that prepares social workers to face this reality is important (Griffin, 1995). Unfortunately, studies have shown that communication about safety is often a weak link in agencies (Brown, Bute, & Ford, 1986; Mace, 1989).

In the CV Study, more than one-half of the social workers had participated in some kind of safety training, particularly those social workers who worked in high-risk settings. Although one-half of the social workers said the training they received met their needs, one-half said it did not. Those whose needs were not met often commented that they had no input in planning or choosing the training. Respondents who received training at their agencies, however, were significantly more likely to report that training met their needs than were respondents who had received training during their formal social work education, both their classes and their field placements.

> **Strategy 4:** *Agency administrators and supervisors, in coopera-tion with line workers, should establish policies regarding how to respond to workers who have experienced client violence.*

For example, procedures for debriefing the worker who has experienced a violent incident should be developed and implemented, and opportunities should be provided for other staff members to discuss the incident. In addition, such policies should include guidelines for providing medical, disability, and liability coverage, availability of counseling, and provisions for paid leave.

When incidents occur, staff should be given the opportunity to analyze the incident with the goal of identifying any factors that could be addressed clinically or by the agency to minimize the probability of a similar incident occurring in the future. The Violent Incident Report Form at the end of this chapter asks for a step-by-step description of the incident. This kind of description permits a clear analysis of the sequence of actions that occurred during the incident. Staff members can then identify junctures in the sequence at which intervention could have been provided to prevent escalation of the aggression into violence. Participants in such a discussion should include the worker involved in the incident, his or her colleagues, and other individuals representing the various levels and departments in the agency. This way, any suggestions for change will include input from all key individuals, which will enhance the probability of successful implementation. Prompt and supportive assistance from administrators and supervisors is critical in the aftermath of these events. As one of the respondents from my study commented:

> "It wasn't the incident itself that was so upsetting ultimately—it was the fact that my supervisor didn't take me seriously and showed no interest in talking about it with me that was so demoralizing."

Flannery, Fulton, Tausch, and DeLoffi (1991) have developed a prototype for a program to help staff cope with the psychological sequelae of experiencing client violence, with the goal of preventing the development of trauma reactions such as posttraumatic stress disorder. This program, titled "The Assaulted Staff Action Program (ASAP)," provides debriefing services to assaulted staff to help the victimized staff member work through his or her feelings and make sense of the incident.

Strategy 5: *Social work practitioners, with support from supervisors, must advocate for the institution of at least minimum safety precautions in their practice settings.*

Red emergency buttons could be installed on agency telephones and silent alarms could be installed under desks. All such alarms should be tested monthly, and the test results should be documented. Any defective alarms should be *immediately* repaired. Interview rooms should be strategically located so that help can be accessed quickly and designed so as not to aggravate agitated clients or provide them with access to potential weapons. Decisions about the use of metal detectors or security personnel should involve a benefit–risk analysis that weighs the degree of safety gained against potential negative outcomes for clients (e.g., intimidation) or staff (e.g., morale; Newhill & Wexler, 1997).

Strategy 6: *Agencies must develop a user-friendly means of reporting and tracking all incidents of violence toward staff and must strongly encourage and support workers in documenting and reporting incidents that occur.*

It is extremely important that agencies have an accurate picture of the incidence and prevalence of violence toward staff. Using a violent incident report form can accurately document and track the incidence and prevalence of violent incidents within the agency and ensure that such incidents are responded to constructively (Griffin, 1995; Langmeyer, 1995).

The problem of the underreporting of violent incidents toward social workers is echoed throughout the literature, and there are many reasons for this underreporting. One common reason is the lack of an appropriately designed reporting form that specifically addresses the kinds of data that are important to gather when reporting incidents of violence toward staff. An inappropriately designed form, coupled with bureaucratic red tape, often discourages workers from making reports (Crane, 1986). Others have suggested that underreporting occurs because workers simply do not want to make the effort to fill out the cumbersome forms (Huff, 1999). In addition, some workers think that violent behavior is routine, and so only unusually severe incidents are reported (Star, 1984). The notion that violence "goes with the territory" was a common comment made by CV Study respondents, especially male social workers in high-risk settings. There seemed to be a kind of resignation that in the kind of work they do, assault has to be accepted as an inevitable part of the job.

Another major reason that violence toward social workers is not reported is that the victim of the violence is often blamed. Social workers who experience violence may be labeled as "provocative, incompetent, authoritarian and inexperienced" by colleagues (Rowett, 1986, p. 136). Fear of stigma and the concern that reporting a violent incident would reflect poorly on their work performance record also discourage social workers from reporting incidents (Star, 1984; Tutt, 1989).

Finally, Rowett (1986) argues that poor supervisory and administrative response to victimized workers further encourages underreporting. For example, in a survey of social service organizations, the British Association of Social Workers found that social services managers do little to confront and reduce the risk of violence, with less than one-fourth of the organizations having any staff guidelines for coping with violence (Crate, 1986; Tonkin, 1986). In fact, researchers concluded that it seemed as though a significant response from those with the power to make changes occurs only in cases of deaths or other major incidents. Thus a vicious circle is created in which "stereotypes of [client] assault as victim-precipitated promote under-reporting which, in turn, may endorse unsympathetic agency cultures which fail to recognize the frequency and effects of aggressive client behavior on workers and, in turn, sustain the stereotypes" (Leadbetter, 1993, p. 624). For example, a respondent in the CV Study commented:

> "I was assaulted by a client who I had to evaluate for involuntary civil commitment. When I told my colleague about it, hoping to get at least a little support, he literally said to me, 'Look, if it's too hot, get out of the kitchen. Anyway, what did you do to the guy to make him hit you?' I felt I was to blame and also that I was weak to let it bother me. I never reported it to our administration."

Strategy 7: *Agencies must employ a risk management approach to home visiting and outreach work.*

The term "risk management" is often used by federal and state regulating agencies on workplace safety and refers to strategies aimed at conducting work productively within certain safety parameters, for example, using safety precautions on heavy machinery. The same principle, however, can be applied to human services work in which services are delivered without compromise in quality but within safety parameters. Risk management strategies must include all staff members who work in the agency, including support staff, paraprofessional staff, and professional staff.

As noted in Chapter 9, home visiting and outreach work carries specific risks due to the context of how and where services are provided.

Here, social workers must advocate for agencies to institute a policy of workers never making home visits alone in situations that may be dangerous. Instead, a team approach should be utilized, and, for home visits that clearly pose a high probability of violence, social workers must be able to request accompaniment by law enforcement officers. As I noted in Chapter 6, obtaining information about the neighborhood in which the client lives is critical. Identifying collateral supports within the community, such as churches, storefront services, and so forth, can also be helpful in fostering worker safety. Similarly, providing staff members with cell phones, beepers, or other means of mobile communication can enhance security in the field.

Strategy 8: *Agencies must establish clear protocols with other organizations with which they have interdependent relationships in the area of safety and risk management.*

I cannot emphasize too strongly how important it is to nurture a good working relationship with the local police department that serves the same area that the agency serves. Developing and nurturing a cooperative relationship with the police, particularly the "beat" police who are out in the streets and are most likely to be those you call on for assistance, is absolutely mandatory to achieve safety goals. Police officers and social workers often hold incorrect assumptions about each other's work, work pressures, abilities, and service parameters. They should have an opportunity to discuss such issues together. Police may underestimate how dangerous many social work practice situations are, and social workers may overestimate the time that police officers have for non-crime-related community demands. Several years ago, I worked for a psychiatric emergency service, and we created a task force that included social workers and police officers with the goal of improving our working relationships. We learned a lot from each other, and our work together from that point on was much more cooperative.

Strategy 9: *Philosophically, we must teach ourselves to accept that it is okay to ask for help.*

Many a violent incident has occurred because a practitioner felt that he or she should be able to handle it alone and believed that asking for help somehow meant that he or she was an incompetent, inadequate practitioner. Many of the CV Study respondents reported that, prior to the occurrence of the violent incident, their "gut feelings" told them that a particular situation was becoming dangerous, but they dismissed their feelings as silly or somehow indicative of personal failure and, therefore, did not ask for assistance until it was too late. Prevention measures such as peer support groups and a general atmosphere of acceptance of help from colleagues is extremely important. Again, support for this strategy must be communicated from the top down by the agency administrators.

> **Strategy 10:** *As part of the overall violence prevention plan, formal agency strategies for accessing help should be implemented and clearly outlined in the agency's safety policy.*

Such strategies outline who should be called in an emergency, how they can be reached, and who is responsible for what duties. Furthermore, this plan should be routinely reviewed, and regular practice drills should be held. Here is an example of what can happen otherwise:

> I remember what turned out, fortunately, to be a funny story about our first violence prevention plan. We were a small agency, but a couple of workers had been threatened, and we realized we needed to put a safety plan into place. So we scrounged around for money to pay for silent alarms, cell phones, and a metal detector. And we all had safety training and learned certain code words to use to access help. Well, we were very proud of ourselves and decided to test our new system with a practice drill. One of us pretended we had a threatening client in our office and hit the silent alarm. Nothing happened. Turns out the one thing we forgot was to identify who would respond. Everyone thought it was somebody else and so nobody came! We felt pretty stupid, but that drill was invaluable in pointing out a major "bug" in our system (Newhill, 1995b).

> **Strategy 11:** *The National Association of Social Workers (NASW) and its state chapters, social work educators, and the Council on Social Work Education must acknowledge the violence risks faced by social work students, field instructors, and other social work practitioners and respond by requiring content on risk assessment, practice with involuntary and violent clients, and risk management strategies in both undergraduate and MSW curricula and in continuing education programs. Furthermore, field faculty should ensure that field placement agencies have a safety policy in place and a plan for student orientation to the policy.*

Our national professional organization, NASW, and social work education have generally lagged behind agencies, other disciplines, and the business community in recognizing that client violence toward social workers is a critical practice concern. Furthermore, training must be an ongoing process. As one respondent in the CV Study commented: "You can't get training just once and be done with it. You need to have periodic reviews and keep practicing it or you won't remember what to do." In the formal social work education curriculum, content on risk assessment and safety can be infused across courses or can be offered as a single course. A model syllabus for such a course is provided in Appendix 2. The syllabus is based on the content of this book and emphasizes case analysis and skill-building exercises as application tools. The course has 15 sessions, which can be taken sequentially as a single course or delivered in modules. The latter may be a more feasible option for agency use.

Social work practicum education must also address the issue of risk reduction and safety for students in field placement (Dunkel, Ageson, & Ralph, 2000). Field education departments should have a school policy, and this policy should be coordinated with placement agencies. Every field placement agency should be required to have a safety policy and every student should be provided with orientation to that policy and training on risk assessment and safety. Dunkel, Ageson, and Ralph (2000) have developed a risk reduction model for field education that incorporates all of the basic requirements.

Strategy 12: *We must give a clear, consistent message to our clients that using violence to solve problems is not acceptable.*

Many of the CV Study respondents reported that learning to set clear fair limits, working with clients to develop nonviolent alternatives, and following through on initiating consequences for violent behavior were helpful in lowering the level of recurrent incidents. Taking such preventive steps can serve to empower us in our future work with clients.

Table 10.1 summarizes the 12 strategies presented. At the end of the chapter are a model for a violent incident report form, a model for an agency safety plan, and a bulleted summary of these strategies to prevent violence. These materials can be duplicated and posted on an agency bulletin board as a reminder of the importance of staff safety and can be used as starting points for agency staff members to develop their own risk management plans.

CONCLUSION

In today's world of social work practice, client violence is increasingly regarded as a common occupational hazard. Every day across the coun-

TABLE 10.1. General Strategies for the Prevention of Violence

- We as social work professionals must raise our consciousness, recognize, and openly acknowledge that client violence is a realistic and legitimate practice concern.

- Agency administrators and supervisors must take the lead in facilitating the development of a safe workplace, which is a fundamental component of the obligation that agencies have toward their social workers and other staff.

- Within the agency setting, staff members should be offered regular high-quality in-service safety training that meets workers' self-identified needs, along with agency priorities.

- Agency administrators and supervisors, in cooperation with line workers, should establish policies regarding how to respond to workers who have experienced client violence.

- Social work practitioners, with support from supervisors, must advocate for the institution of at least minimum safety precautions in their practice settings.

- Agencies must develop a user-friendly means of reporting and tracking all incidents of violence toward staff and must strongly encourage and support workers in documenting and reporting incidents that occur.

- Agencies must employ a risk management approach to home visiting and outreach work.

- Agencies must establish clear protocols with other organizations with which they have interdependent relationships in the area of safety and risk management.

- Philosophically, we must teach ourselves to accept that it is okay to ask for help.

- As part of the overall violence prevention plan, formal agency strategies for accessing help should be implemented and clearly outlined in the agency's safety policy.

- Social work educators and the Council on Social Work Education must acknowledge the violence risks faced by social work students, field instructors, and other social work practitioners and respond by requiring content on risk assessment, practice with involuntary and violent clients, and risk management strategies in both undergraduate and MSW curricula and in continuing education programs. Furthermore, field faculty should ensure that field placement agencies have a safety policy in place and a plan for student orientation to the policy.

- We must give a clear, consistent message to our clients that using violence to solve problems is not acceptable.

try, family stresses and problems, magnified by worsening economic conditions and scarcer benefits and services, boil over into acts of violence directed at individuals within and outside the family. Agencies must acknowledge this reality within which staff members practice and take definitive preventive action to foster worker safety both on and off site, and social work education must follow suit. Social workers who are prepared with the resources and skills to meet the unexpected are in the best position to protect themselves and, ultimately, to provide the best services for their clients.

SKILL DEVELOPMENT EXERCISE

Implementation Exercise

1. Take the Model for the Agency Safety Plan and draft a plan for your agency by employing the model and each of the 12 general strategies for the prevention of violence.

2. If you have experienced an incident of client violence at any point in your career, pick the most serious one, and fill out the Model for a Violent Incident Report Form. Look at what you have written and evaluate whether the form should be modified in any way to fully document what happened to you.

3. Show the Strategies to Prevent Client Violence checklist to your co-workers, supervisor, and agency management and solicit their feedback about each strategy. Such feedback can serve as an opening for discussion about developing an agency safety plan, if one does not exist, or reviewing an existing plan.

Model for a Violent Incident Report Form

The purpose of this form is to document all violent incidents by clients toward staff. **The form must be completed within three business days after the incident occurred.** The information will be used in planning risk reduction procedures for Agency X and in tracking the incidence and prevalence of violence in the agency to guide such procedures. All information will be kept confidential and only aggregate data will be publicly reported.

Date of incident: _____ Time incident occurred: _____ A.M./P.M.

Place the incident occurred: _____

Employee's name: _____

Agency division that employee works in: _____

Relationship that employee has with the client involved (e.g., therapist, case manager, supervisor, etc.):_____

Agency division telephone number: _____ Employee's telephone number: _____

Type of Incident: (because some incidents involve more than one type of violence, please circle all that apply and describe briefly)

1. *Damage to agency property*   Yes   No

Briefly describe what happened: _____

2. *Damage to employee's property*   Yes   No

Briefly describe what happened: _____

3. *Threat (written or verbal, in person or by telephone)*   Yes   No

Briefly describe what happened: _____

4. *Attempted physical attack*   Yes   No

Briefly describe what happened: _____

5. *Actual physical attack **without injury***   Yes   No

Briefly describe what happened: _____

6. *Actual physical attack **with injury***   Yes   No

Briefly describe what happened: _____

Please give details of the injury, treatment, and outcome: _____

_____

7. *Other type of violence* :   Yes   No

Briefly describe what happened: _____

Action Taken: (circle all that apply)

Client was hospitalized *involuntarily*	Yes	No	Client was hospitalized *voluntarily*	Yes	No
Medication administered	Yes	No	Behavioral limits set	Yes	No
Police were involved	Yes	No	Legal charges pressed	Yes	No
Client was jailed	Yes	No	Clinical follow-up plan	Yes	No
Crisis intervention provided	Yes	No	Client terminated from agency services	Yes	No
Client referred to other agency/services	Yes	No	Clinic Safety Policy was revised	Yes	No
Restraint and/or seclusion	Yes	No	Staff member provided with counseling or other help	Yes	No
Other outcome occurred	Yes	No			

(please describe) _____

_____

Information about the Client Involved in the Incident:

Client's name: _____

Client's gender: M / F   Client's age: _____

Client's diagnosis (if applicable): _____

Was client intoxicated on alcohol or drugs?   Yes   No

Was client accompanied by anyone (family, friends, police, other staff members, etc.)?

Description of the Incident: describe, step by step, what led up to the incident, what seemed to specifically trigger the incident, who was present, exactly what happened, who did what, how each person involved in the incident responded during it, and how the incident was resolved. Finally, for future risk reduction planning, identify any thoughts in retrospect about what you think could have been done, if anything, to prevent the incident from occurring.

_____

_____

_____

_____

_____

_____

Administration/Management Action Taken: (to be completed by employee's supervisor, division head, or other agency administrator)

What support and help was given to the employee(s) involved in the incident? (Please be specific)

_____

_____

_____

_____

_____

_____

Describe the follow-up plan for the employee and the agency safety committee:

_____

_____

_____

_____

_____

Form completed by: Employee: _____ Date: _____

Management: _____ Date: _____

Model for an Agency Safety Plan

The following model is a prototype that can serve as a starting point for an agency to develop a staff safety plan. Not all aspects of the plan are appropriate for all agencies, and, obviously, each agency should tailor the components to fit its particular needs.

A critical *first step* for implementation of the safety plan is for the agency administration to issue a position statement to all staff members that outlines their commitment to the plan. Here is an example of such a statement:

All of us at [Agency X] recognize and openly acknowledge that client violence is a realistic and legitimate practice concern and that our primary obligation to staff is to create a fair and safe workplace. We encourage and support the reporting of all incidents of client violence toward staff and will proactively assist workers who are victims of violence. In doing this we promise to:

- Take workers' concerns seriously at all times.
- Establish a climate in which safety is an ongoing topic of discussion.
- Develop a safety policy that will be a collaborative effort of administration and line workers regarding how to respond to workers who have experienced client violence.
- Take the responsibility of broaching the issue of safety in staff meetings and supervisory sessions to allow any concerns or actual incidents that have happened over the past week to be discussed.
- Provide you with the training you need to develop skills in working with violent clients and to reduce your risk of becoming a victim.

The *second step* is for the agency to appoint a safety committee composed of representatives from all staff levels. This committee should also be representative of the staff composition in terms of discipline, race, gender, and age. The charge for the safety committee is to develop the agency's safety policy, which will include the following:

- Guidelines for developing a staff training program that meets workers' identified needs.
- Procedures for debriefing and assisting the worker who has experienced an incident of client violence.
- Guidelines for providing medical, disability, and liability coverage; availability of counseling; and provisions for paid leave.
- Procedures for providing opportunities for other staff members to discuss the incident.
- Guidelines for analyzing incidents that have occurred to identify factors that can be addressed by the agency to reduce the probability of similar incidents occurring in the future.

- Specific plans for the development and implementation of safety precautions, which may include any or all of the following: (1) panic buttons; (2) silent alarms; (3) emergency code words; (4) metal detectors; (5) security guards; (6) emergency response team or network; (7) strategically locating interview rooms for easy access to help in an emergency; (8) designing interview rooms to reduce risk. Regular maintenance and drills will be part of these plans.
- Guidelines for conducting periodic benefit–risk analyses that weigh the degree of safety gained against potential negative outcomes for clients (e.g., intimidation) or staff (e.g., morale) and modifying the safety plan accordingly if needed.
- Use of a violent incident report form with procedural manual to accurately track the incidence and prevalence of violent incidents within the agency.
- Identification of a staff person to keep records on incidents reported and analyze trends over time, which shall be reported to the agency every 6 months.
- Implementation of an access control policy that will control who can access the clinical areas. Such a policy could include the following requirements: (1) All staff members must wear an employee ID badge. This can be a deterrent to violence because, particularly in a large clinic, you will immediately be able to identify who is and who is not on staff; (2) staff members should always maintain key control to their facility or suite; (3) only authorized personnel are allowed in offices; (4) public areas of the agency should be used for "social visits"rather than work areas in the agency.
- Development of a risk reduction home visit–field visit policy.
- Identification of a staff person to serve as a liaison with the local police department to facilitate communication and cooperative collaboration. If serious problems arise, that individual would be responsible for facilitating an agency–police department task force to resolve the problem.
- Encourage a work philosophy that emphasizes and values openly asking for help when needed and supporting others who need help without criticism, put-downs, or retaliation.
- Establishment of formal agency policies for accessing help. Such policies would include who should be called and how and who is responsible for what duties. Furthermore, this policy should be routinely reviewed by the safety committee and tested via safety drills.
- Encourage staff to give a clear, consistent message to clients that using violence to solve problems is not acceptable. All staff members must be trained in clinical skills to help clients develop nonviolent alternatives.

Strategies to Prevent Client Violence

❑ Acknowledge client violence as a serious practice concern.

❑ Recognize that everyone deserves a safe workplace.

❑ Appoint a safety committee.

❑ Develop an agency safety plan.

❑ Employ a violent incident report form.

❑ Offer high-quality in-service safety training addressing risk assessment and risk management strategies.

❑ Establish specific policies to help victimized workers.

❑ Implement specific safety precautions in the office and field.

❑ Employ a risk management approach to home visiting and outreach.

❑ Establish safety protocols with other cooperative organizations.

❑ Ask for help when needed.

❑ Give a clear, consistent message to clients that using violence to solve problems is not acceptable.

Chapter 11

When Client Violence Occurs
The Multidimensional Impact on Social Workers

Experiencing a threat or an assault or having one's property damaged at the hands of a client can affect a social worker in many ways. The extent of the impact depends on a variety of factors, including the severity of the physical and psychological damage inflicted, the context of the incident, the relationship between the victim and the perpetrator, the personality and temperament of the victim, previous exposure to traumatic events, and the coping strategies of the victim (Joseph, Williams, & Yule, 1995; Resnick et al., 1993; True et al., 1993). As with all stress reactions, one cannot predict how any one individual will react based on the event alone. Stress and trauma reactions are very individual (Weinger, 2001). This chapter looks at the various ways that client violence affects individual social workers, including the immediate emotional impact of client violence (in particular, how we tend to blame ourselves) and the emotional stages that victimized social workers go through in the aftermath of a violent incident; what kinds of injuries social workers suffer as a result of client assaults; the impact of client violence on social workers' feelings about their professional work; and, finally, how experiencing client violence affects social workers' practice conduct.

BLAMING OURSELVES

One of the primary obstacles to effectively addressing client violence toward social workers is the fact that social workers tend to blame themselves and each other when an incident occurs. Why do we social workers so readily accept culpability when one of us is threatened or injured by a client? Victor Schwarz (1987), whose daughter Isabel was murdered by a client, suggests three reasons for this phenomenon. One possibility relates to the way many social workers see themselves, that is, as the "caring mother [or father] figure who believes herself capable of assuaging all worldly woes in her children" (Schwarz, 1987, p. 14). This idealistic, albeit unrealistic, perception of self can function as a setup for failure and blame. None of us can permanently sustain such an ideal, yet this kind of professional vision is to some extent encouraged because it is reflected in our cardinal values and our code of ethics. When an adverse event, such as violence, occurs in practice, this vision can influence us to believe we have failed and thus that we should be blamed.

A second factor that contributes to this assumption of blame is related to how social work education and training is provided and the messages that are often transmitted to social work students. Schwarz (1987) suggests that sometimes social work teachers and trainers, often with the best of intentions but with limited direct work experience with violent clients, tell students that prevention of violence is a task requiring finely tuned proficiency. If violence occurs, therefore, it is because the social worker did not possess adequate professional expertise, which can lead to profound feelings of shame for the social worker when an incident occurs. In reality, most of the steps that are actually effective in preventing violence involve simple common sense, logic, and basic clinical skills rather than specialized professional expertise. Every social worker can learn how to reduce risk and promote safety.

Finally, the third reason for guilt and blame taking relates to the erroneous assumption that clients never constitute a threat if the social worker "handles them properly" and uses the "correct" intervention. If violence occurs, therefore, it is because the social worker chose the wrong approach. I recall conducting a risk assessment seminar for a group of social work educators and practitioners during which I disseminated some of the findings from the CV Study. One of the audience participants offered the following comment: "Well, those workers who experienced violence must have done something wrong. The solution to client violence is for social workers to correct their mistakes. Maybe such workers shouldn't be in the field to begin with." What is interesting about this comment is that, traditionally, social workers have always been careful to avoid "blaming the victim," arguing that social problems should not be blamed on those suffering from them (W. Ryan, 1976). However, when it comes to ourselves, our colleagues, and client violence, we seem to be all too willing to blame the victim. Part of this probably has to do with collective denial. If I believe that I am a competent social worker, then blaming a violent incident on another worker's lack of competence helps me to feel safe, that is, safety is guaranteed as long as one practices competently. Unfortunately, this belief can lead social workers to avoid taking steps to develop actual prevention strategies and to avoid acknowledging violence as a legitimate practice risk. It is similar to saying that a rape victim was raped because "she asked for it." The corollary is that if one doesn't "ask for it," one won't be raped, which, of course, isn't true. The mental health and medical care system also may collaborate in blaming the victimized worker for assaults, thus leading to an institutional risk management approach that has "only the patient in mind" (Engel & Marsh, 1986, p. 160). An additional component of this explanation is the commonly held belief that violent clients are "sick people" and thus should be exempt from responsibility for their actions, even to the point of suggesting that workers who accept certain jobs have given implicit permission to be assaulted. For example, St. Paul's Hospital in Vancouver filed a charge against a client who assaulted a nurse (Schwarz & Greenfield, 1978). During the trial, the defense argued that the charges should be dismissed because "by accepting a position in psychiatry, the employee had given permission to be assaulted" (Engel & Marsh, 1986, p. 160). The judge in that case did not agree and held the client accountable for her actions. Miller and Maier (1987) argue that staff members have rights, too, and should not be expected to excuse and accept violent and illegal behavior that clients are able to control. Normalizing violence and victimization is never healthy in one's personal or professional life. We give this message to our clients all the time. Even in settings in which the selection criteria for clients includes dangerousness, such as involuntary psychiatric inpatient units or forensic settings, safety can still be a priority.

SOCIAL WORKERS' EMOTIONAL REACTIONS TO CLIENT VIOLENCE

The Stages of Trauma Resolution

Along with blaming ourselves, what other kinds of emotional reactions do social workers who encounter client violence experience? Atkinson (1991) reports that social workers who are assaulted by clients undergo emotional reactions similar to those experienced by other victims of assault. Typically, assault victims go through three stages of trauma resolution (Bard & Sangrey, 1986). The first stage, termed *disorganization of self*, or what Clark and Kidd (1990) refer to as *numbness and chaos*, involves feelings of shock, dismay, and disbelief. The victim may emotionally detach, which enables him or her to handle the assault itself and the immediate aftermath. The individual may appear to others as if he or she is adjusting and managing the incident without difficulty:

"At first, I was shocked and angry—I couldn't believe that the client had attacked me. I felt detached—like I was watching myself in a movie. I responded to the client calmly, eased my way out of the room, and got help. I thought I was fine, that the whole incident was no big deal, until several days later when I fell apart. I was shaky, cried, couldn't sleep . . . I called in sick for two days. It took me several weeks before I felt okay. I felt it was my fault and my faith in my own skills was shaken."

The second stage, *period of struggle,* is distinguished by feelings of fear, anxiety and anger (Bard & Sangrey, 1986). In the previous example, the worker's period of detachment evolved into fear (shakiness, crying) and anxiety (crying, sleeplessness). The worker doesn't note anger, but this is not surprising given that social workers often blame themselves following incidents of client violence and that any anger experienced is directed toward oneself. Sometimes victims of assault will become hypervigilant and fearful of seeing the assailant again and will suffer from intrusive thoughts that compel the individual to relive the incident:

"I became very fearful—afraid I would see the client again even though I knew he was in the hospital. I parked away from the clinic. I changed my home phone number to an unlisted number, used my maiden name at work, and put another lock on my front door at home. When I would drive home from work, I was very careful to keep an eye on my rearview mirror to be sure I wasn't being followed."

On the positive side, victims of violence often take steps to protect themselves in ways that can be helpful and constructive in keeping them safe. In that process, they may be able to find meaning in the incident by recognizing that the probability of being victimized in the future can be reduced, which helps to restore feelings of self-efficacy (Bard & Sangrey, 1986; Davis & Friedman, 1985; Janoff-Bulman & Frieze, 1983). In the preceding example, the social worker took specific steps to protect herself, such as putting another lock on the front door. Another social worker, in commenting about his experience being assaulted by a client in the client's home, stated:

"I will never go out to a client's home alone again if the client has a history of violence. I will take much more care in questioning the family about the events leading up to the crisis and will ask for police backup if I have any concerns. Forget trying to be a hero. I'm a lot more humble now."

This social worker's newfound humility enabled him to assert control over potentially dangerous situations in the future. His previous victimization provided both justification and incentive for him to establish appropriate parameters in his outreach work methods that will serve to promote his safety.

The final stage of trauma resolution, which often takes several months to achieve, is *readjustment of self* (Bard & Sangrey, 1986). Here the circumstances and meaning of the violent incident are put into perspective. Feelings of fear, anxiety, and anger diminish, and the memories of the event are integrated into the individual's life history. Obviously, there are individual differences in how and when each of these stages is experienced, influenced by characteristics of both the event and the individuals involved. Access to family, friends, and professional help can also mitigate the response to an assault and the subsequent resolution.

The most effective assistance for a victim is help that is immediate, empathic, sensitive, individually tailored, and confidential (Clark & Kidd, 1990). Some individuals, particularly those who are not provided with appropriate timely help, may be unable to resolve the trauma and may remain stuck in the period-of-struggle stage. For example, one respondent in the CV Study noted that, even years after the assault, she still felt strong emotions whenever she thought of the incident, feeling "like it was yesterday." Although this individual acknowledged that she had never really resolved the feelings, she also accepted that lack of resolution and did not feel that it had negatively affected her life.

Incidence of Posttraumatic Stress Disorder

The DSM-IV-TR (American Psychiatric Association, 2000), defines posttraumatic stress disorder (PTSD) as an anxiety disorder consisting of certain characteristic symptoms that develop following exposure to an extreme traumatic stressor. These characteristic symptoms include persistent reexperiencing of the traumatic event, persistent avoidance of stimuli associated with the traumatic stressor, numbing of general responsiveness, and persistent symptoms of increased arousal, with the full symptom picture present for at least 1 month and causing clinically significant distress or impairment in functioning (American Psychiatric Association, 2000, p. 463).

Similar to victims of other types of violence, such as street crimes and natural disasters, staff victims of client violence can develop PTSD. Caldwell (1992) conducted a survey of the incidence of trauma and

PTSD among the staff victims of client violence in two mental health facilities. Sixty-two percent of the clinical staff members who responded to the survey reported having experienced a critical incident involving a threat to their personal safety or having witnessed a serious injury or death, with the majority of them reporting symptoms of PTSD. Of that group, 10% met the criteria for a DSM-III-R (American Psychiatric Association, 1987) diagnosis of PTSD. Of those clinicians reporting critical incidents, only 15% reported any subsequent external review of the incident, and for those who did report a review, the majority involved supervisory or disciplinary actions rather than stress debriefing sessions to help the clinician recover from the trauma. Caldwell concludes by commenting that "one of the most hazardous work settings for employee mental health is the local mental health facility" (p. 839), which is a sad commentary on the state of management responses to employee work-related trauma.

Immediate Emotional Impact

In the CV Study, the immediate emotional impact generated from experiencing an incident of client violence differed considerably depending on the type of violence involved. The predominant feeling following an incident of property damage was anger, followed by feelings of anxiety, fear, sadness, and guilt. In contrast, workers who were threatened felt predominantly fearful and anxious. Although those experiencing attacks often reported fear, anger, and anxiety, victims of client attacks, unlike those of property damage and threats, often reported feeling shocked or shook up, helpless, inadequate, drained, exhausted, or frustrated, and they blamed themselves. The issue of self-blame is a critical one, as discussed previously, and can lead to painful feelings of shame:

> "I blamed myself after the attack. I should have seen it coming, I shouldn't have seen the client alone, I shouldn't have stood so close to her, I didn't pay enough attention to the cues. I look back on it and I know I made mistakes but I didn't see it at the time."

Also, victims of attacks were most likely to report feeling concerned about the client and what the outcome would be for him or her as a result of the incident. Finally, although no workers reported lengthy emotional trauma after property damage and only 1% reported it after threats, 8% of the victims of attacks reported lengthy emotional trauma. For example, one respondent stated:

"I could not go back to work for weeks, I had nightmares, anxiety attacks, and what can best be described as emotional flooding. Why did this have to happen to me? I finally had to leave the agency."

The descriptions of trauma offered by these respondents are consistent with the kinds of symptoms typically reported by individuals who evidence PTSD. This similarity underlines the importance of providing trauma debriefing sessions to social workers who experience client violence, particularly to those who experience physical attacks.

PHYSICAL INJURIES TO THE SOCIAL WORKER AS A RESULT OF CLIENT VIOLENCE

Almost all incidents of client violence exact some kind of emotional toll. Physical assaults, however, can also lead to physical injury, as well as emotional trauma. Several studies have been done on the incidence, characteristics, and costs of staff injuries, particularly on psychiatric inpatient units (see, e.g., Carmel & Hunter, 1989, 1993; Hanson & Balk, 1992; Hill & Spreat, 1987; Hillbrand, Foster & Spitz, 1996; Hunter & Carmel, 1992). Carmel and Hunter (1993) reported on data collected from 1984 through 1988 on staff injuries at a large state hospital. During that period, a total of 209 employees suffered 236 injuries from patient attacks, the majority (71%) of which were head injuries. Ward nursing staff were most at risk, suffering 78% of the injuries, whereas professional staff members sustained only 7% of the injuries. Male nursing staff members had a 50% higher injury rate than female nursing staff members.

Hillbrand and colleagues (1996) looked at the characteristics and costs of staff injuries at a maximum security forensic hospital over a 3-year period. During the study period, 79 patients were involved in 157 staff injuries. Staff members were absent from work for an average of 85 days as a result of the injuries, which, collectively, constituted the cost equivalent of 2% of the hospital's total budget. These statistics suggest that violence toward staff contributes significantly to hospital administrative costs (Hunter & Carmel, 1992). As in Carmel and Hunter's (1993) study, Hillbrand and colleagues found that nursing staff members had the highest injury rates, with male staff members about twice as likely as female staff members to be injured. Staff members were equally likely to sustain injuries from a battery attack (i.e., direct patient attack) as they were when containing the patient (i.e., putting the patient into restraints). The costs incurred as a result of battery attacks, however, tend to be higher than those for containment injuries. Hunter and Carmel (1992) reported from a study of staff injuries at an all-male maximum security forensic hospital that the average cost for a battery injury ($7,573) was 64% higher than that for a containment injury ($4,615). The most common clinical signs associated with injury attacks by clients were florid psychotic behavior, nonpsychotic agitation, recent use of restraints, nonadherence to medication, and a history of assault. Forensic hospitals appear to be the settings with the highest rates of staff injury, followed by nonforensic psychiatric inpatient units. Here is a typical example of an injury sustained by a social worker on a forensic unit:

> "I was working in a maximum security correctional medical facility and was with the patients in the workshop. An inmate became angry and lunged at me with a large board and then grabbed my arms. The guards immediately restrained him and I got out of the way. I had bruises on my arms but it wasn't serious. I was angry."

In the CV Study, the vast majority of respondents who suffered client attacks either did not need medical attention, as illustrated by the previous example, or did not make clear in their responses whether medical care was needed. In four cases the injuries reported were categorized as severe or extreme. In the three cases of severe injuries, the social workers were attacked without warning from behind. In the first case, the social worker was thrown to the floor by the client, sustaining three cracked ribs, a dislocated jaw, and a sprain to the wrist. In the second case, the client threw the social worker to the ground and put his fingers in the worker's eyes in an attempt to gouge them out. The social worker in this case believed that the client intended to kill him. In the third case, the social worker was hit over the head from behind with a chair, which knocked him unconscious. He sustained a severe cut above his right eye that required many stitches, a concussion, and a bone chip in his elbow as a result of the fall. All three cases involved male clients and male social workers in forensic mental health settings. One of the respondents commented:

> "I no longer work in forensic settings. I still, however, work with violent clients, and I make it a point to do a thorough violence assessment with the clients directly. I now work with gang members in high schools and also conduct groups for men involved with spouse abuse, and I have never had a problem. I have also made a personal decision after watching many staff be injured by clients and then treated badly by the disability board that I will not tolerate being injured again."

The case in which the injuries were categorized as extreme involved a serious sexual assault that was highly traumatic, both physically and emotionally, for the social worker:

> "Since the incident, some of the joy of the profession has been lost to me. I no longer have the unrealistic perception that I will remain physically inviolate and unscathed by the chaos and unreasoning violence in our society. I still have my basic belief in the possibility for human growth and change but I no longer work with [the population I used to work with]."

IMPACT ON SOCIAL WORKERS' FEELINGS ABOUT THEIR PROFESSION

Traumatic events can have an impact that goes beyond the immediate emotional reaction. For more than one-half of the social workers in the CV Study, the violent incidents they experienced affected their feelings about their professional work. The most prevalent feeling was a rise in awareness of how violent clients can be, in spite of the social worker's best intentions. This was especially true for those respondents who reported physical attacks. As one respondent put it: "it [the attack] made me realize that social work can be a dangerous profession, and no matter how well we do our work, we can still become targets for a client's rage."

The next most common feeling was the realization that one must be more cautious and careful, which, for some respondents, resulted in enhanced feelings of fear, anxiety, and hypervigilance. Sometimes, respondents directed their feelings of caution toward certain defining aspects of the particular incident they had experienced. For example, one respondent commented that she was particularly cautious around male adolescents, because the individual who threatened her was a male adolescent. Many respondents saw the source of the incident as the practice setting rather than the client, and thus their caution was directed toward the setting. For example, one respondent commented, "I am particularly cautious when I am out in the field. I don't have the same protections there as I do in the agency." Other respondents indicated that their increased caution was broadly directed toward all aspects of their practice as a whole.

Experiencing client violence can also affect social workers' idealism and how they choose to approach their clients. Social workers in the CV Study reported that, following the violent incident, they were more guarded and wary around clients, found themselves keeping clients at a distance, were less empathic toward clients, and were becoming less involved with clients emotionally as a means of self-protection. For example, a respondent said:

> "When I got out of school I really thought I could change the world and clients would want my help. That was pretty naive, I guess. After the incident, I felt more cynical about my work, feeling like I was a fool for being so optimistic. I think I can still be a good social worker, but I see things differently now and I *feel* differently about my work."

Many workers expressed anger at the agency, system, or type of practice. Sources of the anger included feeling that efforts to obtain safety measures "are ignored by the powers that be until someone gets hurt" and feeling that one's supervisor or agency was unsupportive. Finally, many respondents express anger that, given the danger faced by social workers, salaries were not higher. As one respondent put it, "we should be paid more, at least as much as the police or other professionals in high-risk settings." As noted before, a poor supervisory or administrative response to victimized social workers encourages underreporting of incidents and can be emotionally damaging to the social worker involved. Some respondents even indicated that they had thought of leaving the field of social work altogether. Touching on a number of these issues, a respondent commented:

> "After I was threatened, my supervisor just shrugged and told me to make a note of it in the client's record and that there was nothing else that could be done. I thought to myself—why am I doing this for what I get paid? Why do those of us in the most dangerous types of practice—for me it's child welfare—why do we get paid the least? No wonder there's a constant revolving door. Social workers just don't get any respect from the public or from our agencies."

Not all of the changes in feelings reported by the respondents were negative. Six to ten percent of respondents, depending on type of violence experienced, indicated that the incident resulted in furthering the respondent's commitment to help troubled clients and made the respondent more sensitive to clients' situations. These respondents indicated that they were still committed to their profession and liked the work they did. For example:

> "Although the incident made me feel more committed to the importance of training staff in violence prevention, my feelings about my

profession haven't changed. I like social work but I know that I need more training on how to intervene effectively with violent clients."

"I felt sorry for the client. The staff didn't handle the situation well. The incident made me realize even more how much our clients suffer with their problems and how we must maintain our empathy to that and be fair, consistent, and honest. The client didn't mean to hurt me; he was just very frustrated and scared."

IMPACT OF CLIENT VIOLENCE ON SOCIAL WORKERS' PRACTICE CONDUCT

In terms of changes in practice conduct, most of the social workers in the CV Study who had experienced client violence reported that they made very appropriate changes that reduced their risk of experiencing future violence but did not compromise services to clients. Most indicated that they became more cautious and careful, avoided placing themselves in risky situations, and tried to be more aware of their surroundings. Many reported that they avoided violent clients or avoided seeing clients under certain circumstances that might enhance risk, such as alone, on a home visit, without backup, and so forth. Table 11.1 summarizes the various practice conduct changes reported by the social workers.

Many respondents noted that they made efforts to improve their practice skills as a result of the incident, including doing better assessments, approaching clients with empathy and authenticity, allowing clients an opportunity to save face, setting limits, and intervening quickly to prevent violence. Many respondents also indicated that they worked with their colleagues and agency to develop and improve safety measures and advocated for the use of consultation and supervision for assessment and management of violent clients. The issue of safety during home visits was frequently mentioned, and many respondents indicated that they worked on developing safety protocols and better assessment tools.

Taking precautions, such as seeing clients as a team, employing police backup, and letting others know where one is, represent positive safety-enhancing strategies. Avoidance of violent clients, however, is a concern in terms of the social work commitment to provide services to all clients in need. Clients who have problems with violence need good services delivered by competent practitioners. If too many practitioners avoid such clients, they will be left without the help they so desperately

TABLE 11.1. Changes in Practice Conduct Reported by Social Workers Who Have Experienced an Incident of Client Violence

- *I am more cautious and careful*; try to avoid putting myself at risk; I try to be more aware of my surroundings.

- *I do a better assessment*, that is, check the client's history and do a thorough clinical screening; *I am also more vigilant about observing escalating violence* and intervening quickly when it occurs.

- *I am careful about my own behavior*; I word things with clients carefully to avoid appearing threatening, I have conditioned myself to keep calm and attempt to deal rationally with client anger, and I am clear at the beginning what the "rules" are in the therapy room or situation.

- *I am more likely to set firm and clear limits* with clients and to use physical or chemical restraint.

- *I made efforts to learn new skills* for working with violent clients.

- *I have improved the quality of my interventions*, that is, I try to empower my clients and help them take responsibility for their behavior; I am more cautious about confrontation and look for ways to allow clients to save face; and I try to establish a treatment environment of safeness and trust.

- *I refuse to see clients under certain circumstances*, such as alone; I take police, security, or another coworker with me to see the client, and I let others know where I am and who I am with when I am concerned about the possibility of violence.

- *Individually, I advocated for and implemented certain safety measures* to protect myself: having only unbreakable objects in office, leaving office door open, making sure I have a quick exit, having an unlisted phone number, and so forth.

- *With coworkers or agency, I developed a plan for anticipating and handling violent clients*, including improvement of security measures and using more consultation or supervision.

- *I am particularly careful or have altered my protocol to ensure safety during home visits*.

- *I will not tolerate violent behavior* and am prepared to protect myself.

- *I avoid seeing potentially violent clients* anymore in my practice and keep my distance, and I'm less likely to intervene in violent situations involving clients.

- *I get less emotionally involved with clients* so that I'm not caught with my defenses down.

- *I left this type of practice setting* for a completely different setting (or client population) to lower my risk of harm by clients.

need. This possibility illustrates one of the significant negative consequences for clients of not taking action to prevent client violence. As noted before, once a client has behaved violently, he or she will be labeled as a "violent client," and his or her care will be modified from that point on, including who is willing to provide services and under what circumstances.

CONCLUSION

The previous findings clearly show that experiencing an incident of client violence can have a significant impact on social workers in a number of ways, including the immediate emotional impact, physical injuries, feelings about their professional work, and how they subsequently conduct their practice. Some of these changes were positive, others were negative. On the positive side, many respondents indicated that the incident served to raise their awareness about violence, furthered their commitment to help troubled clients, and led to taking action individually and with colleagues to enhance safety. Furthermore, recognizing that an incident of client violence can represent a traumatic stressor for the social worker who is targeted can be a helpful first step in moving away from blaming the victim and toward seeing the victim as someone who has suffered a trauma and deserves appropriate help and support.

On the negative side, however, many respondents reported anger at the agency, system, or type of practice and a disillusionment with the social work profession. Some respondents indicated that they decided to avoid seeing potentially violent clients in their practice and deliberately avoided certain types of clients, most typically clients with certain diagnoses (e.g., personality disorders, schizophrenia, or substance abuse) and within certain demographic groups (e.g., males or adolescents).

Some respondents stated that they left the practice setting in which the incident occurred, and some even reported thinking about leaving the social work profession altogether. Client violence appears to be one factor influencing social worker staff turnover, along with losing public service social workers to private practice positions. The majority of workers who left stated that they chose private practice as the best alternative because they perceived it as safer than the public arena. The emotional and physical impact of client violence can have far-reaching effects on how the individual sees his or her future as a professional social worker. Allowing client violence to occur can result in the loss of services to clients who have problems with violence and loss of individual social workers from our professional ranks.

SKILL DEVELOPMENT EXERCISE

Discussion Questions

1. Why do social workers so readily accept culpability when one of us is threatened or injured by a client? Do you agree with Victor Schwarz's analysis that self-blame stems from the idealistic but unrealistic image we hold of ourselves as social workers, from the way social work education and training is provided, and from the erroneous assumption that clients never constitute a threat if the social worker "handles them properly"? Or do other factors play a role in self-blame?

2. Chapter 11 presents a model of the stages of trauma resolution. Does this model seem to fit the experiences you have had as a social worker? How might the model be modified to fit your experience?

3. If you have personally encountered client violence, what were the immediate and long-term emotional reactions that you experienced?

4. Examine the list of changes that social workers have reported in terms of how they conduct their practice following an incident of client violence. Do you think these changes are positive or negative? Why or why not?

Chapter 12

Future Directions for Practice and Policy

This book has addressed the topic of client violence toward social workers from a prevention perspective rooted in an empirical base. Violence by clients toward social workers is, in part, a reflection both of our violent society and of certain key elements of the modern workplace. Violence is also a staple of our news media and popular entertainment, communicating an underlying message to the public at large that violence is an effective and acceptable means to solve problems. Guns also play a pivotal role in the high level of violence in the United States. Lethal weapons often make the difference between simply thinking violent thoughts or making threats or even injuring someone and action that leads to a fatality. Violence exacts a heavy toll on our society, including pain and suffering for the victims and victims' families, medical expenses to victims, lost productivity due to injuries, expenditures for mental health services to deal with trauma reactions, and expenditures for police, social services, courts, investigations, and incarcerations.

What is it that supports and feeds our violent society? Some have argued that part of it is that we are living in an angry culture that has been evolving for decades. Societal trend watchers have suggested that certain aspects of late 20th-century life, for example, communication overload, disconnectedness, and accelerated competition, have contributed to this development. The answer is not that simple, however. Violence is a multifaceted multidimensional phenomenon resulting from the interaction of a combination of individual, clinical, historical, and environmental factors. An angry culture may play a role, but there is no simple unidimensional answer. Fortunately, we have come a long way in un-

236

derstanding what factors are associated with enhanced risk for violence and which factors serve to protect against violence.

VIOLENCE AND SOCIAL WORK PRACTICE

Most of us choose social work as our profession because we want to help other people and make the world a better place. We do not anticipate that we may become targets of violence by the very individuals we want to help, but today risk is a reality of work life for many practicing social workers. Furthermore, as we begin the 21st century, a variety of indicators suggest that physical and verbal violence by clients toward social workers is increasing across settings. As noted earlier, the answer to why social workers are likely to be targets for a client's violent behavior is complex. Part of the answer probably lies in the unique nature of the social work role, that is, that our work is both caring and controlling. We often control the dwindling supply of resources that our clients desperately need. Many of our clients are very angry because they are living extraordinarily difficult lives and must struggle with multiple challenges and problems every day even while they are aware that others in our country are living lives of phenomenal wealth. They may be coping with poverty, mental illness, drug addiction, family troubles, legal hassles, and living in dangerous and disintegrating neighborhoods. All of these factors can enhance risk for violence. Society uses social workers as agents of both social care and social control, charging us to protect our clients from society but also to protect society from our clients.

Another issue that plays a role in understanding client violence is the fact that in many ways social work practice has changed from earlier times. Late 20th-century politics and policy shifts have created conditions that place social workers at risk. The number of those needing assistance and social services in both the private and public sectors has increased as the federal and state governments have cut back on certain types of institutional support. Budget cuts and the ensuing understaffing of social service agencies have led to increased vulnerability for social workers. Furthermore, social workers today handle client situations on the front lines that previous generations of workers did not encounter as frequently, often involving volatile issues and highly unstable desperate clients who may see violence as their only recourse. Thus the concern about violence and social work practice has not increased because social workers are less able to cope today than in earlier times but because today's social workers are exposed to a greater number of violent situations as a result of changes in our roles and the evolving organization of the social welfare state.

THE EMPIRICAL BASIS OF OUR
UNDERSTANDING OF CLIENT VIOLENCE

This book has reported a variety of findings from the Client Violence Toward Social Workers (CV) Study (Newhill, 1996, 1997), which had the overall goal of examining the nature, degree, and impact of violence perpetrated by clients toward social workers across practice specializations and settings. The study found that the majority of social workers consider violence toward social workers to be a significant issue for the social work profession, and they often worry about their own safety when working with clients. This concern is rooted in experience, as the majority of the sample had experienced one or more types of client violence. Not all social workers are at equal risk, however; the primary influences are gender, practice setting, and the population served. Male social workers have a significantly higher risk for experiencing violence from clients, and, although several theories have been advanced as to why this is the case, we still do not have a definitive answer. Practice settings also vary in risk, although no practice setting was free from reports of violence. Based on the proportion of respondents reporting violence, the highest risk settings, not surprisingly, were criminal justice services, drug and alcohol services, and child welfare services, with mental health services following closely behind. Social workers who work in agencies that serve clients with histories of repetitive violent behavior, such as many psychiatric inpatient services and residential treatment facilities, are more at risk for being victimized by violence.

The CV Study also found that experiencing client violence has a significant impact on victimized social workers in terms of emotional trauma, feelings about their professional work, and how they subsequently conduct their practice. As noted previously, the nature of the immediate emotional impact reported by respondents differed depending on the type of violence they experienced, and the issue of self-blame continues to be a critical one for us as social workers because it can lead to painful feelings of shame if not responded to supportively and constructively by the agency and coworkers.

Not only do social workers suffer immediate emotional trauma following an incident of client violence, but also their feelings about their professional work often change as a result of experiencing violence at the hands of a client. Respondents in the CV Study indicated that experiencing client violence served to raise their awareness of violence in social work practice, resulting in their beliefs that they must be more cautious and careful, but they also felt less trusting of clients. Many of those reporting physical attacks said they believed that assaults go with the territory, that part of a social worker's job in certain settings is being assaulted, implying that they did not feel they had the right to be safe. Normalizing violence and victimization is never healthy in one's personal or professional life, and thus this finding was quite disturbing. We tell our clients who are victims of domestic violence that such violence is not acceptable and that they have a right to be safe. Why are we unable to say the same thing to ourselves?

A significant proportion of the social workers who experienced attacks also reported that they were angry at the system, their supervisors, or the type of practice they were involved in; that they were tired of violence; and that they did not like social work as much as they used to. Thus, although some social workers may accept violence as part of the job, it still affects their feelings about their work. The good news is that some of the respondents indicated that the incident did not result in negative feelings; rather, it made them more committed to helping troubled clients and increased their sensitivity to clients' situations. Although these social workers were more careful in their practice, they did not distance themselves from clients but, in fact, were more sensitized to their clients' needs as a result of their personal experience with violence.

Across types of violence, the social workers reported remarkably similar changes in practice conduct. Most respondents indicated that, after the incident, they became more cautious and careful, avoided placing themselves in risky situations, and tried to be more aware of their surroundings. Some, however, reported that they avoided seeing violent clients, which is a concern because of the social work commitment to provide services to all clients in need. Clients who have problems with violence need good services delivered by competent practitioners. If too many practitioners avoid such clients, they will be left without the help they so desperately need. This possibility illustrates one of the negative consequences of not taking action to prevent client violence. On the positive side, many respondents changed how they conducted their practice by making efforts to improve their practice skills, including doing better assessments, conscientiously approaching clients with empathy and authenticity, and intervening quickly to prevent violence. Other respondents stated that they left the setting in which the incident occurred, and some even reported thinking about leaving social work altogether.

IMPLICATIONS FOR THE FUTURE

The findings from the CV Study, in combination with other existing literature, suggest that client violence can have a wide-ranging impact on social workers beyond the immediate emotional or physical damage. Allowing client violence to occur can result in the loss of services to clients who have problems with violence and loss of individual social workers from our professional ranks. In response, all social workers, social service agencies, social work educators, social welfare policy makers, and client advocacy groups must join together in taking steps to reduce the incidence of client violence toward social workers. Violence harms practitioners, and violence harms clients.

This goal can be accomplished by, first, acknowledging openly that client violence is a legitimate practice concern that affects both clients and practitioners and, second, by committing the time and resources to providing appropriate risk assessment and risk management training and services along with high-quality prevention measures. Every social services agency should have a safety policy that is developed and regularly reviewed by a standing safety committee composed of representatives from *every* staff level and service area. Safety must be a *collective inclusive effort*. Every new employee should be briefed on the contents of the safety policy, and regular emergency drills should be conducted, particularly after new staff members have been hired. Accomplishing this does not require a huge outlay of time or money. What it does require is serious commitment and follow-through. No longer can we afford to wallow in collective denial of the reality of practice risks.

Many prevention measures cost very little to implement. Developing a system of code words to signal the need for help, for example, costs nothing. Determining who will make a "show of force" or arranging one's office contents to eliminate objects that can be used as weapons cost nothing. Being supportive, caring, and nonblaming toward colleagues who are victimized costs nothing. The one thing that is required, however, is an overt recognition that violence is a legitimate practice issue, along with a commitment to plan in advance how to reduce the risk of violence. High-quality training in risk assessment, intervention, and management may cost some money but the cost is minuscule in comparison with the human and economic costs of allowing staff members to be emotionally and physically injured. Agencies can band together in cooperative arrangements to share training sessions and exchange expertise, which can lower cost. The primary obstacle to a safe workplace for all social workers is our denial that a problem exists. Agencies must acknowledge the reality within which staff members practice and take action to preserve worker safety, both in the office and in the field. Social workers who are prepared with the resources and skills to meet the unexpected are in the best position to protect themselves and, ultimately, to provide the best services for their clients.

Appendix 1

Client Violence toward Social Workers Survey Questionnaire

1. Under *each* of the statements presented below, please circle whether you Strongly Agree (SA), Agree (A), Disagree (D), Strongly Disagree (SD), or are Neutral (N), that is, you neither Agree or Disagree.
   a. I consider client violence toward social workers to be a significant issue for the social work profession in general.   (SA) (A) (D) (SD) (N)
   b. Client violence toward social workers is a significant issue *in my practice*.   (SA) (A) (D) (SD) (N)
   c. I sometimes worry about *my own safety* while working with clients.   (SA) (A) (D) (SD) (N)
   d. I prefer to not work with clients who *are or may be* violent.   (SA) (A) (D) (SD) (N)

Please answer the following questions by circling or filling in the appropriate answer.

2. Has a client ever intentionally damaged your property or agency property that you were using?
   (a) No
   (b) Yes   *If Yes*: Please answer the questions under "PROPERTY DAMAGE" section.

3. Have you ever been threatened by a client? "Threat" is defined as a verbal threat of harm or a threatening physical gesture.
   (a) No
   (b) Yes *If Yes*: Please answer the questions under "THREAT" section.

241

4. Has a client ever actually attacked or attempted to physically attack you?
   (a) No
   (b) Yes   *If Yes*: Please answer the questions under "PHYSICAL ATTACK" section.

5. Do you know of any *social work colleagues or social work coworkers* who have been threatened, attacked, or had property damaged by a client?
   (a) No
   (b) Yes   *If Yes*: How many have had these experiences?
             Had property damaged: #__
             Been threatened: #__
             Been physically attacked: #__

6. Have you ever received any training in how to intervene with violent and potentially violent clients?
   (a) No
   (b) Yes
        b1. *If Yes*, where was the training provided? (check as many as apply)
            __ as part of my social work academic coursework
            __ as part of my student field placement
            __ at my agency
            __ it was training I sought out independently
            __ other (please specify) _____
        b2. *If Yes*, to what extent did the training meet your needs? (if you have participated in more than one, please answer about the most recent training)
            __ Fully met my needs
            __ Mostly met my needs
            __ Somewhat (or partially) met my needs
            __ Not at all
        b3. *If Yes*, did you find the training helpful in working effectively with violent or potentially violent clients?
            (a) No
            (b) Yes   (Please go directly to question #8)

7. If you answered *No to question #6*, would you want to take part in a training program if it were available?
   (a) No
   (b) Yes
   Why/Why not?_____

Finally, I would like to ask you a few questions about yourself to help interpret the results. Please circle or fill in each appropriate answer.

8. Your gender:
   (a) Male
   (b) Female

9. Your age (as of last birthday):
   _____ years

10. Your ethnic/racial origin:
    a. American Indian/Alaska Native
    b. Asian or Pacific Islander
    c. Black/African American (non-Hispanic)
    d. Chicano(a)/Mexican American
    e. Puerto Rican
    f. Other Hispanic
    g. White (non-Hispanic)
    h. Other (please specify): _____

11. Please circle all degrees you have earned:
    a. BSW/BASW   c. DSW or PhD in social work
    b. MSW   d. Other degrees (please specify): _____

12. Year highest degree was awarded: _____

13. Primary area of practice: (please circle one)
    a. Medical/health care services
    b. Alcohol/drug/substance abuse services
    c. Developmental disabilities/mental retardation
    d. Corrections/criminal justice
    e. Community organization and planning
    f. Children and youth/child protective services
    g. Family services
    h. Group services
    i. School social work
    j. Services to aged
    k. Occupational
    l. Mental health services
    m. Public assistance/welfare
    n. Other (please specify): _____

14. Total number of years in practice: _____

15. Primary practice function:
   a. Direct services
   b. Supervision
   c. Management/administration
   d. Policy development/analysis/planning
   e. Consultant/education/training/research
   f. Other practice function (please specify): _____

End of Questionnaire   THANK YOU!!

A. PROPERTY DAMAGE Section

1. How many times has your property, or property of your agency that you were using, been intentionally damaged by a client?
   _____ Number of times

For the following questions, please choose the most serious incident of property damage:

2. What was the client's:
   a. Gender: _____
   b. Age: _____
   c. Length of relationship with you: _____

3. What was your role with the client (e.g., therapist, case manager, etc.)?
   _____

4. The incident of property damage occurred at:
   a. My office
   b. Other area of agency (please specify): _____
   c. Client's home
   d. Other site in community (please specify): _____
   e. Other (please specify): _____

5. Please describe the nature and extent of the property damage:
   _____
   _____

6. How did you and/or others respond to the incident?
   _____
   _____

7. How did you feel emotionally after the incident occurred? (check all that apply)
    (a) Angry   (e) Sad or depressed
    (b) Scared   (f) Embarrassed or humiliated
    (c) Anxious   (g) Other (please specify): _____
    (d) Guilty

8. As a result of the incident, how, if at all, have your feelings about your professional work changed?

    _____
    _____
    _____

9. As a result of the incident, have the ways in which you conduct your practice changed?
    (a) No
    (b) Yes   *If Yes*, Please specify below:

    _____
    _____

B. THREAT Section

1. How many times have you been threatened by a client?
    _____ Number of times

For the following questions, please choose the most serious threat:

2. What was the client's:
    a. Gender: _____
    b. Age: _____
    c. Length of relationship with you: _____

3. What was your role with the client (e.g., therapist, case manager, etc.)?

    _____

4. Please describe the content and nature of the threat.

    _____
    _____

5. The threat occurred at:
    a. My office
    b. Other area of agency (please specify): _____

    c. Client's home

    d. Other site in community (please specify): _____

    e. Other (please specify): _____

6.   How did you and/or others respond to the threat:

    _____

    _____

7.   How did you feel emotionally during and following the threat? (check all that apply)

    (a) Angry   (e) Sad or depressed

    (b) Scared   (f) Embarrassed or humiliated

    (c) Anxious   (g) Other (please specify): _____

    (d) Guilty

8.   As a result of the threat, how, if at all, have your feelings about your professional work changed?

    _____

    _____

9.   As a result of the threat, have the ways in which you conduct your practice changed?

    (a) No

    (b) Yes   *If Yes*, Please specify below:

    _____

    _____

C. PHYSICAL ATTACK Section

This section includes both actual attacks and attempted attacks.

1.   How many times have you been physically attacked by a client?

    _____ Number of times actually attacked

    _____ Number of times of attempted attacks

For the following questions, please choose the most serious attack or attempted attack:

2. The incident I have chosen was: _____ an attempted attack

                                              _____ an actual attack

3. What was the client's:
    a. Gender: _____
    b. Age: _____
    c. Length of relationship with you: _____

4. What was your role with the client (e.g., therapist, case manager, etc.)?
    _____

5. The attack or attempted attack occurred at:
    a. My office
    b. Other area of agency (please specify): _____
    c. Client's home
    d. Other site in community (please specify): _____
    e. Other (please specify): _____

6. Was a weapon involved?
    (a) No
    (b) Yes   _If Yes:_ What type of weapon was involved? _____

7. Please describe the nature of the incident:
    _____
    _____
    _____

8. How did you and/or others respond to the client's attack or attempted attack?
    _____
    _____

9. Did you require medical attention as a result of the attack?
    a. _Yes,_ I required hospitalization.
    b. _Yes,_ I required outpatient medical care.
    c. _No,_ I did not require medical attention.

If you answered Yes, please describe the nature and extent of your injuries:
    _____
    _____

10. Please describe your emotional reaction to the attack:
    _____
    _____
    _____

11. What was the outcome for the client who attacked you? (circle either Yes or No for all that apply)

a. Were police called?	No	Yes
b. Were charges pressed?	No	Yes
c. Was client jailed?	No	Yes
d. Was client removed from premises but *not* jailed?	No	Yes
e. Was client hospitalized?	No	Yes

> *If Yes*, was the hospitalization:
> e1. voluntary
> e2. involuntary as:
>   e2a. danger to self
>   e2b. danger to others
>   e2c. gravely disabled

f. Did the client experience an outcome *other than* the above?
No   Yes   *If Yes*, please describe below:

_____

_____

11. As a result of the incident how, if at all, have your feelings about your professional work changed?

_____

_____

_____

12. As a result of the incident, have the ways in which you conduct your practice changed?
(a) No
(b) Yes *If Yes*, please specify below:

_____

_____

_____

Appendix 2

A Model Syllabus for a Course on Understanding and Managing Violence and Safety in Social Work Practice

Session 1:   Violence and our Society
A historical perspective on violence in America
Social and individual costs of violence
Role of guns and the gun culture
Role of the media
Are we an angry culture?
Lab exercise: Small-group discussion

Session 2:   Family and School Violence
Family violence
  Domestic violence
  Child abuse and neglect
Violence in our schools
Community violence
Lab exercise: Small-group discussion

Session 3:   Violence in the Workplace
Prevalence of workplace violence—who is at risk?
Classifying workplace violence
Causes of violence in the workplace
Corporate responses to incidents of workplace violence

Session 4:   Violence and Social Work Practice
Why this is an issue for us as social workers
Incidence and prevalence of violence
Nature and degree of violence

Impact of violence on social work practice conduct
Lab exercise: Small-group discussion

Session 5:   The Prediction of Violence
Can we predict violence?
Why should we predict violence?
Dangerousness and the systems approach
Defining dangerousness as related to crime and mental illness
Using a systems approach to predict violence
A model to predict violence

Session 6:   Risk Factors for Violent Behavior, Part 1:
Individual/Clinical Risk Factors
Demographic risk factors
Clinical risk factors
Biological risk factors

Session 7:   Risk Factors for Violent Behavior, Part 2:
Historical and Environmental
Historical risk factors
Environmental and contextual risk factors
Developing a risk assessment model and protocol
Lab exercise: Case analysis

Session 8:   Working with Involuntary and/or Resistant Clients
Reactance theory and resistance
Clinical response strategies
Socialization strategies
The legally involuntary client
The socially involuntary client
Conducting the initial session
Effective contracting strategies
Lab exercise: Role plays for working with involuntary or resistant clients

Session 9:   Clients, Practitioners, and Settings at Risk
Characteristics of clients involved in violent incidents
Practice settings at risk for violence: How and why
Practitioners at risk for violence: How and why
Lab exercise: Case analyses in different practice settings

Session 10: Understanding the Emotional Sequelae of Experiencing Violence
Blaming ourselves
Social workers' immediate and long-term reactions to client violence

Understanding posttraumatic stress disorder and other trauma-induced
   disorders
Critical stress debriefing
Lab exercise: Critical stress debriefing role plays

Session 11: The Risk Assessment of Violent Clients
Encountering a violent client
The person-in-the-environment perspective
Aspects to be considered when making a risk assessment across client
   populations and practice settings
   Background information
   Clinical status of the client
      Physical appearance and behavior
      Assessment of biological risk factors
      Diagnostic assessment
      Inquiring about violence
      Inquiring about violence with quiet, guarded clients
   Environmental assessment
      Environmental assessment of the client's situation
      Environmental assessment in preparation for a client evaluation in
         the field or home visit
Summary of the Guidelines for Risk Assessment of the Violent Client
Lab exercise: Case analysis

Session 12: Intervention Approaches with Violent Clients, Part 1:
         Approaching and Engaging the Violent Client
How do we respond to incidents of client violence?
Appropriate and inappropriate responses
Client outcomes following incidents of violence
Interventions with violent clients
   Choosing an interviewing environment
   Talking with the violent client
   The role of empathy in working with violent clients
   Role of the strengths perspective
Lab exercise: Role plays with violent clients in a range of contexts

Session 13: Intervention Approaches with Violent Clients, Part 2:
         Intervention Modalities
Medication
When to hospitalize
Psychotherapy with violent clients
Behavior therapy
Intervention strategies when a client makes a threat

The duty to protect
Lab exercise: Case analysis

Session 14: Individual and Agency Strategies to Prevent Violence
Education and training
Prevention recommendations for the clinic physical environment
Preventing injury from weapons
Introduction to physical maneuvers by the clinician
Twelve general strategies for the prevention of violence

Session 15: Wrap-Up
How to develop an agency safety policy
Future directions for the profession

References

Abt E (Producer/Director) (2001, August 1). *Point of View: Take It from Me* [Television broadcast]. New York and Washington, DC: Public Broadcasting Service.

Adler DA (1990) Treating personality disorders. *New Directions for Mental Health Services* (Vol. 47). San Francisco: Jossey-Bass.

American Humane Association, Children's Division (1997, January). *Child Protection Leader*. Englewood, CO: Author.

American Psychiatric Association (1987). *Diagnostic and Statistical Manual of Mental Disorders, Third Edition, Revised*. Washington, DC: Author.

American Psychiatric Association (2000). *Diagnostic and Statistical Manual of Mental Disorders, Fourth Edition Text Revision*. Washington, DC: Author.

American Psychological Association Commission on Violence and Youth (1993). *Violence and Youth: Psychology's Response*. Washington, DC: Author.

Anderson E (1997). Violence and the inner-city street code. In J. McCord (Ed.). *Violence and Childhood in the Inner City*. Cambridge, UK: Cambridge University Press.

Appelbaum KA, & Appelbaum PS (1991). A model hospital policy on prosecuting patients for presumptively criminal acts. *Hospital and Community Psychiatry*, 42(12): 1233–1237.

Appelbaum PS (1985). Tarasoff and the clinician: Problems in fulfilling the duty to protect. *American Journal of Psychiatry*, 142: 425–429.

Appelbaum PS (1994). New directions in the assessment of dangerousness of the mentally ill. *Japanese Journal of Psychiatry and Neurology*, 48: 77–83.

Associated Press (2000, July 26). Health groups link media, child violence. *Pittsburgh Post-Gazette*, p. A12.

Astor RA, Behre WJ, Fravil KA, & Wallace JM (1997). Perceptions of school violence as a problem and reports of violent events: A national survey of school social workers. *Social Work*, 42(1): 55–68.

Astor RA, Behre WJ, Wallace JM, & Fravil KA (1998). School social workers and school violence: Personal safety, training, and violence programs. *Social Work*, 43(3): 223–232.

Atkinson, JC (1991). Worker reaction to client assault. *Smith College Studies in Social Work*, 62(1): 34–42.

Ault A (1999, July 8). A virtual reality that's best escaped. *New York Times*, p. D5.

Barash DP (2002, May 24). Evolution, males and violence. *Chronicle of Higher Education*, pp. B7–B9.

Bard M (1969). Family intervention: Police teams as a community mental health resource. *Journal of Criminal Law, Criminology and Police Science*, 60: 247–250.

Bard M, & Sangrey D (1986). *The Crime Victim's Book* (2nd ed). New York: Brunner/Mazel.

Barratt ES (1972). Anxiety and impulsiveness: Toward a neuropsychological model. In C Spielberger (Ed.), *Anxiety: Current Trends in Theory and Research* (pp. 195–222). New York: Academic Press.

Barratt ES (1994). Impulsiveness and aggression. In J Monahan & HJ Steadman (Eds.), *Violence and Mental Disorder: Developments in Risk Assessment* (pp. 61–79). Chicago: University of Chicago Press.

Beaver HW (1999). Client violence against professional social workers: Frequency, worker characteristics, and impact on worker job satisfaction, burnout and health. *Dissertation Abstracts International Section A: Humanities and Social Sciences*, 60(6-A): 2227.

Beck J (Ed.) (1985). *The Potentially Violent Patient and the Tarasoff Decision in Psychiatric Practice*. Washington, DC: American Psychiatric Press.

Behrer S, & Evans JK (1988, February 18). Slain social worker told mother not to worry. *Pittsburgh Post-Gazette*, pp. A1, A4.

Beigler JS (1984). Tarasoff vs. confidentiality. *Behavioral Sciences and the Law*, 2(3): 272–286.

Bell CC, & Fink PJ (2000). Prevention of violence. In CC Bell (Ed.), *Psychiatric Aspects of Violence: Issues in Prevention and Treatment*. Vol. 86: *New Directions for Mental Health Services* (pp. 37–47). San Francisco: Jossey-Bass.

Bellesiles MA (2000). *Arming America: The Origins of a National Gun Culture*. New York: Knopf.

Berg AZ, Bell CC, & Tupin J (2000). Clinician safety: Assessing and managing the violent patient. In CC Bell (Ed.), *Psychiatric Aspects of Violence: Issues in Prevention and Treatment*. Vol. 86: *New Directions for Mental Health Services* (pp. 9–29). San Francisco: Jossey-Bass.

Bernay LJ, & Elverson DJ (2000). Managing acutely violent inpatients. In ML Crowner (Ed.), *Understanding and Treating Violent Psychiatric Patients* (pp. 49–68). Washington, DC: American Psychiatric Press.

Bernstein HA (1981). Survey of threats and assaults directed toward psychotherapists. *American Journal of Psychotherapy*, 35: 542–549.

Bizjak T (1988, February 19). ESL employees tour scene of massacre. *San Francisco Chronicle*, p. A2.

Bjorkqvist K (1994). Sex differences in physical, verbal and indirect aggression: A review of recent research. *Sex Roles: A Journal of Research*, 30(3–4): 177–188.

Black KJ, Compton WM, Wetzel M, Minchin S, Farber NB, & Rastogi-Cruz D (1994). Assaults by patients on psychiatric residents at three training sites. *Hospital and Community Psychiatry*, 45(7): 706–713.

Black, T, & Spinks P (1985). Predicting outcomes of mentally disordered and dangerous offenders. In DP Farrington & R Tarling (Eds.), *Prediction in Criminology* (pp. 174–192). Albany: State University of New York Press.

Boxer S (1999, May 1). When fun isn't funny: Evolution of pop gore. *New York Times*, pp. A17, A19.

Bridges-Parlet S, Knopman D, & Thompson T (1994). A descriptive study of physically aggressive behavior in dementia by direct observation. *Journal of the American Geriatric Society*, 42, 192–197.

Brizer, DA, & Crowner ML (1989). *Current Approaches to the Prediction of Violence*. Washington, DC: American Psychiatric Press.

Brooke J (1999, May 1). Officials admit failure to spot plot in Littleton. *New York Times*, pp. 1, 10.

Brown A (1987). *When Battered Women Kill*. New York: Free Press.

Brown GL, Goodwin FK, Ballenger JC, Goyer PF, & Major LF (1979). Aggression in humans correlates with cerebrospinal fluid amine metabolites. *Psychiatry Research*, 1: 131–139.

Brown R, Bute S, & P Ford (1986). *Social Workers at Risk: The Prevention and Management of Violence*. London: Macmillan.

Brownmiller S (1975). *Against Our Will: Men, Women and Rape*. New York: Simon & Schuster.

Caldwell MF (1992). Incidence of PTSD among staff victims of patient violence. *Hospital and Community Psychiatry*, 43(8): 838–839.

Carmel H, & Hunter H (1989). Staff injuries from inpatient violence. *Hospital and Community Psychiatry*, 40: 41–46.

Carmel H, & Hunter M (1993). Staff injuries from patient attack: Five years' data. *Bulletin of the American Academy of Psychiatry and Law*, 21(4): 485–493.

Carson RC, Butcher JN, & Mineka S (1998). *Abnormal Psychology and Modern Life* (10th ed.). New York: Longman.

Catalano R, Dooley D, Novaco RW, Wilson, G, & Hough, R (1993). Using ECA survey data to examine the effect of job layoffs on violent behavior. *Hospital and Community Psychiatry*, 44(9): 874–879.

Charles CL (1999). *Why Is Everyone So Cranky?* New York: Hyperion Press.

Chermack ST, Fuller BE, & Blow FC (2000). Predictors of expressed partner and non-partner violence among patients in substance abuse treatment. *Drug and Alcohol Dependence*, 58(1–2): 43–54.

Clark S, & Kidd B (1990). Part of the job. *Social Work Today*, 21(45): 20–21.

Cleckley H (1976). *The Mask of Sanity* (5th ed.). New York: Mosby.

Cocozza JJ, & Steadman HJ (1978). Prediction in psychiatry: An example of misplaced confidence in experts. *Social Problems*, 25(2): 265–278.

Cole D, & Lamberth J (2001, May 13). The fallacy of racial profiling [Editorial]. *New York Times*, p. 13.

Collins JJ (1989). Alcohol and violent behavior: Less than meets the eye. In NA

Weiner & ME Wolfgang (Eds.), *Pathways to Criminal Violence* (pp. 49–67). Newbury Park, CA: Sage.

Corder BF, Ball BC, Haizlip TM, Rollins R, & Beaumont R (1976). Adolescent parricide: A comparison with other adolescent murder. *American Journal of Psychiatry*, 133(8): 957–961.

Counseling session ends in shootings (1997, June). *NASW News*, 42(6): 1, 8.

Counts DC, Brown J, & Campbell JC (Eds.) (1972). *Sanctions and Sanctuary: Cultural Perspectives on the Beating of Wives*. Boulder, CO: Westview Press.

Craig TJ (1982). An epidemiological study of problems associated with violence among psychiatric inpatients. *American Journal of Psychiatry*, 139: 1262–1266.

Crane D (1986). *Violence on Social Workers* (Social Work Monograph No. 46). Norwich, UK: University of East Anglia.

Crate R (1986, November). Social workers and violent clients: Management response. *Social Work Today*, 10: 1–3.

Crowner ML (2000). A brief guide to the assessment and pharmacological treatment of violent adult psychiatric inpatients. In ML Crowner (Ed.), *Understanding and Treating Violent Psychiatric Patients* (pp. 3 19). Washington, DC: American Psychiatric Press.

Davis RC, & Friedman LN (1985). The emotional aftermath of crime and violence. In CR Figley (Ed.), *Trauma and Its Wake: The Study and Treatment of Post-Traumatic Stress Disorder* (pp. 90–112). New York: Brunner/Mazel.

Death penalty upheld in arson death. (1990, April 6). *Sacramento Bee*, p. A4.

De Becker G (1997). *The Gift of Fear: Survival Signals That Protect Us from Violence*. Boston: Little, Brown.

Department of Health and Social Security (1988). *Violence to Staff: Report of the DHSS Advisory Committee on Violence to Staff*. London: HMSO.

DeWolfe AS, & Ryan JJ (1984). Wechsler performance IQ verbal IQ index in a forensic sample: A reconsideration. *Journal of Clinical Psychology*, 40: 291–294.

Diamond RJ (1998). *Instant Psychopharmacology*. New York: W.W. Norton.

Dillon S (1992, November 18). Social workers: Targets in a violent society. *New York Times*, pp. A1, C18.

Dionne EJ (1999, September 20). Face it: This is a violent society. *Pittsburgh Post-Gazette*, p. A21.

Dobash RE, & Dobash RP (1979). *Violence Against Wives: A Case Against the Patriarchy*. New York: Free Press.

d'Orban PT (1990). Female homicide. *Irish Journal of Psychological Medicine*, 7: 64–72.

Doyle R, & Cave J (Eds.). (1992). *Serial Killers: Ted Bundy*. Alexandria, VA: Time-Life Books.

Drifter is judged guilty in slaying of social worker (1991, March). *NASW News*, p. 12.

Dubin WR (1981). Evaluating and managing the violent patient. *Annals of Emergency Medicine*, 10: 481 484.

Dubin WR (1995). Assaults with weapons. In BS Eichelman & AC Hartwig (Eds.), *Patient Violence and the Clinician* (pp. 53–72). Washington, DC: American Psychiatric Press.

Dubin WR, & Lion JR (Eds.) (1992). *Clinician Safety: Report of the American Psychiatric Association Task Force on Clinician Safety.* Washington, DC: American Psychiatric Association.

Dubin WR, & Lurie HJ (Producers). (1982). *Management and Treatment of the Violent Patient* [Videotape]. (Available from IEA Productions, Inc., 520 East 77th Street, New York, NY, 10021.)

duBois R (1997). The action film "Terminator": Gateway to aggressive fantasies in adolescence? In HJC van Marle (Ed.), *Challenges in Forensic Psychotherapy: Forensic Focus No. 5* (pp. 63–69). London: Jessica Kingsley.

Duenwald M (2002, September 10). Some friends, indeed, do more harm than good. *New York Times,* p. D-5.

Duncan JW, & Duncan GM (1971). Murder in the family: A study of some homicidal adolescents. *American Journal of Psychiatry,* 127(11): 1498–1502.

Dunkel J, Ageson AT, & Ralph CJ (2000). Encountering violence in field work: A risk reduction model. *Journal of Teaching in Social Work,* 20(3/4): 5–18.

Dunkel T (1994, August). Danger zone: Your office. *Working Woman,* pp. 39–42, 70, 72.

Eccles K, & Tutt N (1987, December). Coping with violence an issue for trainers. *Insight,* p. 8.

Ehrenreich B (2001). *Nickel and Dimed: On (Not) Getting By in America.* New York: Henry Holt.

Elam SM, Rose LC, & Gallup AM (1994, September). The 26th annual Phi Delta Kappa/Gallup poll of the public's attitudes toward the public schools. *Phi Delta Kappan,* pp. 42–56.

Else L, Wonderlich S, Beatty W, Christie D, & Staton R (1993). Personality characteristics of men who physically abuse women. *Hospital and Community Psychiatry,* 44(1): 54–58.

Engel F, & Marsh S (1986). Helping the employee victim of violence in hospitals. *Hospital and Community Psychiatry,* 37(2): 159–162.

Englander EK (1997). *Understanding Violence.* Mahwah, NJ: Erlbaum.

Ennis BJ, & Litwack TR (1974). Psychiatry and the presumption of expertise: Flipping coins in the courtroom. *California Law Review,* 62: 693–752.

Eronen M, Angermeyer MC, & Schulze B (1998). The psychiatric epidemiology of violent behaviour. *Social Psychiatry and Psychiatric Epidemiology,* 33(Suppl 1): S13–S23.

Eronen M, Tiihonen J, & Hakola P (1997). Psychiatric disorders and violent behavior. *International Journal of Psychiatry in Clinical Practice,* 1(3): 179–188.

Ervin F, & Lion J (1969). Clinical evaluation of the violent patient. In D Mulvihill & M Tumin (Eds.), *Crimes of Violence: Staff Report Submitted to the National Commission on the Causes and Prevention of Violence* (Vol. 13, pp. 1163–1188). Washington, DC: U.S. Government Printing Office.

Estroff SE, & Zimmer C (1994). Social networks, social support, and violence among persons with severe, persistent mental illness. In J Monahan & HJ

Steadman (Eds.), *Violence and Mental Disorder: Developments in Risk Assessment* (pp. 259 295). Chicago: University of Chicago Press.

Euster S (1992, December 4). Societal barometer [Letter to the editor]. *New York Times*, p. A14.

Ewing C (1987). *Battered Women Who Kill*. New York: Lexington Books.

Fagan J (1993). Set and setting revisited: Influences of alcohol and illicit drugs on the social context of violent events. In SE Martin (Ed.), *Alcohol and Interpersonal Violence: Fostering Multidisciplinary Perspectives* (NIAAA Research Monograph No. 24; pp. 161–191). Rockville, MD: National Institutes of Health.

Fagan J, & Chin K (1990). Violence as regulation and social control of distribution of crack. In M de la Rosa, E Lambert, & B Gropper (Eds.), *Drugs and Violence* (pp. 8 43). Rockville, MD: National Institute of Drug Abuse.

Faludi S (1999, August 16). *Rage of the American male*. Newsweek, p. 31.

Fauman MA (1994). *Study Guide to DSM-IV*. Washington, DC: American Psychiatric Press.

Fellin P (1996). *Mental Health and Mental Illness*. Itasca, IL: Peacock.

Felthous AR (1980). Aggression against cats, dogs and people. *Child Psychiatry and Human Development*, 10(3): 169–177.

Felthous AR (1981). Childhood cruelty to cats, dogs and other animals. *Bulletin of the American Academy of Psychiatry and Law*, 9(1): 48–52.

Felthous AR, & Kellert SR (1986). Violence against animals and people: Is aggression against living creatures generalized? *Bulletin of the American Academy of Psychiatry and Law*, 14(1): 55–69.

Fisher WA (1994) Restraint and seclusion: A review of the literature. *American Journal of Psychiatry*, 151: 1584–1591.

Flannery RB, Fulton P, Tausch J, & DeLoffi AY (1991). A program to help staff cope with psychological sequelae of assaults by patients. *Hospital and Community Psychiatry*, 42: 935–938.

Flannery RB, Hanson MA, & Penk WE (1994). Risk factors for psychiatric inpatient assaults on staff. *Journal of Mental Health Administration*, 21: 24–30.

Freud S (1930/1962). *Civilization and Its Discontents* (J Strachey, Ed. & Trans.). New York: W.W. Norton.

Friedman TL (1999, April 27). Judgment not included [Editorial]. *New York Times*, p. A31.

Furlong MJ, Babinski L, Poland S, & Munoz J (1996). Factors associated with school psychologists' perceptions of campus violence. *Psychology in the Schools*, 33: 28–37.

Gilligan J (1996). *Violence: Reflections on a National Epidemic*. New York: Random House.

Glassner B (1999). *The Culture of Fear*. New York: Basic Books.

Gleick J (1999). *Faster: The Acceleration of Just About Everything*. New York: Pantheon.

Goetting A (1988a). Patterns of homicide among women. *Journal of Interpersonal Violence*, 2: 3–20.

Goetting A (1988b) When females kill one another: The exceptional case. *Criminal Justice and Behavior*, 15: 179–189.

Goldstein AP, Monti PJ, Sardino TJ, & Green DJ (1979). *Police Crisis Intervention*. New York: Pergamon.

Goldstein PJ (1985). The drugs–violence nexus: A tri-partite conceptual framework. *Journal of Drug Issues*, 15: 493–506.

Good guys down show support for those who remain. (1997, April 29). *Journal Gazette* (Fort Wayne, IN), p. 6A.

Goode E, & Eakin E (2002, September 11). Threats and responses: Treating the traumatized. New York Times, pp. A1, A16–17.

Goodwin DW, Alderson P, & Rosenthal R (1971). Clinical significance of hallucinations in psychiatric disorders. *Archives of General Psychiatry*, 24(1): 76–80.

Gordon RA (1977). A critique of the evaluation of Patuxent Institution, with particular attention to the issues of dangerousness and recidivism. *Bulletin of the American Academy of Psychiatry and the Law*, 5: 210–255.

Gove PB (Ed.) (1971). *Webster's Third New International Dictionary*. Springfield, MA: Merriam.

Grafman J, Schwab K, Warden D, et al. (1996). Frontal lobe injuries, violence, and aggression: A report of the Vietnam Head Injury Study. *Neurology*, 46: 1231–1238.

Greenfield LA (1992). *Prisons and prisoners in the United States* (No. NCJ-137002). Washington, DC: U.S. Department of Justice.

Greenhouse L (2002, May 8). U.S., in a shift, tells justices citizens have a right to guns. *New York Times*, p. 30.

Gresswell DM (1991). Psychological models of addiction and the origin and maintenance of multiple murder. *Issues in Criminological and Legal Psychology*, 2(17), 86–91.

Griffin W (1997). Staff safety in human services agencies. *Protecting Children*, 12(4), 13(4): 4–7.

Griffin WV (1995). Social worker and agency safety. In R Edwards & J Hopps (Eds.), *Encyclopedia of Social Work* (19th ed., pp. 2293–2305). Washington, DC: National Association of Social Workers Press.

Grimsley KD (1998, July 20). Surprise! The U.S. lags in workplace violence. *Pittsburgh-Post Gazette*, p. A4.

Grosz DE, Lipschitz DS, Eldar S, & Finkelstein G (1994). Correlates of violence risk in hospitalized adolescents. *Comprehensive Psychiatry*, 35: 296 300.

Guterman NB, Jayaratne S, & Bargal D (1996). Workplace violence and victimization experienced by social workers: A cross-national study of Americans and Israelis. In GR VandenBos & EQ Bulatao (Eds.), *Violence on the Job: Identifying Risks and Developing Solutions* (pp. 175 188). Washington, DC: American Psychological Association.

Gutheil TG (1985). Prosecuting patients. *Hospital and Community Psychiatry*, 36: 1320–1321.

Haffke EA, & Reid WH (1983). Violence against mental health personnel in Nebraska. In JR Lion & WH Reid (Eds.), *Assaults within Psychiatric Facilities* (pp. 91–102). New York: Grune & Stratton.

Hafner H, & Boker W (1973a). *Crimes of Violence by Mentally Abnormal Offenders* (H Marshall, Trans.). Cambridge, UK: Cambridge University Press.

Hafner H, & Boker W (1973b). Mentally disordered violent offenders. *Social Psychiatry*, 8: 220–229.

Hall RCW, & Frankel BL (1996). The value of consultation-liaison interventions to the general hospital. *Psychiatric Services*, 47(4): 418–420.

Hanson RH, & Balk JA (1992). A replication study of staff injuries in a state hospital. *Hospital and Community Psychiatry*, 43(8): 836–837.

Hare RD, & McPherson LM (1984) Violent and aggressive behavior by criminal psychopaths. *International Journal of Law and Psychiatry*, 7: 35–50.

Harman H (1990). Forward. In D Norris, *Violence Against Social Workers: The Implications for Practice* (pp. 7–8). London: Jessica Kingsley.

Harman P, & Davis M (1997). Personal safety for human services professionals: A law enforcement perspective. *Protecting Children*, 12(4), 13(4).

Harrison R, & Gillen M (1996). Surveillance and investigation of homicides at work: California fatality assessment and control evaluation program. *Occupational Medicine: Violence in the Workplace*, 11: 243–255.

Hart SD, & Hare RD (1997). Psychopathy: Assessment and association with criminal conduct. In DM Stoff, J Breiling, & JD Maser (Eds.), *Handbook of Antisocial Behavior* (pp. 22–35). New York: Wiley.

Hasch M, & Guggenheim K (1988, February 17). Slaying triggers hostage siege at St. Francis. *Pittsburgh Press*, pp. A1, A8.

Hatti S, Dubin WR, & Weiss KJ (1982). A study of circumstances surrounding patient assaults on psychiatrists. *Hospital and Community Psychiatry*, 33: 660–661.

Heilbrun AB (1990). The measurement of criminal dangerousness as a personality construct: Further validation of a research index. *Journal of Personality Assessment*, 54: 141–148.

Hellman DS, & Blackman S (1966). Enuresis, firesetting and cruelty to animals: A triad predictive of adult crime. *American Journal of Psychiatry*, 122: 1431–1435.

Hepworth DH, Rooney RH, & Larsen JA (1997). *Direct Social Work Practice: Theory and Skills* (5th ed.). Pacific Grove, CA: Brooks/Cole.

Herbert B (2002, May 9). More guns for everyone! *New York Times*, p. 32.

Hess TH, Hess KD, & Hess AK (1999). The effects of violent media on adolescent inkblot responses: Implications for clinical and forensic assessments. *Journal of Clinical Psychology*, 55(4): 439–455.

Hill J, & Spreat S (1987). Staff injury rates associated with the implementation of contingent restraint. *Mental Retardation*, 25(3): 141–145.

Hillbrand M, Foster HG, & Spitz RT (1996). Characteristics and costs of staff injuries in a forensic hospital. *Psychiatric Services*, 47(10): 1123–1125.

Hiratsuka J (1988, September). Attacks by clients threaten social workers. *NASW News*, p. 3.

Hixon J, & Schwartz J (Producers) (1989). *Better Assessment and Treatment of*

Violent and Aggressive Patients [Videotape]. (Available from McIntyre Media, 75 First St., Suite 203, Orangeville ON L9W 5B6, Canada.)

Holmes RM (1991). *Sex Crimes*. Newbury Park, CA: Sage.

Horejsi C, Garthwait C, & Rolando J (1994). A survey of threats and violence directed against child protection workers in a rural state. *Child Welfare*, 73(2): 173–179.

Hoy K (1993, February 20). It's a tough job but...we social service workers need extra pay, not extra praise. *Pittsburgh Post-Gazette*, p. B-3.

Huber GA, Roth LH, Appelbaum PS, & Ore TM (1982). Hospitalization, arrest and discharge: Important legal and clinical issues in the emergency evaluation of persons believed to be dangerous to others. *Law and Contemporary Problems*, 45: 99–123.

Hudgins A (1999, May 1). When bullies ruled the hallways. *New York Times*, p. A22.

Huff DL (1999). Promoting worker safety in a changing society. *The New Social Worker*, 6(3): 12–13, 24.

Hughes R (1992). *Culture of Complaint: The Fraying of America*. New York: Oxford University Press.

Hunter M, & Carmel H (1992). The cost of staff injuries from inpatient violence. *Hospital and Community Psychiatry*, 43(6): 586–588.

Hunter ME, & Love CC (1993). Types of weapons and patterns of use in a forensic hospital. *Hospital and Community Psychiatry*, 44(11): 1082–1085.

Jaffe P, Wolfe D, & Wilson SK (1986). Similarities in behavioral and social maladjustment among child victims and witnesses to family violence. *American Journal of Orthopsychiatry*, 56(1): 142–146.

James B (1994). School violence and the law: The search for suitable tools. *School Psychology Review*, 23: 190–204.

Janoff-Bulman R, & Frieze IH (1983). A theoretical perspective for understanding reactions to victimization. *Journal of Social Issues*, 39: 1–17.

Jayaratne S, Vinokur-Kaplan D, Nagda BA, & Chess WA (1996). A national study on violence and harassment of social workers by clients. *Journal of Applied Social Sciences*, 20, 1–14.

Johnson D, & Brooke J (1999, April 22). Two suspects hadn't been taken seriously. *New York Times*, pp. A1, A22.

Johnson D, & Kinney J (1993) *Breaking Point: The Workplace Violence Epidemic and What To Do about It*. Chicago: National Safe Workplace Institute.

Johnston D (1999, August 29). It may not feel true, but gunshot deaths are down. *New York Times*, p. 5.

Jones A (1981). *Women Who Kill*. New York: Holt, Rinehart & Winston.

Joseph S, Williams R, & Yule W (1995). Psychosocial perspectives on post-traumatic stress. *Clinical Psychology Review*, 15: 515–544.

Kaminer W (1995). *It's All the Rage: Crime and Culture*. New York: Addison-Wesley.

Kandel E, Mednick SA, Kirkegaard-Sorenson L, Hutchings B, Knop J, Rosenberg R, & Schulsinger F (1988). IQ as a protective factor for subjects at high risk for antisocial behavior. *Journal of Consulting and Clinical Psychology*, 56: 222–226.

Kaplan HJ, & Sadock, BJ (1989). Psychiatric report. In HJ Kaplan & BJ Sadock (Eds.), *Comprehensive Textbook of Psychiatry/V* (Vol. I, pp. 462–467). Baltimore: Williams & Wilkins.

Kaplan SG, & Wheeler EG (1983). Survival skills for working with potentially violent clients. *Social Casework*, 64: 339–346.

Kay SR, Wolkenfeld F, & Murrill LM (1988). Profiles of aggression among psychiatric inpatients. II: Covariates and predictors. *Journal of Nervous and Mental Disease*, 176: 547–557.

Keidan, B. (2002, July 28). Man's best friend is sometimes rarely his enemy. *Pittsburgh Post-Gazette*, pp. C1, C4.

Kelleher, MD (1997). *Profiling the Lethal Employee: Case Studies of Violence in the Workplace*. Westport, CT: Praeger.

Kim JS, Choi S, Kwon SU, & Seo YS (2002). Inability to control anger or aggression after stroke. *Neurology*, 58, 1106–1108.

Klassen D, & O'Connor WA (1987, October). *Predicting violence in mental patients*. Paper presented at the annual meeting of the American Public Health Association, New Orleans, LA.

Klassen D, & O'Connor WA (1988). A prospective study of predictors of violence in adult male mental health admissions. *Law and Human Behavior*, 12(3): 143–158.

Klassen D, & O'Connor WA (1989). Assessing the risk of violence in released mental patients: A cross-validation study. *Psychological Assessment: A Journal of Consulting and Clinical Psychology*, 1(2): 75–81.

Klassen D, & O'Connor WA (1994). Demographic and case history variables in risk assessment: In J Monahan & HJ Steadman (Eds.), *Violence and Mental Disorder: Developments in Risk Assessment* (pp. 229–257). Chicago: University of Chicago Press.

Klaus K (1994). Crime statistics. *Congressional Digest*, 73(6–7): 167–169.

Kozol HL (1982). Dangerousness in society and law. *University of Toledo Law Review*, 13: 241–267.

Krakowski M, Volavka J, & D. Brizer (1986). Psychopathology of violence: A review of the literature. *Comprehensive Psychiatry*, 27: 131–148.

Kraus JF, & McArthur DL (1996, April-June). Epidemiology of violent injury in the workplace. *Occupational Medicine: Violence in the Workplace*, 11: 201–217.

Kronberg ME (1983). Nursing interventions in the management of assaultive patients. In J Lion & W Reid (Eds.), *Assaults within Psychiatric Facilities* (pp. 225–238). New York: Grune & Stratton.

Labig CE (1995). *Preventing Violence in the Workplace*. New York: American Management Association.

Lang AR (1993). Alcohol-related violence: Psychological perspectives. In SE Martin (Ed.), *Alcohol and Interpersonal Violence: Fostering Multidisciplinary Perspectives* (NIAAA Research Monograph No. 24; pp. 121–147). Rockville, MD: National Institutes of Health.

Langmeyer DB (1995). A critical incident report for capturing violent acts: The North Carolina experience. In BS Eichelman & AC Hartwig (Eds.), *Patient Violence and the Clinician* (pp. 125–138). Washington DC: American Psychiatric Press.

Lanza ML (1983). The reactions of nursing staff to physical assault by a patient. *Hospital and Community Psychiatry*, 43: 44–47.

Lau MA, & Pihl RO (1995). Provocation, acute alcohol intoxication, cognitive performance, and aggression. *Journal of Abnormal Psychology*, 104: 150–155.

Leadbetter D (1993). Trends in assaults on social work staff: The experience of one Scottish department. *British Journal of Social Work*, 23: 613–628.

Leonard KE (1993). Drinking patterns and intoxication in marital violence: Review, critique and future directions for research. In SE Martin (Ed.) *Alcohol and Interpersonal Violence: Fostering Multidisciplinary Perspectives* (NIAAA Research Monograph No. 24; pp. 253–280). Rockville, MD: National Institutes of Health.

Levin J, & Fox JA (1985). *Mass Murder: America's Growing Menace*. New York: Plenum Press.

Levinson RM, Briggs RP, & Ratner CH (1984). The impact of a change in commitment procedures on the character of involuntary psychiatric patients. *Journal of Forensic Sciences*, 29(2): 566–573.

Levy P, & Harticollis P (1976) Nursing aides and patient violence. *American Journal of Psychiatry*, 133: 429–431.

Lewin T (1998a, March 26). Experts note access to guns and lack of ties to adults. *New York Times*, p. A21

Lewin T (1998b, March 25). Study finds no big rise in public school crimes. *New York Times*, p. A18.

Lewis DO, Shanok SS, & Pincus JH (1983). Homicidally aggressive young children: Neuropsychiatric and experiential correlates. *American Journal of Psychiatry*, 140: 148–153.

Liberman RP, & Bedell JR (1989). Behavior treatment. In HJ Kaplan & BJ Sadock (Eds.), *Comprehensive Textbook of Psychiatry/V* (Vol. II, pp. 1462–1482). Baltimore: Williams & Wilkins.

Liberman RP, & Mueser KT (1989). Schizophrenia: Psychosocial treatment. In HJ Kaplan & BJ Sadock (Eds.), *Comprehensive Textbook of Psychiatry/V* (Vol. II, pp. 792–806). Baltimore: Williams & Wilkins.

Liberman RP, & Wong SE (1984). Behavior analysis and therapy procedures related to seclusion and restraint. In K Tardiff (Ed.), *The Psychiatric Uses of Seclusion and Restraint* (pp. 35–67). Washington, DC: American Psychiatric Press.

Lidz CW, Meisel A, Zerubavel E, Carter M, Sestak R, & Roth L (1984). *Informed Consent: A Study of Decision Making in Psychiatry*. New York: Guilford Press.

Lidz CW, Mulvey EP, & Gardner WP (1993). The accuracy of predictions of violence to others. *Journal of the American Medical Association*, 269: 1007–1011.

Lindgren C (1990). *Justice Expenditure and Employment*. Washington, DC: U.S. Department of Justice.

Linehan MM (1993). *Cognitive-Behavioral Treatment of Borderline Personality Disorder*. New York: Guilford Press.

Link BG, Andrews H, & Cullen FT (1992). The violent and illegal behavior of mental patients reconsidered. *American Sociological Review*, 57: 275–292.

Link BG, & Stueve A (1994). Psychotic symptoms and the violent/illegal behavior of mental patients compared to community controls. In J Monahan & HJ Steadman (Eds.), *Violence and Mental Disorder: Developments in Risk Assessment* (pp. 137–159). Chicago: University of Chicago Press.

Lion J, & Pasternak SA (1973). Countertransference reactions to violent patients. *American Journal of Psychiatry*, 130: 207–210.

Lion JR (1972). *Evaluation and Management of the Violent Patient*. Springfield, IL: Charles C Thomas.

Lion JR (1995). Verbal threats against clinicians. In BS Eichelman & AC Hartwig (Eds.), *Patient Violence and the Clinician* (pp. 43–52). Washington, DC: American Psychiatric Press.

Lion JR, Snyder W, & Merrill LG (1981). Underreporting of assaults in a state hospital. *Hospital and Community Psychiatry*, 32: 497–498.

Lisa's law. (1998, May 29). *Waterloo/Cedar Falls Courier*, p. A8.

Loewenberg F, & Dolgoff R (1985). *Ethical Decisions for Social Work Practice* (2nd ed.). Itasca, IL: Peacock.

Loranger AW (1999). Categorical approaches to assessment and diagnosis of personality disorders. In CR Cloninger (Ed.), *Personality and Psychopathology* (pp. 201–244). Washington, DC: American Psychiatric Press.

Lorenz K (1966). *On Aggression*. New York: Harcourt Brace Jovanovich.

Lucas C, Sainsbury P, & Collins J (1962). A social and clinical study of delusions in schizophrenia. *Journal of Mental Science*, 108: 747–758.

Lyter SC, & Martin M (2000, February). *Playing it safe: A survey addressing dangers in the field*. Paper presented at the annual program meeting of the Council on Social Work Education, New York.

MacDonald G, & Sirotich F (2001). Reporting client violence. *Social Work*, 46: 107–114.

Mace, P. (1989). The effect of attitude and belief on social workers' judgments concerning potentially dangerous clients. *Dissertation Abstracts International*, 50(2-A): 544.

MacFadden RJ (1980). *Stress, support and the frontline social worker*. Toronto: University of Toronto.

Madden DJ, Lion JR, & Penna MW (1976). Assaults on psychiatrists by patients. *American Journal of Psychiatry*, 133: 422–425.

Martin D, & Fine GA (1991). Satanic cults, satanic play: Is "Dungeons and Dragons" a breeding ground for the devil? In JT Richardson, J Best, & D Bromley (Eds.), *The Satanism Scare: Social Institutions and Social Change* (pp. 107–123). New York: Aldine de Gruyter.

Maxey B (1997). Violence in the workplace is a serious problem. In D Bender & B Leone (Eds.), *Violence: Opposing Viewpoints* (pp. 30–44). San Diego, CA: Greenhaven Press.

McCarthy K (1991, November). Threat of violence leaves its mark: Analysts concerned about safety. *APA Monitor*, 22(11): 22–23.

McCulloch LE, McNiel DE, Binder RL, et al. (1986). Effects of a weapon-screening program in a psychiatric emergency room. *Hospital and Community Psychiatry*, 37(8): 837–838.

McNiel DE (1994). Hallucinations and violence. In J. Monahan & HJ Steadman (Eds.), *Violence and Mental Disorder: Developments in Risk Assessment* (pp. 183–202). Chicago: University of Chicago Press.

McNiel, DE, Eisner, JP, & Binder RL (2000). The relationship between command hallucinations and violence. *Psychiatric Services*, 51(10): 1288–1292.

McPeak W (1979). Family disputes. In AP Goldstein, PJ Monti, TJ Sardino,& DJ Green (Eds.), *Police Crisis Intervention* (pp. 37–52). New York: Pergamon.

Mead M (1968). Cultural factors in the cause and prevention of pathological homicide. In JM MacDonald (Ed.), *Homicidal Threats*. Springfield, IL: Charles C Thomas.

Meloy JR (Presenter) (Menninger Video Productions, Producer) (1994). *Assessing Violence Risk* [Videorecording]. (Available from Menninger Video Productions, The Menninger Foundation, P.O. Box 1829, Topeka, Kansas 66601-0829.)

Meyers CJ (1984, Spring). The legal perils of psychotherapeutic practice (Part II): Coping with Hedlund and Jablonski. *The Journal of Psychiatry and Law*, 12: 39–47.

Miczek KA, DeBold JF, Haney M, Tidey J, Vivian J, & Weerts EM (1994). In AJ Reiss & JA Roth (Eds.), *Understanding and Preventing Violence, Volume 3: Social Influences* (pp. 377–468). Washington, DC: National Academy Press.

Miller RD, & Maier G (1987). Factors affecting the decision to prosecute mental patients for criminal behavior. *Hospital and Community Psychiatry*, 38(1): 50–55.

Millon T, Simonsen E, Birket-Smith M, & RD Davis (1998). *Psychopathy: Antisocial, Criminal, and Violent Behavior*. New York: Guilford Press.

Mills M, Phelan L, & Ryan J (1985). Prosecuting patients. *Hospital and Community Psychiatry*, 36: 1321–1322.

Minkoff K (2000). *Dual diagnosis: An integrated model for the treatment of people with co-occurring psychiatric and substance disorders in managed care systems* [Videotape]. Brookline Village, MA: Mental Illness Education Project.

Monahan J (1981). *Predicting Violent Behavior: An Assessment of Clinical Techniques* (Vol. 114, Sage Library of Social Research). Beverly Hills, CA: Sage.

Monahan J (1984). The prediction of violent behavior: Toward a second generation of theory and policy. *American Journal of Psychiatry*, 141: 10–15.

Monahan J (1988). Risk assessment of violence among the mentally disordered: Generating useful knowledge. *International Journal of Law and Psychiatry*, 11: 249–257.

Monahan, J (1992). Mental disorder and violence behavior: Perceptions and evidence. *American Psychologist*, 47: 511–521.

Monahan J, & Steadman H (Eds.) (1994). *Violence and Mental Disorder: Developments in Risk Assessment*. Chicago: University of Chicago Press.

Morin R, & Deane C (2000, May 14). Poll shows 1 in 4 threatened with a gun. *Pittsburgh Post-Gazette*, p. A22.

Morris T, & Blom-Cooper L (1964). *A Calendar of Murder: Criminal Homicide in England since 1957*. London: Michael Joseph.

Moss HB, & Tarter RE (1993). Substance abuse, aggression and violence: What are the connections? *American Journal of Addictions*, 2: 149–160.

Mulvey EP (1994). Assessing the evidence of a link between mental illness and violence. *Hospital and Community Psychiatry*, 45(7): 663–668.

Mulvey EP, & Lidz CW (1998). Clinical prediction of violence as a conditional judgment. *Social Psychiatry and Psychiatric Epidemiology*, 33: S107–S113.

Mulvihill D, & M Tumin (Eds.) (1969). *Crimes of Violence: Staff Report Submitted to the National Commission on the Causes and Prevention of Violence* (Vol. 13). Washington, DC: U.S. Government Printing Office.

Murdach AL (1980). Bargaining and persuasion with non-voluntary clients. *Social Work*, 25(6): 456–460.

Neathery MM (1992). Assaults on staff: Letter to the editor. *Hospital and Community Psychiatry*, 43(3): 286.

Ness C (2000, April 16). When women turn to violence [Letter to the editor]. *New York Times*, p. 14.

Newhill CE (1991). Parricide. *Journal of Family Violence*, 6(4): 375–394.

Newhill CE (1992). Assessing danger to others in clinical social work practice. *Social Service Review*, 66(1): 64–84.

Newhill CE (1995a). Client violence toward social workers: A practice and policy concern for the 1990's. *Social Work*, 40(5): 631–636.

Newhill CE (1995b). *A Crisis Casebook*. Unpublished manuscript.

Newhill CE (1996). Prevalence and risk factors for client violence toward social workers. *Families in Society*, 77(8): 488–495.

Newhill, CE (in press). Client threats toward social workers: Nature, motives and response. *Journal of Threat Assessment*.

Newhill CE, & Mulvey EP (2002). Emotional dysregulation: The key to a treatment approach for violent, mentally ill individuals. *Clinical Social Work Journal*, 30: 157–171.

Newhill CE, Mulvey EP, & Lidz CW (1995). Characteristics of violence in the community by female patients seen in a psychiatric emergency service. *Psychiatric Services*, 46(8): 785–789.

Newhill CE, & Wexler S (1997). Children and youth services social workers' experiences with client violence. *Children and Youth Services Review*, 19(3): 195–212.

Nieves E (1999, July 29). Yosemite suspect says killing women was a fantasy. *New York Times*, p. A12.

Nolan KA, Volavka J, Mohr P, & Czobor P (1999). Psychopathy and violent behavior among patients with schizophrenia or schizoaffective disorder. *Psychiatric Services*, 50(6), 787–792.

Norris D (1990). *Violence against Social Workers: The Implications for Practice.* London: Jessica Kingsley.

Northwestern National Life Insurance Company (1993). *Fear and Violence in the Workplace: A Survey Documenting the Experience of American Workers.* Minneapolis, MN: Author.

Novaco RW (1994). Anger as a risk factor for violence among the mentally disordered. In J Monahan & HJ Steadman (Eds.), *Violence and Mental Disorder: Developments in Risk Assessment* (pp. 21–59). Chicago: University of Chicago Press.

Novaco RW (1997). Remediating anger and aggression with violent offenders. *Legal and Criminological Psychology,* 2 (Part 1): 77–88.

Novaco RW, & Renwick SJ (1998). Anger predictors of the assaultiveness of forensic patients. In E Sanavio (Ed.), *Behavior and Cognitive Therapy Today: Essays in Honor of Hans J. Eysenck.* Oxford, UK: Anonima Romana.

Osgood DW (1994, November). *Drugs, alcohol and adolescent violence.* Paper presented at the annual meeting of the American Society of Criminology, Miami, FL.

Pagelow MD (1984). *Family Violence.* New York: Praeger.

Paradiso S, Robinson RG, & Arndt S (1996). Self-reported aggressive behavior in patients with stroke. *Journal of Nervous and Mental Disease,* 184, 746–753.

Parker RN, & Auerhahn K (1998). Alcohol, drugs and violence. *Annual Review of Sociology,* 24: 291–311.

Parton N, & Small N (1989). Violence, social work and the emergence of dangerousness. In M Langan & P Lee (Eds.), *Radical Social Work Today* (pp. 64–81). London: Unwin Hyman.

Perlman B (1987). Prosecuting patients. *Hospital and Community Psychiatry,* 38: 673.

Pernanen K (1991). *Alcohol in Human Violence.* New York: Guilford Press.

Perry JC, & Vaillant GE (1989). Personality disorders. In HJ Kaplan & BJ Sadock (Eds.), *Comprehensive Textbook of Psychiatry/V* (Vol. 2, pp. 1352–1395). Baltimore: Williams & Wilkins.

Petrie WM, Lawson EC, & Hollender MH (1982). Violence in geriatric patients. *Journal of the American Medical Association,* 248(4): 443–444.

Phelan LA, Mills MJ, & Ryan JA (1985). Prosecuting psychiatric patients for assault. *Hospital and Community Psychiatry,* 36: 581–582.

Poster EC, & Ryan JA (1989). Nurses' attitudes toward physical assaults by patients. *Archives of Psychiatric Nursing,* 3: 315–322.

Prentky RA, Burgess AW, Rokous F, Lee A, Hartman C, Ressler R, & Douglas J (1989). The presumptive role of fantasy in sexual serial homicide. *American Journal of Psychiatry,* 146(7): 887–891.

Prins H (1975). A danger to themselves and to others: Social workers and potentially dangerous clients. *British Journal of Social Work,* 5(3): 297–309.

Psychiatrist identifies physical clues for predicting patient violence. (1986, October 3). *Psychiatric News,* pp. 5–7.

Public Broadcasting Service (2001). *Local News* [Television broadcast]. New York: Author.

Quinsey VL, Harris GT, Rice ME, & Cormier CA (1998). *Violent Offenders: Appraising and Managing Risk*. Washington, DC: American Psychological Association.

Quinsey VL, Warneford A, Pruesse M, & Link N (1975). Released Oak Ridge patients: A followup study of review board discharges. *British Journal of Criminology*, 15: 264–270.

Ray CL, & Subich LM (1998). Staff assaults and injuries in a psychiatric hospital as a function of three attitudinal variables. *Issues in Mental Health Nursing*, 19, 227–289.

Record number of adults in prison or on parole (2000, July 25). *New York Times*, p. A21.

Resnick HS, Kilpatrick DG, Dansky BS, Saunders B, & Best CL (1993). Prevalence of civilian trauma and posttraumatic stress disorder in a representative national sample of women. *Journal of Consulting and Clinical Psychology*, 61: 984–991.

Rey, L (1996). What social workers need to know about client violence. *Families in Society*, 77(1): 33–39.

Richmond JS, & Ruparel MK (1980). Management of violent patients in a psychiatric walk-in clinic. *Journal of Clinical Psychiatry*, 41: 370–373.

Robins LN, Tipp J, & Przybeck T (1991). Antisocial personality. In LN Robins & D Regier (Eds.), *Psychiatric Disorders in America* (pp. 258–290). New York: Free Press.

Robins S, & Novaco RW (1999). Systems conceptualization and treatment of anger. *Journal of Clinical Psychology*, 55(3): 325–337.

Rooney RH (1992). *Strategies for Work with Involuntary Clients*. New York: Columbia University Press.

Rossi A, Jacobs M, Monteleone M, Olsen R, Surber R, Winkler E, & Wommack A (1986). Characteristics of psychiatric patients who engage in assaultive or other fear-inducing behaviors. *Journal of Nervous and Mental Disease*, 174(3): 154–160.

Rowett C (1986). *Violence in Social Work*. Cambridge: Institute of Criminology.

Ruben I, Wolkon G, & Yamamoto J (1980). Physical attacks on psychiatric residents by patients. *Journal of Nervous and Mental Disease*, 168: 243–245.

Rubin B (1972). Prediction of dangerousness in mentally ill criminals. *Archives of General Psychiatry*, 72: 397–407.

Ryan W (1976). *Blaming the Victim*. New York: Vintage.

Sack K (1999, July 31). Killer confessed in a letter spiked with rage. *New York Times*, p. A1, A8.

Sampson RJ, Raudenbush SW, & Earls F (1997). Neighborhoods and violent crime: A multilevel study of collective efficacy. *Science*, 277, 918–924.

Sarbin T (1967). The dangerous individual: An outcome of social identity transformations. *British Journal of Criminology*, 7: 285–295.

Scalera NR (1995). The critical need for specialized health and safety measures for child welfare workers. *Child Welfare*, 74: 337–350.

Schultz LG (1987). The social worker as a victim of violence. *Social Casework: The Journal of Contemporary Social Work*, 68(3): 240–244.

Schultz LG (1989). The victimization of social workers. *Journal of Independent Social Work*, 3(3): 51–63.

Schwartz TL, & Park TL (1999). Assaults by patients on psychiatric residents: A survey and training recommendations. *Psychiatric Services*, 50, 381–383.

Schwarz CJ, & Greenfield GP (1978). Charging a patient with assault of a nurse on a psychiatric unit. *Canadian Psychiatric Association Journal*, 23: 197–200.

Schwarz V (1987). Social worker, heal thyself. *Community Care*, 442: 14–15.

Seeck SL (1998). *Violence in the Workplace: A Study of Violence by Clients Directed toward Psychologists and Social Workers in Los Angeles*. Unpublished dissertation, California State University, Long Beach.

Segal SP, Watson MA, Goldfinger SM, & Averbuck DS (1988). Civil commitment in the psychiatric emergency room II: Mental disorder indicators and three dangerousness criteria. *Archives of General Psychiatry*, 45: 753–758.

Shah S (1977) Dangerousness: Some Definitional, Conceptual and Public Policy Issues. In BD Sales (Ed.), *Perspectives in Law and Psychology, Volume 1: The Criminal Justice System* (pp. 91–119). New York: Plenum Press.

Shah S (1981). Dangerousness: conceptual, prediction and public policy issues. In J Hays, R Ray, K Thomm,& K Solway (Eds.), *Violence and the Violent Individual* (pp. 151–178). New York: SP Medical and Scientific Books.

Shanker T (2001, August 20). Global arms sales rise again, and the U.S. leads the pack. *New York Times*, p. A-3.

Shapiro D (1965). *Neurotic Styles*. New York: Basic Books.

Silver E, Mulvey EP, & Monahan J (1999). Assessing violence risk among discharged psychiatric patients: Toward an ecological approach. *Law and Human Behavior*, 23(2): 237–255.

Silver JM, & Yudofsky SC (1987). Documentation of aggression in the assessment of the violent patient. *Psychiatric Annals*, 17: 375–384.

Simmons R (2002). *Odd Girl Out: The Hidden Culture of Aggression in Girls*. New York: Harcourt.

Simon R (1989). Social worker stabbed to death by patient in Santa Monica clinic. *California NASW News*, 15(7): 1, 5.

Simon RI (1998). Psychiatrists' duties in discharging sicker and potentially violent inpatients in the managed care era. *Psychiatric Services*, 49(1): 62–67.

Simonsen E, & Birket-Smith M (1998). Preface. In T Millon, E Simonsen, M Birket-Smith, & RD Davis (Eds.), *Psychopathy: Antisocial, Criminal and Violent Behavior* (pp. vii–xi). New York: Guilford Press.

Skeem JL, & Mulvey EP (2001). Psychopathy and community violence among civil psychiatric patients: Results from the MacArthur Violence Risk Assessment Study. *Journal of Consulting and Clinical Psychology*, 69(3): 358–374.

Skiba JT, & Cosner RE (1990). In harm's way: A study of client assaults on Pennsylvania children and youth workers. *Protective Services Quarterly*, 5, 1–11.

Skolnik-Acker E, Atkinson JC, Frost AK, Kaplan B, & Pelavin A (1993). *Violence against Social Workers*. Unpublished manuscript.

Slayings stir on-job fears. (1993, June). *NASW News*, p. 7.

Snow K (1994). Aggression: Just a part of the job? The psychological impact of aggression on child and youth workers. *Journal of Child and Youth Care*, 9: 11–29.

Snyder S, Pitts WM, & Pokorny AD (1986). Selected behavior features of patients with borderline personality traits. *Suicide and Life-Threatening Behavior*, 16: 28–39.

Sobel R (1982, January 8). Man held in fire at his psychotherapist's home. *Los Angeles Times*, pp. 1, 6.

Star B (1984). Patient violence/therapist safety. *Social Work*, 29: 225–230.

Steadman HJ (1980). The right not to be a false positive: Problems in the application of the dangerousness standard. *Psychiatric Quarterly*, 52(2): 84–93.

Steadman HJ (1982). A situational approach to violence. *International Journal of Law and Psychiatry*, 5: 171–186.

Steadman HJ, Cocozza JJ, & Melick ME (1978). Explaining the increased crime rate of mental patients: The changing clientele of state hospitals. *American Journal of Psychiatry*, 135, 816–820.

Steadman HJ, Monahan J, Appelbaum PS, Grisso T, Mulvey EP, Roth LH, Robbins PC, & Klassen D (1994). Designing a new generation of risk assessment research. In J Monahan & HJ Steadman (Eds.), *Violence and Mental Disorder: Developments in Risk Assessment* (pp. 297–318). Chicago: University of Chicago Press.

Steadman HJ, Mulvey EP, Monahan J, Robbins PC, Appelbaum PS, Grisso T, Roth LH, & Silver E (1998). Violence by people discharged from acute psychiatric inpatient facilities and by others in the same neighborhoods. *Archives of General Psychiatry*, 55(5): 393–401.

Stolberg SG (1999, May 9). Science looks at Littleton, and shrugs its shoulders. *New York Times*, pp. 1,4.

Stone A (1976). The Tarasoff decision: Suing psychotherapists to safeguard society. *Harvard Law Review*, 90(2): 358–378.

Stone MH (1990). Abuse and abusiveness in borderline personality disorder. In PS Links (Ed.), *Family Environment and Borderline Personality Disorder* (pp. 131–148). Washington, DC: American Psychiatric Press.

Stone MH (1998). The personalities of murderers: The importance of psychopathy and sadism. In A Skodol (Ed.), *Psychopathology and Violent Crime: Review of Psychiatry* (Vol. 17, pp. 29–52). Washington, DC: American Psychiatric Press.

Stone MH, Stone DK, & Hurt SW (1987). The natural history of borderline patients treated by intensive hospitalization. *Psychiatric Clinics of North America*, 10, 185–206.

Swanson JW (1994). Mental disorder, substance abuse, and community violence: An epidemiological approach. In J Monahan & HJ Steadman (Eds.), *Violence and Mental Disorder: Developments in Risk Assessment* (pp. 101–136). Chicago: University of Chicago Press.

Swanson JW, Holzer CE, Ganju VK, & Jono RT (1990). Violence and psychiatric disorder in the community: Evidence from the Epidemiological Catchment Area surveys. *Hospital and Community Psychiatry*, 41(7): 761–770.

Swartz MS, Swanson JW, Hiday VA, Borum R, Wagner HR, & Burns BJ (1998). Violence and severe mental illness: The effects of substance abuse and nonadherence to medication. *American Journal of Psychiatry*, 155(2): 226–231.

Tarasoff v Regents of the University of California, Cal 3d 425, 131 Cal Rptr 14, 551 P12d 334 (1976).

Tardiff K (1984). Characteristics of assaultive patients in private hospitals. *American Journal of Psychiatry*, 142: 1409–1413.

Tardiff K (1989). A model for the short-term prediction of violence potential. In DA Brizer & M Crowner (Eds.), *Current Approaches to the Prediction of Violence* (pp. 3–12). Washington, DC: American Psychiatric Press.

Tardiff K (1996). *Concise Guide to Assessment and Management of Violent Patients* (2nd ed.). Washington, DC: American Psychiatric Press.

Tardiff K, & Maurice WL (1977). The care of violent patients by psychiatrists: A tale of two cities. *Canadian Psychiatric Association Journal*, 22: 83–86.

Tardiff K, & Sweillam A (1980). Assault, suicide and mental illness. *American Journal of Psychiatry*, 37: 164–169.

Tardiff K, & Sweillam A (1985). Assaultive behavior among chronic inpatients. *American Journal of Psychiatry*, 139: 212–215.

Taylor PJ, Dalton R, & Fleminger JJ (1982). Handedness and schizophrenic symptoms. *British Journal of Medical Psychology*, 55: 287–291.

Taylor PJ, Garety P, Buchanan A, Reed A, Wesseley S, Ray K, Dunn G, & Grubin D (1994). Delusions and violence. In J Monahan & HJ Steadman (Eds.), *Violence and Mental Disorder: Developments in Risk Assessment* (pp. 161–182). Chicago: University of Chicago Press.

Teplin L (1994). Psychiatric and substance abuse disorders among male urban jail detainees. *American Journal of Public Health*, 84: 290–293.

Thackrey M (1987). *Therapeutics for Aggression*. New York: Human Sciences Press.

Thornberry TP, & Jacoby JE (1979). *The Chronically Insane*. Chicago: University of Chicago.

Tonkin B (1986, November). Quantifying risk factors. *Community Care*, 440: 13.

Townsend D (1985, May 1). Letter to the editor. *The Guardian*, p. 16.

True WR, Rice J, Eisen SA, Heath AC, Goldberg J, Lyons MJ, & Nowak J (1993). A twin study of genetic and environmental contributions to liability for posttraumatic stress symptoms. *Archives of General Psychiatry*, 50: 257–264.

Tully CT, Kropf NP, & Price JL (1993). Is field a hard hat area? A study of violence in field placements. *Journal of Social Work Education*, 29(2): 191–199.

Turner JT (1984). *Violence in the Medical Care Center: A Survival Guide*. Rockville, MD: Aspen.

Tutt N (1989, Spring). Violence to staff. *Practice*, 1: 80–91.

University of Southampton Department of Social Work Studies (1989). *Social Work in Crisis: A Study of Conditions in Six Local Authorities*. London: National and Local Government Officers Association.

U.S. Department of Justice, Bureau of Justice Statistics (1992). *Drugs, crime and the justice system.* Washington, DC: U.S. Department of Justice.

U.S. Department of Labor, Bureau of Labor Statistics (1994). *Workplace Homicides in 1993. Compensation and Working Conditions.* Washington, DC: U.S. Department of Labor.

Vaillant GE, & Perry JC (1985). Personality disorders. In HJ Kaplan & BJ Sadock (Eds.), *Comprehensive Textbook of Psychiatry* (4th ed., pp. 958 986). Baltimore: Williams & Wilkins.

Vallianatos C (2001). Security training helps deflect assaults. *NASW News,* 46: 3.

Violence and the public's health [Special issue] (1993). *Health Affairs,* 12(4).

Violence and the social worker. (1986, September 26). *New Society,* p. 1.

Virkkunen M, & Linnoila M (1993). Brain serotonin, type II alcoholism, and impulsive violence. *Journal of Studies on Alcohol,* 11(Suppl.): 163–169.

Volavka J (1995). *Neurobiology of Violence.* Washington, DC: American Psychiatric Press.

Walker L (1989). *Terrifying Love: Why Battered Women Kill and How Society Responds.* New York: Harper & Row.

Walsh E, Leese M, Taylor PJ, Johnston I, Burns T, Creed F, Higgitt A, & Murray R (2002). Psychosis in high-security and general psychiatric services. *British Journal of Psychiatry,* 180: 351–357.

Webster CD, Douglas KS, Eaves D, & Hart SD (1997). Assessing risk of violence to others. In CD Webster & MA Jackson (Eds.), *Impulsivity: Theory, Assessment and Treatment* (pp. 251–277). New York: Guilford Press.

Weeks JC (1982, September 23). Cherry pie. [Letter to the editor]. *New York Review of Books,* p. 15.

Weiden PJ, Scheifler PL, Diamond RJ, & Ross R (1999). *Breakthroughs in Antipsychotic Medications: A Guide for Consumers, Families and Clinicians.* New York: W.W. Norton.

Weinger S (2001). *Security risk: Preventing client violence against social workers.* Washington, DC: National Association of Social Workers.

Wertham F (1954). *Seduction of the Innocent.* New York: Rinehart.

White HR (1990). The drug use-delinquency connection in adolescence. In R Weisheit (Ed.), *Drugs, Crime and Criminal Justice* (pp. 215–256). Cincinnati, OH: Anderson.

White HR (1997). Alcohol, illicit drugs, and violence. In DM Stoff, J Breiling, & JD Maser (Eds.), *Handbook of Antisocial Behavior* (pp. 511–523). New York: Wiley.

White JL, Moffitt TE, & Silva P (1989). A prospective replication of the protective effects of IQ in subjects at high risk for juvenile delinquency. *Journal of Counseling and Clinical Psychology,* 57: 719–724.

White TW (1996). Research, practice and legal issues regarding workplace violence: A note of caution. In GR VandenBos & EQ Bulatao (Eds.), *Violence on the Job: Identifying Risks and Developing Solutions* (pp. 87 100). Washington, DC: American Psychological Press.

Whitman RM, Armao BB, & Dent OB (1976a). Assaults on the therapist. *American Journal of Psychiatry,* 133: 426–431.

Whitman RM, Armao BB, & Dent OB (1976b, May). *Assaults on the therapist, III: Coping and disposition.* Paper presented at the 129th annual meeting of the American Psychiatric Association, Miami, FL.

Widiger TA, & Trull TJ (1993). Borderline and narcissistic personality disorders. In PB Sutker & HE Adams (Eds.), *Comprehensive Handbook of Psychopathology* (2nd ed., pp. 371–394). New York: Plenum Press.

Wiener R, & Crosby I (1986). *Handling Violence and Aggression* [Training manual and videotape]. London: National Council for Voluntary Child Care Organizations.

Wilson JQ, & Hernstein RJ (1985). *Crime and human nature.* New York: Simon & Schuster.

Wise TP (1978). Where the public peril begins: A survey of psychotherapists to determine the effects of Tarasoff. *Stanford Law Review,* 31: 165–190.

Wolfgang ME (1958). *Patterns in Criminal Homicide.* Philadelphia: University of Pennsylvania.

Wolfgang ME, & Ferracuti F (1967). *The Subculture of Violence.* London: Tavistock.

Wong SE, Woolsey JE, Innocent AJ, & Liberman, RP (1988). Behavioral treatment of violent psychiatric patients. *Psychiatric Clinics of North America,* 11: 569–580.

Young J (1992, December 4). Violence on the job is a growing threat [Letter to the editor]. *New York Times,* p. A14.

Zuckerman DM (1996). Media violence, gun control, and public policy. *American Journal of Orthopsychiatry,* 66(3): 378–389.

Index